DEAN INGE

DEAN INGE

Adam Fox
Canon of Westminster
Hon. D.D., St Andrews

JOHN MURRAY

FIFTY ALBEMARLE STREET LONDON

By the same author

JOHN MILL AND RICHARD BENTLEY

PLATO FOR PLEASURE

PLATO AND THE CHRISTIANS

GOD IS AN ARTIST

Printed in Great Britain
by Unwin Brothers Limited
Woking and London

Contents

Illustrations

Acknowledgements

In the course of writing this book I have made many extracts from Dean Inge's writings, and I gratefully acknowledge the permissions given to me to do so.

The biggest debt is to Messrs Longmans who published so many of the Dean's works: I have quoted from *The Church and the Age*, *Outspoken Essays* I and II, *Personal Idealism and Mysticism*, *The Philosophy of Plotinus*, *The Platonic Tradition in English Religion*, *Types of Christian Saintliness*, *Vale*.

I have also to thank Messrs Ernest Benn & Co., publishers of *England*; Messrs Cassell & Co., publishers of *Assessments and Anticipations*. Messrs Duckworth & Co., publishers of *Faith and its Psychology*; Messrs Hodder and Stoughton, publishers of *Christian Ethics and Modern Problems*; Messrs Hutchinson, publishers of *Mysticism in Religion*; Dr H. D. A. Major, the editor and proprietor of *The Modern Churchman*; Messrs Macmillan & Co., publishers of *All Saints' Sermons*; Messrs Methuen & Co., publishers of the *Bampton Lectures*, 1899; Messrs John Murray, publishers of *Contentio Veritatis*, *Society in Rome under the Caesars*, *Truth and Falsehood in Religion*; Messrs Putnam, publishers of *The End of an Age*; the proprietors of the *Evening Standard* and of the *Sunday Express*; and the proprietors of the *Taranaki Daily News*, New Zealand, for an extract from *The Briton at Home*.

I have further to thank Messrs Longmans for extracts from two of George Tyrrell's books, *Lex Orandi* and *A Much Abused Letter*.

To many others I owe a sentence here and there. To all I tender my thanks.

Note

The re-issues and editions of Dean Inge's Works are numerous. I have used what I thought were probably the most widely circulated and therefore the most readily accessible. The references for the *Plotinus* are to the 2nd edition (1923).

Where extracts are not inset in the page I have aimed at enclosing within double inverted commas all that can be attributed directly to the Dean or Mrs Inge in printed volumes, articles, diaries or letters; and within single inverted commas whatever I took from other sources. I do not feel certain that my vigilance has been equal to the achievement of this aim.

I have tried to make the references to the notes at the end of the book (pp. 281–5) as few as possible. In the Index I have briefly described the persons named.

Preface

William Ralph Inge, Dean of St Paul's, was the most famous ecclesiastic and one of the most famous writers of his time, and this was due to a combination of brains and personality which is seldom met with. It is inevitable that his life should be written, and although he deprecated any memoir of himself, he left in very good order a great deal of material for much more than a memoir. Moreover, he wrote and published a good deal about himself, and often so modestly that his own account of things would not give a fair or full impression of him.

There is, however, one great difficulty in the way of attempting his biography; it is the absence of events in his long career of ninety-three years. His appointment to the Deanery of St Paul's is the one great event; the half-century before this occurred is by way of preparation: the rest is all authorship, character and celebrity, but no really great occasions. Lord Oxford and Asquith's impression of him at the age of sixty-five is pointed: 'November 10, 1925. We have had at lunch the Dean of St Paul's and his wife. He is a strange, isolated figure, with all the culture in the world, and a curiously developed gift of expression, but with kinks and twists both intellectual and temperamental. Still, he is one of the few ecclesiastics in these days who is really interesting.'[1]

This suggests a fascinating study, but scarcely a dramatic narration. Fortunately for the study the Dean kept diaries, sometimes very full ones, for more than sixty years. From them most of this book has been compiled. Every page of them is revealing, and it has been cruel work to make no use of so many amusing, delightful, and important entries. The Dean on re-reading the diaries in his old age thought them as interesting as the Creevey Papers, and they certainly will be found so, when they are published, perhaps fifty years hence. At present publication would be impossible.

I have given a good deal of attention to the earlier years, on the general ground that the first part of a biography is almost

always the best part, but also because the gradual development
of this shy child and odd young man into a national character
is something near to a romance. In the latter part I have tried
to present the private life and private thoughts, at any rate to
a much greater extent than is apparent in his printed *Diary of
a Dean* which devotes itself rather too severely to externals. The
relation of that book to the manuscript diaries is not quite
simple. There is a good deal in the book which is not in the
diaries, mainly by way of later reflection on public events.

All the time I have been writing I have felt it was impossible
that his should be like other ecclesiastical biographies. It could
not for example be like that of Dean Church, the most distinguished of his more recent predecessors at St Paul's, less still
like the life of Bishop Westcott, great scholar as he was. If it
was to be anything like a picture of Dean Inge, it would not be
the picture of an administrator nor a contribution to chance
history, but a glimpse (is more ever possible?) into a mind and
heart in its own setting and circumstances. The psychology I
leave to others.

Without the generous help of the Dean's children it would
have been useless to attempt this life. All the diaries and other
family papers have been at my disposal, and I have been entertained most kindly by Mr Craufurd Inge at Brightwell and by
Mrs Wigram at Monkton Combe. To this I must add my
gratitude to Sir John Murray for his encouragement.

Among others who have helped I mention particularly
Prebendary A. F. Judd; Dr W. R. Matthews, the present Dean
of St Paul's; Sir John Sheppard, formerly Provost of King's;
Mr Justice Vaisey; Mr Norman Whatley; and Dr H. D. A.
Major who provided me with a full list of Dean Inge's contributions to *The Modern Churchman*. I have had information on
special points from many correspondents to whom I have
applied, and some have done me a valuable service in confirming
opinions which I had already formed for myself. I am grateful
to Canon J. S. Bezzant, Lady Blackett, Miss Agatha Bowlby,
Mr Jack Breslan, Dr Spence Burton, Bishop of Nassau, the
late Mrs Violet Carruthers, Sir Hugh Cholmeley, Dr C. H. Dodd,
the Revd. Gordon Girling, the late Mrs Walter How, Mr A. L.
Irvine, Mr Donald Lindsay, the present Headmaster of Malvern,

and one of his predecessors Mr F. S. Preston, Dr Thomas Loveday, Miss Blenda and Miss Gerda Morgan, the Rev. R. E. Mugliston, Miss Ruth Spooner, Mr Edward Stapleton, the Bishop of Winchester, Dr E. G. Selwyn, the late Dean of Winchester, Mr Warner Allen, Bishop H. H. Williams; last and not least, at Eton to the Provost, two of the masters, Mr F. W. How and Mr R. C. Martineau, the Librarian, Mr Tom Lyon, and two former masters Mr M. D. Hill and Mr F. E. Robeson. The Editors and Librarians of the *Evening Standard* and the *Sunday Express* have readily granted me facilities for reading back numbers of these publications. I must thank Miss Torres for being indefatigable in procuring me copies of Dean Inge's works, small items as well as great. Mrs K. Rogers of Oxford has typed my crabbed manuscript with skill and patience.

PART ONE

Preparations
1860–1911

I

Childhood

It may be that nothing has changed the face of England and our way of life in the last hundred years so much as the decay of the village. The villages of England standing unfortified among their fields gave the life of the English a particular character of its own and the place of their habitation a particular appearance. Although no two villages were alike, yet they had, when they were self-contained communities, a certain common character, as can be seen when in the sprawling cities of today we come across a few houses, or an open space, or even a group of trees, which we recognise at once as the nucleus of a former village.

In the village of a hundred years ago or more life was in some ways primitive. Professor C. S. Lewis put this in his own striking way when he said that the manner of life of Jane Austen differed less from that of Homer than from ours today! Even towards the end of the last century the wells were of the utmost importance in the village; the horses, whether they drew the plough or the carrier's cart, were the ultimate source of all well-being; almost all food was seasonal, a good harvest meant a great deal, though a hard winter was not unwelcome. Only perhaps in fuel was the situation better than now. In 1814 at Foston near York Sydney Smith built himself a new parsonage, and he had eleven coal fires burning in it day and night for two months before he went into it and for some days after.[1]

But primitive or not, the village was much more civilised than now in the sense of being an ordered community, where each man had his place and a traditional way of doing his job. The squire might be a tyrant, but he was often a benevolent one, and his wife felt some responsibility for the sick; and if the big house neglected its duties, the parson performed them, if he could, while careful to perform his own as laid down for him by law. Life was not very eventful, but neither was it dull.

The age-long satisfactions of food and home and love were to be had, and occasional diversions. Slow thinking was prevalent, but at least it was a quiet life. Only towards the end of the nineteenth century did agricultural depression bring real want, for which the remedy has been industrial expansion; but this, if it saved the individual, seriously damaged the village community. The motor car, the cinema, and huge taxation completed its downfall, though of course they have brought their own blessings with them. For better and for worse the village has changed.

In the village of Crayke besides the Castle and the Manor House there are several fair-sized residences. One of these and by no means the smallest of them is called The Cottage. 'Here,' as a plaque on the wall informs you, 'on 6 June, 1860, was born William Ralph Inge, scholar, philosopher, writer and Dean of St Paul's.' He was not only born there, but the house and village were to be his home for the first fourteen years of his life. He retained a lively and affectionate remembrance of them, and no wonder, for our earliest years are usually the most impressionable, and Crayke is rather a striking place.

It lies about twelve miles north of York to the east of the road to Thirsk on the southern slope of a spur on what the maps call the Howardian Hills, which are themselves a detached portion of the Cleveland Hills. Where the parish begins, it borders the plain of York at a height of about one hundred and forty feet above the sea, and so far the road from York has been almost completely level. But now it rises to some two hundred feet where the houses begin, and another hundred feet and more up the village street to where the church stands on a knoll, and a little higher still and quite on top to what remains of the castle or what seem to have been two separate castles in the same enclosure. The Rectory is opposite the church, and The Cottage about two hundred and fifty yards below. The parish is entirely agricultural. The population in 1861 was five hundred and eighty-five.

The Rector from 1835 to 1874 was Dr Edward Churton, a theologian, and a Spanish scholar of some distinction; from 1846 he was Archdeacon of Cleveland. The living in his time was worth about £900 a year, and he had private means. He is said to have thought himself fortunate. In 1854 there came from Oxford to be tutor to his nephew, and then to his sons, a certain William Inge, a Fellow of Worcester College, who had a First in Greats and had once played cricket for the University against Cambridge, when he took six wickets. He must have been an effective teacher, for three of the sons got scholarships at Eton. The youngest of them, Henry, got the first scholarship and subsequently won the Newcastle. Presently the young tutor was attracted by the boys' sister; he took orders and became curate of Crayke, and after some delays he married Susan Mary Churton on 30 June 1859. The Archdeacon should have favoured his aspirations, for he too had been curate to his father-in-law, Archdeacon Watson of Hackney.

The future Dean of St Paul's, William Ralph Inge, was the first child of this marriage. He was born on 6 June 1860. His sister Agnes Sophia followed two years later, in 1866 Mary Caroline, and in May 1868 Charles Cuthbert, while two other children died in infancy. To house this growing family a sub-stantial wing was added to The Cottage in 1868, and there Mr. Inge was content to remain as curate until 1874, when the Archdeacon died and he removed to Alrewas, near Burton-on-Trent, on the nomination of Dr G. A. Selwyn, Bishop of Lichfield.

The Cottage at Crayke in which Ralph Inge spent his child-hood is rather a handsome house, but the handsomest rooms are those which the Inges added, making hardly justifiable the name of The Cottage. The garden is attractive in an unusual way. It slopes steeply down, but the view is now restricted by trees which may have been non-existent or scarcely noticeable a hundred years ago. The Rectory has a similar garden, and from its southern windows there is a very clear view of the Minster twelve miles away across the plain of York. Dean Inge wrote of this as one of his early recollections. In these pleasant surroundings the curate's children were brought up. Ralph, destined to be the most distinguished of them, was almost eight years older than his brother, who could not therefore be much of a playmate for him, and in Ralph's earliest years it was his sister Sophy who was his dear companion. Their mother set

down every year some record of them in the way of occupa-
tions, interests, and temperament, with a note of their daily
time-table, lessons, and books read. Ralph was educated at home
until five months before he went to Eton, when he was sent to
a preparatory school for one term, presumably to acclimatise
him to boarding school life. He tells us that both his parents
were excellent teachers: they were at times assisted by a
governess, and at times a cousin or two joined the party as
pupils. One of these, Walter How, afterwards Fellow and Tutor
of Merton, went on to Stoke House, Mr Parry's school at
Slough, and this was where Ralph went too for his one term.

Mr Inge was as successful with his son as he had been with
his wife's brothers. Ralph got the second scholarship at Eton,
when Eton scholarship was at a very high level. His path to
this success can be traced in his mother's note-book and in a
number of letters which have been preserved.

In December 1864 Mrs Inge and three children joined her
husband at Bournemouth, and they did not return to Crayke
till the middle of the following May. The youngest child,
Edward, died on 15 March after a short illness, and was buried
in St Peter's Churchyard. The Dean visited the grave sixty-five
years later. A whole series of Mrs Inge's letters to her mother
during the stay at Bournemouth have survived with some lively
details about Ralph at four years old. On 13 February she writes
of him:

> We do not stimulate his eager thoughts—even with the very
> little food we give him his little mind and feelings seem all too
> full. But I am very happy and thankful about him now, though
> of course he is the same wayward difficult child, I am quite sure
> he is improved, and I see that he is now quite happy and loving
> and open with us both.

And on 2 March:

> He is a very delightful little pupil, only somehow he *will* get
> on with *thinking* so fast that I must soon put him to multiplication
> table or 'hic haec hoc' to make a sort of drag chain on his busy
> little mind. . . . You remember how hard it was to get him to
> read or endure to be told 'anything sad,' and how impossible I
> found it to teach him anything about our Lord's sufferings. So

we left it quite alone for a long time, but lately he has been quite different, and this morning he asked to read the hymns about it, saying 'I *do* like *this* sort of sad, because it isn't like other sads, and I think its very *un*-sad too, isn't it Mama?'

Ralph was now three months short of five years old, and in the next few years his mother's letters give further glimpses of him. In the first part of the year 1868 Mr Inge was away in Italy. His wife writes to tell him of her anxiety over Ralph's health and even more over his temperament, and gives a very vivid and very sympathetic picture of a little boy and girl.

Feb: 2nd. [He has been ill.] Here is little Ralph, playing alone with ships, waggons, sea, railways, music, horses without end, and this morning dogs and a fox too, all so real to him, and yet nothing else but a chair and a basket of rubbish to the prosy eyes of other people.

Feb: 5th. His illness has of course fostered his little wilfulnesses and waywardnesses.

Feb: 26th. I am more afraid about Ralph [than about Sophy], for he is very often least good with strangers, and he certainly has more faults of temper than any of the Nearwell children [the How cousins in Shropshire].

March 4th. Did I tell you that the hounds met here last Saturday? Ralph and Sophy went to see all the fun. Little bonny boy was wild with delight: he is growing more boyish in many ways, quite full of merry mischief—tho' more like Willie[2] in thoughtfulness and eager questionings. As his spirit and strength grow stronger, of course he both wants and can bear a stronger hand near him than when he was so weak and excitable.

March 11th. Little Sophy is beginning to show that her sweet temper is not without its accompanying spice of determination. She *fights* for what she wants, and without crying, she makes a complete storm with voice, hands and feet, not in a passion fit, like little Ralph's, nor as if she was hors de soi-même like him, but with more pertinacity than his . . . but she is certainly far less excitable at present.

March 20th. He is fast growing out of a baby into a boy and will soon want you home to keep him in order.

April 3rd. He does try to be good very often.

April 20th. Sophy's little fights never upset or distress her, as poor little W. R.'s always upset him.

April 24th. It is the way of the child never to have his demonstrations of affection ready at command, and if anyone asks him about you with a view to elicit some of his pretty little loving words and ways it never succeeds—he is both too wayward, and I think also too deep in his feelings, to bring them out except when the little fountain is stirred from within.

Thus does his mother's very loving and very penetrating care of the future Dean of St Paul's reveal and to some extent explain him at this and every subsequent period of his life almost to the end. The child is certainly father to the man in his case. The wilful, affectionate, imaginative, unforthcoming little boy did not alter much except in wisdom for the next eighty years.

The foundation of that wisdom was laid securely by the strenuous education the children had had planned for them and carefully carried out by their parents. It was an education in religion, languages, and literature, gradually built up for Ralph to scholarship standard, while indoor or outdoor recreations were provided and fostered, as opportunity occurred, without any forcing. Mrs Inge's accounts of it probably represent the stage reached towards the end of each year. There were rather frequent visits to relations and the seaside, where lessons were sometimes, but not always, discontinued. By 1865 reading and writing had presumably been mastered and 'drawing begins to supersede almost all other quiet amusements.' In 1866 Ralph and Sophy both begin French. In June 1867 a governess is employed part-time, but both children began Latin which Mrs Inge always takes herself. In 1868 they learn the Kings of England and the First History of Rome, also of Greece. They are reading *Contes Faciles* and doing 'a little French on slates.' In Latin a short exercise is written before breakfast and a little bit of grammar or construing done with Mrs Inge afterwards. Ralph did some reading by himself and began to make maps and games of questions and answers.

On his ninth birthday (6 June 1869) Ralph begins the Greek

His mother

"... I'm afraid she never really forgave me."

His father

"... the placid and healthy temperament of a family of athletes."

alphabet 'when he also went into his own room and had his
oak book-case.' About this time 'we began making lists of
flowers and birds seen in walks. Rabbits and gardens not much
cared for, from want of grown-up encouragement. Walks apt
to be unwelcome, but this improves.' 'Cricket much liked, but
too rare a treat to be well-learnt. Hoops and balls the chief
active plays.' But in June and July 'W. R.'s eyes too weak for
reading, writing and drawing. Lessons almost prohibited.
Croquet flourished well.'

The years that follow are a record of continuous progress
towards an Eton scholarship.

But the course of this elaborate home education, though it
might be interesting to teachers, does not get much below the
surface. Fortunately three letters written by his mother during
a visit to relatives at Langton Green near Tunbridge Wells fill
in the picture.

1871. [No further date, but apparently the day of arrival at
Langton Green.]

He will not have much, if any, cricket, I think, but if he can
but be happy without, I shall be glad of the break. He is, I am
afraid, singularly helpless and astray in all common things—he
seems to have not the least notion of finding his own way anywhere, forgetting all about his bearings in the strangest way.

1871. July 26th. He got up early this morning and had an hour of
solitary play in the garden before breakfast, which he seemed to
be enjoying in his own quiet fashion. Then he had some new
milk, and came in to write his history of St Paul till Prayers.

August 4th. Dear little Ralph is very happy today, because there
is another Cricket match on the Green, and he is under the trees
scoring. Last time he sat there nearly five hours, and only grieved
over the shower that made it not quite six hours long. I cannot
arouse anything like spontaneous interest or enjoyment in anything else. He is fairly happy and generally very good, but there
is no alacrity about anything except the cricket; croquet is next
best, he has been playing remarkably well, and enjoys his power—
but the beautiful drives, rides and walks, the farmyard, the new
well that is being made, all seem to have no interest for him, if
he gives his attention to them at all or to any conversation that
is going forward, it is only as being demanded of him, and as

soon as possible his thoughts fly back to 'Daft'[3] and Grace,[4] and the other heroes. I don't see any better chance of giving him wider sympathies and more sensible interests than this visit gives us, but it seems to take very little visible effect upon him at present. We are reading 'Lady Barker' all together . . . but in the most interesting part he begged leave to go and see if the Smarts Hill Eleven had come! Lessons are very much against the grain.

If it was so with this particular boy, it looks as if he was being run too hard.

And then there is also the religious instruction to be taken into account, of which not a little can be known. In 1864 Ralph began to go to church on Sunday afternoons. In 1865 he went frequently to the Litany with his mother when they were away at the seaside. In 1866 he and Sophy are writing Collects on slates. In 1867 they went to the Litany on Wednesdays and Fridays in Advent. They sang out of *Hymns Ancient and Modern*. In 1868 besides the Litany on Wednesdays and Fridays they went to church twice on Sundays. In 1869 they had a lesson on the Epistle and Gospel with Mrs Inge, using reference Bibles. This presumably was on Sundays. On week-days they learnt verses out of the Psalms, and the repetition of them, new and old, was combined with the daily Latin lesson. In 1870 in Lent the children gave up sugar to get pence towards shoes for Ada Bilton whose mother died at Christmas 1869. In 1871 Ralph was confirmed and joined the Sunday School First Class in the afternoon. He began writing his life of St Paul. During the Christmas holidays Mrs Inge read them all she could find about Melanesia, and they were heartily interested in all about Bishop Patteson, who had just been killed by the natives.

There is here obviously a carefully thought out scheme of progressive religious instruction and Christian practice, which the parents must often have discussed between themselves. And for 1873 Mrs Inge gives a more detailed account of a routine which had now become what might almost be called a way of life. This is the programme for Sunday; and there was church as well.

At nine Carol and Charlie [now aged seven and five respectively]. Hymns for little children. Mrs. Barbould.

9.30. Elder children repeat what they had learnt. Texts on the Collect read all together. Denton on the Gospel for the Day.

2 p.m. Sunday School.

4.30. W. R. I. to write his St Paul.
A. Sophy Inge. Texts on the Te Deum.

Evening Carol and Charlie Sunday Pictures and singing Narrative Hymns.
Elder ones read to themselves for half an hour. W. R. I. Life of Bishop Mackenzie (the gift of his Uncle William Ralph Churton).

6.30. Catechism.

[In the week: Greek Testament with Mrs Inge once a week.]
Miss Yonge's Scripture Lesson daily.
Preparation for Lent Catechising in Church.

To modern ears this sounds too much, but in this well-ordered clergyman's home it probably fitted in quite naturally. Sunday was condemned otherwise to be a day of inactivity; and daily lessons without a scripture lesson would have seemed strange to children who had never known anything else. The Dean recollected sixty years after that in his home "religious observances, not to any burdensome extent, were performed as a matter of course." (*Things New and Old*, p. 3.) Nor can it be said that his training in religion was anything but a great success in view of his whole career. It had not quite the effect that was intended, but that it was a great source of strength to him cannot be denied. He never ceased to be grateful for it.

At the same time one can well understand that the boy Ralph was overstrained, and to read of his enthusiasm for cricket rather than for 'Lady Barker' is a pleasant relief. It has the further interest of being an hereditary enthusiasm. The Dean had a father, an uncle, a brother, and a nephew who all played cricket for Oxford, and although he himself never got further than playing for the Collegers at Eton and for his College at Cambridge he enjoyed the game. He could have gone further in all probability, if he had not been obsessed with the need to work as a schoolboy and as an undergraduate. It is easy to imagine him saying that cricket took too much time. But later on he regularly watched the game, and there were large family parties

at Lord's and at the Canterbury cricket week year after year.
In 1939 he thought it worth while to enter in his diary that his
niece Margaret had taken ten wickets for six runs against
Holloway College.

There is no doubt that his mother was formidable, and perhaps too formidable. She was by all accounts a puritan and a
rather advanced Church woman at the same time. A connection
of hers by marriage has said that you felt that if you laughed
at anything in her presence it would have been better not to
have done it. But this was certainly not the impression she
made upon everybody. Her grandchildren knew well what a
remarkable person she was. Yet Ralph's nervous disposition
was probably not much helped by her, and he *was* nervous and
shy. He recalled in some Early Recollections how he could not
bear to look at himself in a mirror long after he was grown up
because, when he was three or four, he had seen a distorted
reflection of himself. When his son Craufurd was eleven years
old he remarked in a letter to his wife that the children were not
shy and timid as he used to be. "They enjoy trying new things
and seeing new people. Craufurd in this way has a much happier
disposition than mine." And a few days later he wrote, "You
and I will have to be careful not to let Craufurd feel that he is
victimised whenever there is trouble. It is what I used to feel."

It is difficult to know whether he took more after his father's
family or his mother's. The Inges came from Staffordshire,
where descendants of the senior branch still lived in considerable affluence. They were steady, plodding, successful people.
The Dean's father was not so much of a personality as his
mother, but of much more than average ability, and an
extremely virtuous person. His self-effacement was remarkable,
as is shown by his remaining curate to his father-in-law for
fifteen years, and then accepting a troublesome living. But in
1881 he was appointed by the Crown to be Provost of Worcester College, Oxford, of which he had been a Fellow until
his marriage. At Oxford he identified himself with many good
works, and lectured for Divinity Moderations, the humblest of
academic employments. To his great surprise he was offered the
Bishopric of Salisbury. He is said to have refused it by return
of post without consulting his family. The Dean of Windsor

(Randall Davidson) wrote to Sir Henry Ponsonby: 'I am very sorry Dr Inge has declined. His appointment would have been good in all ways. He is a scholar, and a man of real intellectual power as well as a good and vigorous man, who would in every way have done credit to Lord Salisbury's very wise selection.'

The Churtons were academically more distinguished, excellent scholars and notable divines. To this the Dean drew attention in his article on Eugenics, the last of the *Outspoken Essays*, Second Series (p. 200). It is an interesting record and well worth studying, but it does not account for the Dean. He was unique.

From the Inge side perhaps he got his diligence, his love of cricket and other games, his diffidence: from the Churtons his scholarship and literary accomplishments, and possibly a way of lapsing into silence, for many of the Churtons were and are notable for being men of few words.[5] From both sides he might have learnt a certain clannishness. He kept up with his relations and he learned the lesson early, for on both sides there was a great array of uncles and aunts and cousins, and children made longer visits to their relations than would now be expected. It was a part of their education not to be foregone, but depending for its effects on the uncles and aunts and not much less on the nurses and governesses. The children often enjoyed themselves, but they learnt to control their feelings in the interests of good manners, and even to write and thank for a visit for which they were not very grateful and express affections which they were not yet old enough to feel. But this of course helped to develop gratitude and make affection conscious.

2

The Eton Colleger

William of Wykeham was the first to realise in a grand way the idea of forming a close connection between a School and a College at the University. Before that the monasteries had provided themselves with houses and halls, to which they sent their scholars, at Oxford and Cambridge, but the close relation between the two St Mary Winton Colleges and the scale of their foundation seemed to be something new, so much so that Wykeham's College at Oxford was and still is called the New College. Fifty years later King Henry VI founded on almost exactly the same lines the College of the Blessed Mary of Eton and the King's College of Our Lady and St Nicholas at Cambridge, and he paid William of Wykeham the posthumous compliment of making the seventh Headmaster of Winchester the first Headmaster of Eton.

It must be allowed even by Wykehamists that 'Eton and King's' is a more familiar form of words than 'Winchester and New College,' but the experiment was in neither case very successful. Both foundations became 'closed shops' of the narrowest kind, and were emancipated only a hundred years ago. In 1860 eight men in all entered King's College : they had all been Eton scholars, and within three years they were all Fellows of King's, and if they did not marry they could retain their Fellowship for life. But these were the last to be elected according to the form prescribed in the statutes of King Henry VI; and although the new statutes which came into force in 1861 did not at once much alter the character of the College, in the 'seventies both Eton and King's showed a new vigour such as comes with reform, and were conspicuous in every way; and in 1879 there were thirty entries into King's of whom only seven were Etonians and two of them Oppidans.

Eton also was flourishing wonderfully when Ralph Inge

tried for a scholarship in 1874. He was almost certainly the oldest candidate, for he had what is called a lucky birthday. The boys had to be under fourteen on the first of June, and he was fourteen on the 6th. Allowance would be made for age in the examination: he would be expected to do better than the others, and he certainly did. When the result was announced he was second. The first six names were:

1. H. F. W. Tatham
2. W. R. Inge
3. H. V. Macnaghten
4. C. P. Pott
5. A. C. Benson
6. R. White Thomson

C. P. Pott was killed in a carriage accident while he was an undergraduate, but it is remarkable that the other five were all of them subsequently assistant masters at Eton, and from 1886 to 1888 they were all masters at the same time. Their immediate destiny, however, was to go into College as scholars, and five others went with them.

The first three were all pupils of the Revd. Francis St John Thackeray, whom the Dean in *Assessments and Anticipations* (p. 17) calls the best of the classical tutors. In class he appears not to have been successful, but an Oppidan pupil corroborates the Dean's estimate. 'Thackeray in the quiet of his study and pupil-room was altogether different from the exasperated "swag" in division. I seem to hear the low tones of his persuasive voice pointing out how much more beautiful and poetical I could have made my crude prose. *There* was the real Thackeray, the scholar and the gentleman, as he appeared to those who saw him apart from the conflict and strife of school-life.' (*Eton in the 'Seventies*, Hon. Gilbert Coleridge. Smith, Elder & Co., 1912, p. 101.)

One odd little difficulty arose at once, the kind of thing which worries a new boy dreadfully, but is in most cases easily set right by a sensible grown-up. Ralph consulted his mother about it a few days after his arrival, and she wrote back (1 October 1874):

I hope your kind fag-master will not put you in such a difficulty often. I think I would venture to ask him not: but you will know best what you can say to him. If you were to say 'I am very much obliged indeed, but I suppose I had better do my own verses, and if you would just look at them and give me a hint where to mend them, I should be "awfully glad" '—I think he wouldn't be angry, or think you ungracious.

I think the kind fag-master was F. H. Rawnsley: later he was fag to H. E. Ryle.

On the whole things did not go too badly. Mrs Inge wrote to her husband at the end of the Easter holidays (25 April 1875):

> I send you dear Ralph's pleasant little notes. These holidays leave a very, very pleasant relish behind them as regards *him*. I feel that this dreadful first year of school-life, as far as human eyes can see, has more than fulfilled our fondest hopes. He is as loving and, I believe, as devout as a home boy could be, and has gained in self-control and strength of character and body.

No doubt Thackeray the master and Inge the boy suited one another admirably. But the boy, like the master, probably did not at first much enjoy the conflict and strife of school life. Though older than the others of his election, he had much less experience of what school demands. Hugh Macnaghten, who came next on the list, was only twelve years old, but he is believed to have said in after life that they bullied Inge and he now much regretted it. At home things had very much changed. When Ralph went off to Mr Parry's at Stoke House for his first term at boarding school his grandfather the Archdeacon had parted from him with the words

> If we do meet again why, we shall smile;
> If not, why then this parting was well made[1]

They never did meet again, for the Archdeacon died in July 1874. The Inge family thereupon migrated from their dear Crayke to Alrewas, described by the Dean fifty years after as "a straggling, difficult, and rather unattractive parish on the banks of the Trent."[2] This must have been a great loss in the holidays, and the incessant talk about parish affairs, so the Dean says, dispelled any wish, if he had ever had it, of becoming a parish priest.

In his second year at Eton his tutor wrote as follows to Mr Inge:

April 10th, 1876.
[No address, Athenaeum note-paper.]

My dear Sir,

I have delayed a few days in writing to you about your boy, but I trust he has brought home the printed list, in which he holds the first place both for School Work and in Collections. This will I hope be a great comfort and pleasure to you; as well as to know that he is an excellent good boy in all matters of behaviour, as far as I know, or have ever heard from all the masters under whose notice he has come.

There is a very nice style about all his written work, and I hope if his health continues good that he may be able to stand a good deal of reading, but at present as he has no examination pending, he should have a thorough good holiday; if any exception be made to what Mr Ainger says at the end of his report, it had perhaps better be in the form of some refreshing English reading—poetry or a Waverley Novel.

With the utmost satisfaction at your boy, and earnest hopes for his future.

I remain
Yours very truly
Francis St John Thackeray.

Mr Ainger's report referred to in the letter ran to this effect:

Div ix. 1st of 34.

Inge K.S.[3] I have nothing but good to say of him. He is very punctual and regular—attentive in school and does excellent work all round. His composition shows great taste and power for a boy and has improved much in the two school terms I have known him. I hope he will not be allowed to open a book in the holidays.

A. C. Ainger.

In a later report, probably at the end of the next term, he was even more highly commended:

Div ix.

Inge K.S. 1st. of 35.

Excellent in all respects—work up to a high standard. Ought to become a distinguished scholar. I have nothing but praise to give him after a tolerably long acquaintance.

A. C. Ainger.

His translations into English verse have frequently been first-rate for a boy.

What being a Colleger was among that brilliant set can be learnt from several sources. The Dean himself in 1922 recalled his school-days in *The Evening Standard*. He says that "the more ambitious Collegers, to whom the school work was child's play, worked by themselves for the Newcastle Scholarship, the blue ribbon of Eton, harder than most of them have ever worked since. We used to read the classics, as they ought to be read, in masses." This impression is supported by Hugh Macnaghten (*Fifty Years of Eton*, Allen & Unwin, 1924, p. 28). 'There was a tradition of strenuousness among the Collegers of the 'seventies. . . . We played football regularly eight or nine times a week; there were no compulsory "times" in the College: tradition sufficed: moreover some of us worked much too hard. Personally I worked like a madman, reading and re-reading the *Poetae Scenici* from end to end. I could construe almost anything.' But these impressions do not tally with what A. C. Benson wrote of himself and his great friend H. F. W. Tatham in a memoir of Tatham, prefixed to *The Footprints in the Snow* (H. F. W. Tatham, Macmillan, 1910, pp. xiii–xv), where we get the impression that they drifted delightfully through their school-days in College. Yet there was very little to choose between the four of them when it came to scholastic achievement. Macnaghten notes incidentally that it was a surprise when in 1877[4] Inge got the Newcastle Medal (the second place in the examination) and 'first leapt into fame.' He got the Scholarship the next year. The *Eton College Chronicle* (15 May 1879) said it was 'after a contest which was probably unusually open, Macnaghten mi. being Medallist.' Thackeray wrote an appreciative letter:

Dear Mr Inge,

I am indeed, as you can well believe, most thankful and heartily glad about your son's success. It is a great honour—the greatest that Eton has to bestow, and your son is thoroughly worthy of it. He is the third of my pupils that has attained it, but of none of them have I been so glad as of him.

Having been Medallist last year, it would have been mortifying not to have kept his place; though I did not feel certain whether the Medallist of this year might not wrest it from him.

It does your son great credit to hold his own against him, as I hear he (Macnaghten) is omnivorous.

However Ralph has shewn that he has digested well what he has read. I could get no particulars from the Examiners, who were anxious to go.

Your son should during these few days rest as far as possible, and after the King's Scholarship take a *thorough holiday*.

With my cordial congratulations to yourself and Mrs Inge believe me to remain

Yours sincerely

Francis St John Thackeray.

In 1883 Thackeray left Eton for the dull but eligible living of Mapledurham in the gift of the Provost and Fellows of Eton —or perhaps 'eligible' is not quite the right word, seeing that it was only offered to him after it had been refused by four other masters—rather call it dull but delightfully so. A hundred of his old pupils made him a presentation. He always kept up with them, and Inge kept up with him. The good old scholar lived till 1919: he had been just the man for Inge, K.S. at Eton.

Of Ralph's last year in College we know something from ten of his own letters, some of them long ones, which have survived out of many.[5] They are to his parents and give some vivid glimpses of work and play. They make it impossible not to think he was enjoying himself.

The following gives a good idea of his standard of attainment in the classics, when there were just two months to the examination for the Newcastle (4 February 1879):

I find much more time to read than last half: I have finished the Demosthenes and the Trachiniae: I think Pretor's notes are very good, and most of his translations of words very spirited. I have just begun to look through the Georgics on my Tutor's recommendation; he is very kind, and takes a great deal of trouble to help me on. I am doing the Agamemnon with him this half: I have done it before rather lately, but I find a great deal which I knew very imperfectly, especially in the Choruses, which I still find rather beyond me, and if I can remember some of Kennedy's phrases it will be very useful. Some of his emendations seem very clever, though I sometimes wonder whether Aeschylus would recognise his play if he saw it as it is edited now: there seems to be hardly a line which has not been emended.

The young scholar came near to the opinion of Henry Jackson, the Professor of Greek at Cambridge, who thought that Aeschylus would be surprised to hear that we got grammar and sense out of his choruses. (*Henry Jackson, O.M.*, R. St John Parry, Cambridge, 1926, p. 127.)

Ralph's account of his studies would be incomplete without what follows in the same letter:

I had one very good day's skating just before the frost went. I made an attempt to play hockey on the ice with about eight other Collegers; we had the pool all to ourselves, and had great fun. There has been splendid skating about here. The good skaters go to the Home Park, which is all flooded, and makes a splendid large piece of ice, but there are many other good places besides.

A month later the mood of despondency which sets in before an examination was upon him. To his mother (2 March 1879):

I am beginning to get rather tired of doing nothing but work, especially as there seems such a small chance of success, but I suppose it will come in useful afterwards, and at all events I shall have the satisfaction of knowing that I have done my best. I am going to begin Divinity this week.

On 6 April he wrote to his father anticipating a failure in the examination, but he came out first, and was able to telegraph to Alrewas on the morning of 10 April: *The Newcastle has just been given out I am scholar expect me by the three thirteen unless I telegraph again.*

On 26 April another telegram arrived, this time from Ralph's uncle and godfather, at King's: *Ralph has done best of all in classics and is chosen for a scholarship.* He had got the first of the Eton Scholarships to King's.

The next term was his last at school. In June answering a birthday letter from his mother he wrote: "It is very melancholy to think it is my last birthday at Eton. Oh that I were two months younger." He meant that in that case he would still have been eighteen at the end of the term and eligible to stay another term. But he was nineteen; it was time to go on to King's. He had got all he could out of Eton as a boy, including a love for the school which never forsook him.

3
King's

Inge was admitted to King's on 11 October 1879, with the other Eton scholars of that year, M. S. Dimsdale, Edward Impey, R. A. Coleridge, and C. W. Chitty. Dimsdale was his best friend among them. They worked and walked together, and by 22 October he had already some picture in his mind of the kind of life he should lead at Cambridge, when he wrote to his mother:

> I am doing my best to get into a routine of working hours. The dons here are most kind, and Cooke gave me some advice as to reading, which must be very valuable. His lectures are very good, and I think I ought to learn a good deal from them. The ordinary plan of a Cambridge day is as follows (for a reading man): Chapel at eight a.m., work from nine to one-thirty. Exercise from two to six, society from six-thirty to eight; work from eight p.m. to [?]. Some men who want to do an extra amount of work read also from four to six. We have a capital dinner in hall, with two courses of solid meat, so that I find I can live very well on bread and butter for the rest of the day. Anything more that one wants is sent up from the kitchen at half an hour's notice, so that one has no trouble in providing for visitors. The freshmen this term are not at all regular at Chapel except Dimsdale and myself, and the proportion of attendants at the daily service is very small. D. and I have formed a classical co-operative society. We did more than half a play of Plautus last night. The Little-go[1] weighs very heavy on my mind, but I must hope for the best. I am doing a mathematical paper every Saturday. I mean to go in for the Carus next month, but I shall not have a chance against the Theological Tripos men.

If he did go in for the Carus Prize (for Greek Testament) he did not get it, but he did pass the Little-go, which had weighed so heavy on his mind because of the mathematics. His thoughts must often have gone back to Eton, where he and

Dimsdale shared a friend in A. C. Benson, still a Colleger. Before October was out Benson sent Inge an account of things in College which was adolescently gloomy. Of the Master in College he observes that 'Broadbent is fairly sociable. He has not been to my room once this half. Wood has been turned down for lighting-up.[2] The Literary is more than ordinarily feeble' and so forth. He ends with a little commission: 'Go and kick Dimsdale and tell him he is a pig not to answer my letter —if you see him.' Towards Christmas Benson wrote again, not less gloomy, but evidently aware that the Cambridge term was ending: 'I wish you would come down and stay for about a week, things in general are so filthy. You really must come down and bring Dimsdale. It will not be necessary to play in College Game unless you are specially anxious,—you could come to breakfast and tea with us always. . . . Everyone (myself included) is relapsing with the snarling growling sort of frame of mind which is the epidemic consequent on the end of the half so you must excuse the highly irritated tone of this effusion and only regard the part about your coming down. Write if you will—It will be quite a comfort.'

Benson did not come up to King's till 1881. The two remained friends, and a quarter of a century later Benson was Inge's best man at his wedding. But school soon recedes into the background as the more engrossing interests of undergraduate life prevail. We do not know much of Inge's social life. He played cricket for his College, and became proficient at lawn tennis which he had already had some opportunity of playing at school and at home. But it looks fairly certain that he became one of those reading men who work between four and six. In after life he felt that he had missed much of what Cambridge had to offer him and recommended undergraduates not to work too hard. But at any rate his work was not in vain. His academic career was most distinguished.

In a letter to his mother on 12 March 1880, that is to say, towards the end of his second term, he announced his first success: "The Bell came out this morning. I got the first. . . . I have just been to the Vice-Chancellor to sign my name in a book, promising to take my degree of B.A. according to the term of the Scholarship. The value appears to be about £55 a year for four years." It is true that the Bell scholarship was confined to the sons of clergymen, but in those days sons of clergymen were always to be found among the best scholars at Oxford and Cambridge. The standard was high. In the following term he shared the Porson Prize for Greek Iambics with C. H. Garland of St John's College. On 19 February 1881 he was able to telegraph to Alrewas that he had won the Porson scholarship, a University award of sixty pounds, open to men of not more than five terms' standing. The examination, according to the Regulations, was 'exclusively classical.' In a letter next day to his father he said: "It is satisfactory to know that I am first of my year at present, though of course the Scholarships are not much of a test in regard to the Tripos."

He was to be strongly confirmed in this view before long, for in the College examinations in the following June, the end of his second year, he experienced the only real set-back of his undergraduate career. His tutor, J. E. C. Welldon, wrote him a long letter on the result, and said he was afraid he would be disappointed.

> *27th June, 1881.* . . . I cannot say your work was so good as it has been before and will, I doubt not, be again. It used to be almost a proverb that Eton men distinguished themselves as Freshmen, then suffered an eclipse and afterwards shone again more brilliantly than ever; perhaps you too are only gathering fresh lustre by retiring for a short time into shade; yet don't suppose you did badly, your actual place is ample proof of your high merit; only we have come to expect things so high of you that what would be great in any one else seems comparatively small in you.

Welldon goes on for three more sides with details of marks and points in scholarship which only Cambridge men perhaps would fully appreciate; but one comment is noticeable: 'Your grammar was very fair; but philosophy is not a strong point of yours, or indeed it seems of any other King's men.' Was Welldon right or wrong about the philosophy? He ends his letter with some advice which Inge had heard before to 'work hard during the Long Vacation and then—for to you this is quite equally important—take a good holiday before you begin your Tripos-year.'

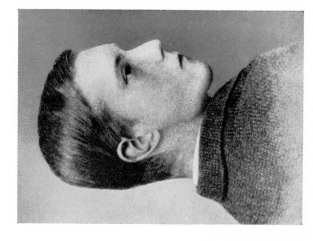

Aged 22
Overwork?

Aged 5
Sitting up and taking notice.

The looked for recovery occurred, and 1882 was quite an exciting time. In February Inge got the Craven scholarship, the best of all the classical awards then open to him. This seems really to have pleased him.

February 18, 1882

My dear Mamma,

I hope you will by this time have got my telegram to say that I have been fortunate enough to get the Craven—Welldon told me immediately after the result was declared a little before two this afternoon. I must have got it pretty easily, as all the six examiners voted for me. There was a great fight for second between Barker of Trinity and young Macnaghten, the former being finally chosen, with Macnaghten "proxime accessit." I have not heard about Dimsdale. I very much wish he had got one of them. I hope, as you say, that I have been given what is best for me, though it seems hardly fair that I should always have the luck when the examination is most important. The dons are very jolly and cordial as usual, but I have only seen two or three of my friends,—as most of them are gone out for the afternoon. I must go and tell Uncle Willy this evening. Many thanks for your letter of this morning and Papa's. I think we should all have been satisfied with less than the Craven this time, but it is of course a very jolly thing to get.

Your very loving son
W. R. Inge.

His parents had evidently written to soften the blow of failure, which was anticipated in view of the previous summer's set-back. That no doubt made it all the jollier.

He now set about to compete for the Browne Medals for Greek and Latin Odes and Epigrams. He was awarded the prizes for Greek Ode, Latin Ode, and Greek Epigram. He sent in two Greek epigrams, and the unsuccessful one is believed to have been the next in merit. His friend Dimsdale got the medal for Latin epigram, which makes it likely that Inge did not compete for it. He did, however, go in again for the Porson Greek Verse Prize, which he had shared in 1880, but here he was not successful. It was awarded to Gardner of Caius, though the Regius Professor of Greek voted for Inge. In the College Examination, in which he had had his disappointment the year before, he was now, as he wrote to his father, "very easily first, 921 marks to the next man's 802, which I hope will mean a £30 prize, which will be useful just now, as I shall have various expenses in taking my degree next term."

The Regius Professor of Greek at this time was Benjamin Hall Kennedy, chiefly famous as a great schoolmaster and the compiler of the *Public School Latin Grammar*, which has been used almost universally for three generations. He had been Headmaster of Shrewsbury when the Dean's father was a boy there, and consequently got to know his old pupil's son when he came up. He took a real interest in the young man's career, and wrote to his father about his successes, and his prospects in the Tripos. A few sentences are worth quoting, as being written from a point of special vantage:

Feb. 18, 1882. I congratulate you cordially on the election of your son to the Craven Scholarship, which has been made to-day by the unanimous votes of the six examiners, three of whom were Salopians, Munro, Prof. Mayor, and myself. One only was a King's man, Welldon. . . . I shall confidently hope to see your son Senior Classic in the summer. Will he then read for the Second Tripos (Classics) or for Theology—or possibly for both these?

Feb. 22nd, 1882. (With an invitation to pay a visit in the first or second week in May.) As your son's examination does not begin till the 22nd of that month, you will not be trenching on his time. As to that, I think I can say with the most perfect safety that he will have no competitor with the faintest chance of endangering his position (as Senior Classic).

June 8, 1882. I must write a line to congratulate you and Mrs Inge most heartily on the splendid addition to your son's academical honours of those Browne medals. I trust next week will show him Senior Classic, as he ought to be, but knowing as I do the 'furore' of many examiners in favour of the 'bracketing' or (as they now prefer to call it) divisional system, I do not feel by any means sure that he will stand as 'Senior Classic': for there is, I know, one very good man at least, Gardner of Caius, who may come near enough to rank with him in a First Division, and (as G comes before I) may precede him in the list alphabetically.

Dr Kennedy's apprehensions were justified. When the Tripos

list was published the First Class was headed by a big Division containing seven names, of whom three were King's men, Dimsdale, Inge, and Rowlatt. So there was no Senior Classic for the first time.

The list came out on 17 June. Inge took his B.A. degree and went home on the 21st. Home had in the previous year become Worcester College, Oxford, a decided change for the better. He modestly or carelessly omitted to bring his Browne Medals with him, and was still promising to do so in the following November. And now he took Dr Kennedy's advice to relax so far as to go a short tour on the Continent. It was the first time (I think) that he had left Britain. He and his cousin Walter (How) and 'Uncle Willy' started on 27 June.

Here 'Uncle Willy,' another William Ralph, but a Churton, deserves some notice. He was young Ralph's godfather—and his mother's eldest brother. He had been tutored by the Dean's father for an Eton scholarship, proceeded in due course to King's, became a Fellow in 1859 and took a first in both Mathematics and Theology in the following year. He was the first Tutor of King's under the new Statutes, and Dean of the College from 1867 to 1879. At his death in 1897 he had lived more than forty years in College. He had the reputation among the dons of being very silent, and he was certainly very studious and very pious, a strong High Church man. He wanted his nephew Ralph to join a society called the S.T.C.[3] when he came up to Cambridge, but Ralph wrote to his mother that he should be very sorry to disappoint Uncle Willy, but he thought it would not be wise for him "to join a society which is at least *supposed* to belong to a very extreme party, until I have given more thought to it." He read a paper to it 28 years later.

The three travellers met for the tour in London. The two young men had time for two hours at Lord's before they left. It was the third day of the University match, and it saw Cambridge beating Oxford by three wickets, joy for Inge and grief for How. The first stage of their journey was via Queenborough and Flushing to Cologne. Thence they made their way via Coblenz and Heidelberg to Lucerne and on to Engelberg, then to Chur, Davos and Schuls in the Engadine. They then began to think of their return. Ralph wrote frequently to his mother.

His long letters on thin paper were of the kind always expected from the Continent in those days. They show a young man's lively interest in 'the sights,' but no peculiarities of taste. On the whole the tour must be judged not entirely successful, largely because of the weather. But apart from that the mountain walks were not very congenial to Ralph or Walter, and Uncle Willy easily overdid it and had no thin clothing. They were accompanied by a brother and sister of the name of Hicks who were very enthusiastic mountaineers and acted as leaders in some rather strenuous expeditions. The others soon came to excuse themselves and eventually went their own way. A few extracts from the letters bring the party to the mind's eye:

Hotel Titlis. Engelberg. July 2. 1882. I think I must reserve my impressions of Switzerland till I have seen it in fine weather, at present I own I wish myself back in Germany. The mountains inspire one with horror, especially at the idea that I shall be expected to climb them. . . . Hicks and his sister evidently intend to scale perpendicular precipices and glaciers and other horrible places, so I rather guess we shall part company before long, as we must not be a drag upon them, and Walter must not and I will not do any very arduous walks. . . . I wish you or Sophy or some of you could have come with us; we really must plan a tour next year for a large party of us . . . to Cologne and the Rhine, for we passed through all this part so quickly that we could not see a quarter of what there was to be seen, and I am sure you would be immensely interested with the German towns and castles. . . . (P.S.) We saw English papers at Heidelberg, with the score of the University match and the Eton and Winchester.

Engelberg. July 4. 1882. I think my last letter was written in a rather gloomy frame of mind, chiefly caused by the weather, so I feel bound to tell you as soon as possible that Switzerland in sunshine is a very different place from Switzerland in rain. I think it requires bright sunshine more than an English landscape, for there is not much colour anywhere and when not lighted up by the sun the bare crags and rocks have a most desolate and depressing effect. Yesterday Hicks took us for a sort of preliminary canter over a pass 7250 feet high, and calmly proposed starting again after four or five hours rest (at midnight!) to ascend the Titlis, a mountain nearly 11,000 feet high and eight hours stiff climbing over snow and ice. But here we all struck. . . .

Hotel Fluella. Davos Dörfli. July 9. 1882. The guide-book calls the distance to Davos from Landquart, where we went by train, 28 miles; we drove the first seven, and walked the rest, which nearly finished all of us, as we were burdened with knapsacks, and I in addition with a stick, umbrella, alpenstock and billycock, most unportable things. . . .

Hotel Belvidere. Schuls. July 12th. 1882. This is a hopelessly wet day, the worst of all the wet days we have had since we came to Switzerland, I must try to write a letter to pass the time. . . . Uncle Willy spends his leisure hours on Tobit.

They returned home shortly after this, and when the Long Vacation was over Ralph went up to Cambridge again. His objective now was the second part of the Classical Tripos in 1883. It was in this year that new Regulations came into effect. There was no individual order; the names in each class were arranged alphabetically with symbols indicating what distinctions, if any, had been gained. There were fourteen men in the First Class, and four of these gained two distinctions each. It was not possible to get more. Dimsdale and Inge were two of these four: they both gained distinction in (*a*) Translation from English into Latin and Greek, and Latin and Greek into English and in (*b*) History. But Inge came out best of all, because he was awarded the first Chancellor's medal.

His Cambridge career as undergraduate and bachelor and examinee was ended. He had been distinguished, but it had perhaps exhausted him a little. Of course his connection with Cambridge and King's was not severed. He won a University Prize, he was elected to Fellowships, he took his Master's degree, he became a Professor, he was an honorary Fellow of two Colleges. But after 1883 he did not come into residence again for twenty-four years, and then only for four years. Instead he began to earn his living, and this, after a short time, brought him back to Eton.

It would be very interesting to know what effect Cambridge had on Inge's religion, but there is not much to go upon. He had been brought up in the High Tractarian tradition, and on arriving at King's, as we have seen, he was a more than usually regular attendant at Chapel. At the same time in his first term he was already unwilling to commit himself to Anglo-Catholicism until he had thought things out for himself. With an undergraduate, if he is capable of thinking (and this undergraduate was) the effect is often a recourse to extremes which may go as far as Rome or as far as atheism. But in this case it was not so. At the end of his third year Dr Kennedy supposed it quite likely that he would read Theology, which does not suggest any great reaction from orthodoxy. The strongest influences in religion at Cambridge at the time were towards sound learning, and Inge put himself under them. He attended E. C. Selwyn's Sunday Greek Testament readings at King's. He heard the famous preachers who visited Cambridge, Thring for example, and Farrar, and Knox Little. But the greatest impression was made upon him by Westcott. Sir John Sheppard describes this as 'a decisive and a happy influence on his career.' Brooke Foss Westcott, afterwards Bishop of Durham, took up his appointment as Regius Professor of Divinity at Cambridge in 1870, and was elected the first Professorial Fellow of King's. He had a weekly meeting of young men to talk informally about Socrates and Plato. One of these young men was Inge, who retained a lively recollection of the meetings, and thirty years after contributed an account of them to the *Life of Bishop Westcott* (by his son Arthur Westcott, Macmillan, 1903, Vol. I, pp. 9–10). The meetings took place on Sunday afternoons, and twelve or fifteen undergraduates were present. Westcott played the part of Socrates, presumably (though Inge does not say so) as a midwife of the mind. He did most of the talking, but not as though he were a teacher instructing his pupils. "He often spoke of human personality, propounding mystical doctrines of the solidarity of human beings, which then seemed to most of us paradoxical and difficult, but which have since come back to me associated with memories of his face and voice." "We always felt that we were in the presence of a saint, and that it did us good to see and hear him." It is easy to think that the young men were impressed and Inge among them, and that this early teaching must have done something towards making Plotinus congenial at a later stage and mysticism the great reality in the Dean's religion.

4
Schoolmastering

Men often come to be schoolmasters who have not the necessary gifts. They think that to be learned and diligent and care for their subject and for the boys justifies a vocation to the class-room. But this is not the exact truth. Most of the masters in a school do not need to be learned; in fact it is often a handicap if their subject has come too easily to themselves. They need to work, but not too hard, for it is important that they should be fresh, and teaching freshly in class is exhausting. They certainly must not dislike the boys; the best thing is that the boys should fear them affectionately, in any case that they should fear them a little. But men will often be too human or too odd or too nice to be frightening and unable to acquire the trick—for trick it is in part—and therefore they cannot 'keep order' and therefore they can never teach in class effectively. It follows from this that inability to keep order is no reflection whatever upon a man's character or talents. It is simply that schoolmastering is not his line, unless he has or can acquire the art of discipline, and it is often acquired by rather rough and ready methods.

By all accounts Inge had it not and did not acquire it. Nor did his tutor Thackeray, as we have seen, successful though he was with individual pupils. Nor did his contemporary Tatham at first, though he did so before long. The great Bishop Westcott never had the gift in his seventeen years at Harrow, and that excellent scholar R. L. A. du Pontet, with all his virtues, never came near it at Winchester. Two famous schoolmasters of forty years ago had the trick at one school and not at another.

Inge took up school work more or less by chance. He was just on the point of going into residence at King's for a fifth year and was preparing to move into new rooms, when events took a different turn and led to his being a schoolmaster for five years, and actually in four different schools. John Kennedy, the Headmaster of Aldenham, a former Captain of the School at Eton, was a Fellow of King's and had applied to the College to send him a temporary composition master. Inge was eminently qualified, recommended accordingly, and accepted. It was his first experience of schoolmastering, and he seems to have enjoyed it. In a letter from Aldenham he wrote:

> I have had a very pleasant week—I am afraid it is almost a week since I last wrote to you, and I think I am getting more into the way of looking over exercises. I providently brought with me a number of College composition papers, so that I have not had to inflict my own productions upon the boys. I shall be interested to see how one of them turns out. He seems to be nearly up to scholarship form already, and he is said to be only just fifteen, though he looks older. They are all a particularly pleasant set of boys, and I should be glad to see any of them again. I actually played football yesterday, after a five years interval, but I found the Association rules rather puzzling. However it gave me some good exercise, which I wanted, and I did not get kicked.

Here is a young schoolmaster, not much different from others. He likes the boys, is tempted into playing games with them, and it might be conjectured that the compositions he gave them were too hard. A young man straight from the University does not realise how much more he knows than his pupils.

The employment at Aldenham had been temporary. But already before he took it up Inge had been in correspondence with Dr Ridding, the Headmaster of Winchester, about work there, and he was engaged for the summer term; meanwhile Ridding was made the first Bishop of Southwell, and W. A. Fearon from Durham School became Headmaster. He confirmed Inge's appointment in March 1884, and expressed the hope that he might possibly hold himself free for the offer of a further appointment if Winchester wanted him. Inge was certainly worth trying out, and this was soon demonstrated. Eton, Harrow, and Winchester were then regarded as the three leading schools in England, and before he took up his work at Winchester he had already done a term's work at Harrow, and had been appointed a master at Eton for the following September.

His plan would have been to go into residence at King's again for the Lent Term, but on 11 January he received a letter from Dr Butler, the Headmaster of Harrow, offering him work immediately.

The offer was accepted, but what Harrow thought of Inge or Inge thought of Harrow has not survived, and seems now to be past enquiry. His thoughts at any rate were diverted before half-term by the unexpected offer of a mastership at Eton. He wrote to ask his mother's advice:

Harrow

[Sunday] Feb. 17th. 1884.

My dear Mother,

I have been spending a very queer Sunday, which may alter my plans considerably. On Saturday evening . . . I found a letter on my table just arrived through Cambridge from Joynes at Eton, saying that Dr Hornby wanted to see me at once, and have some quiet talk with me. I was extremely puzzled to know what it could be, but I thought it best to start off by the first train this morning, which brought me to Eton just too late to go into morning chapel. I went first to Joynes' house, and directly after chapel to the Head's house, meeting Charlie[1] in Weston's yard. When I got in the Head told me that two masters (C. C. James and Stone) are probably going to leave at Easter, and he wanted me to supply one vacancy, and Dimsdale the other. I told him about Winchester, and how matters stood, as well as I could, and he said that if I could not come till September he would keep it open for me, though I should lose a place in seniority. It would be a permanent appointment unless the work plainly did not suit me. It must have been a sudden idea on Hornby's part, for he had never said a word to me, nor to Dimsdale, as far as I know, on the subject, and he had done so to several others. But that of course does not concern me. I suppose you would think it best for me to go. I said I should like it, if no previous engagements stood in the way, and it is obviously a more permanent thing than either of the others. I am going to wait for your answer before I do anything, as I think I was wrong in not mentioning the matter to Dr Butler, and I should like to be advised what to do. I suppose the only thing to do will be to write to Dr Ridding, and ask him whether I am right in supposing that his appointment to a Bishopric will alter plans for next term, and mentioning that I have had this offer from Eton. But please tell me just what you think I ought to do. (Is he a Lord Bishop by courtesy yet?) . . .

Your affec^{ate} son

W. R. Inge.

His mother no doubt concurred in what he supposed he ought to do, and will have answered the last question in the negative. On 2 May he took up his work at Winchester under the new Headmaster. A letter to his mother at this time discusses the question of the training of teachers. "As long as there are parents," he wrote, "who agree with you in preferring the old way of education, there will be no compulsion for those who intend to teach, to go in for examinations, as those who do not will find no difficulty in getting good appointments." This arose out of an article in the *Guardian* advocating training for teachers, and he says about it further: "On the whole I do not think I am quite convinced. Perhaps the unwonted pleasure of agreeing with the majority makes me tenacious of my opinion." He was already conscious of being in the main a minority man.

Only a faint tradition of his teaching at Winchester has survived. He seems to have been conscious himself that he was not getting on too well, and yet in the latter part of the term he wrote several cheerful letters to his parents, showing that he found life at least entertaining, and that Winchester was not without its diversions. One to his father, however, contains an expression of misgivings which were often repeated in one form or another:

Winchester. June 6th. 1884. You make me feel ashamed of myself by speaking of wasted time. I am afraid I have singularly little to show for my 24 years either for others or myself. I wish more and more that I had made more use of the social advantages at Cambridge. I should get on so much better if I could get up more sympathy and sociability with other people. But it is easier to see one's faults than to mend them.

Back at Eton in the autumn of 1884 Inge, as an old Etonian, would fall easily into the routine of the place. There would still be some boys in the school who were there when he was a boy there himself; and many of his old schoolmasters were still on the staff. He stayed till Christmas 1888, but of these ten terms not much that is significant can be told. There were happy days indeed, but, as the Dean himself said later, these were uncomfortable years, and what made them uncomfortable was inability to keep order. This, as always happens in such cases, is remembered in anecdote, and, boys being the humourless (though amusing) creatures they are, the anecdotes largely turn on bringing things into class. Two such may be recorded for a certain originality in their make-up. They are both widely attached to Mr Inge by oral tradition, but possibly of course to other masters too. It is said that on one occasion a considerable number of boys brought tuning-forks into school and proceeded to twang them. Inge asked what the noise was; he probably heard it rather imperfectly. A boy suggested that it was mice in the ceiling. "I don't believe it is mice in the ceiling," said the master. "You all go out of the room and if I still hear the noise I will think it is mice in the ceiling." They went out and did not return. Silence reigned in the class-room. On the whole it might be reckoned that, provided he never referred to the matter again, the master had the better of it here. The other story relates that Mr Inge was asked by another master which school (i.e. which teaching period in the day) he liked best. Laughing at himself, he answered that he liked the Five o'clock school best, because it was such fun when the boys' balloons went into the gas.

It was an uncomfortable and sometimes a depressing experience. But under all circumstances there is much to make a schoolmaster happy in a good school, especially if it is his own old school, and if he plays games. As an Eton master Inge never played football, but he did play cricket and tennis. He also spoke at the Literary Society, and something of the whimsical wit for which he was afterwards noted is easy to detect in a speech he made where another master, J. D. Bourchier, read a paper on *Irish Loyalty*. 'Mr Inge thought that many of the misfortunes in Ireland were due to the introduction of the potato which had the same effect on the Irish that rice had on the Indians. Finding that they could live on very little they had ceased to work hard, and thus the ruin of the nation had gradually been worked.'[2]

One does not know whether the boys thought this serious or not. One cannot even be absolutely certain that the speaker himself knew whether it was, but in 1919 he printed a remark about the bad effect of the potato on Ireland in a very harsh form, and with no uncertainty about it.

These four years at Eton could not have been as stimulating as they might have been for this very intelligent young man in his middle twenties, but they were certainly not years of stagnation. He secured his Fellowship at King's in 1886, and in the same year he won the Hare Prize at Cambridge. This mental activity in the midst of a schoolmaster's preoccupations must have been strenuous. It is likely indeed that a year or two of Cambridge tranquillity might have been better for his health and happiness in the years that followed.

The matter of the Fellowship cost him some pains. He was not successful at his first attempt in 1885: the award went to Dimsdale. He no doubt relied on a magnificent array of University prizes and distinctions, rather superior to Dimsdale's, but he submitted a dissertation on *Scipio Aemilianus*, and the younger Scipio could hardly give any great opportunity for his particular talents, especially if he was busy and not very fresh. The examiners, though they praised its diligence, thought it showed little understanding of the political life of Rome and not much imagination.[3] Dimsdale's dissertation had both these qualities; he was an excellent Latinist, and spent his life as a Tutor of King's; if Hornby's intended offer of a mastership at Eton was ever made to him, he did not accept it. In the following year (1886) Inge was the first of the four Fellows elected; he sent in the same dissertation, or at any rate one on the same subject. He never came into residence, however. He had dropped into the mastership at Eton, and there was not much to lure him away. No lectureship was available for him at King's; Dimsdale had been elected already to the one he might have had, and he was better off financially at Eton. He cared for Eton so much, too, and in the end all this turned out for the best, for it put him into a Fellowship at Oxford, where he was led away almost insensibly from pure scholarship to metaphysics and that idealist philosophy which was then in the ascendant at Oxford. There he found his own line.

The Hare Prize at Cambridge is for a Dissertation on a Classical Subject, and the subject proposed that year was *Society in Rome in the First Century*. The prize was awarded to Inge, and his essay appeared in print in 1888 under the title *Society in Rome under the Caesars*.[4] Except for *The Eton Latin Grammar for use in the Higher Forms*, which is a very thorough piece of scholarship but scarcely literature, and a school edition of selections from Cornelius Nepos, this is the Dean's first published work. It must have been written while he was a master at Eton, and can hardly rank as a piece of original research. But it is, as befits a Prize Essay, a brilliant sketch in its way and deserves more than a cursory perusal not only for its own sake, but to see if anything of its author's mature style and standpoint is to be found in it already.

When he won the prize the Dean was only twenty-six years old. Looked at seventy years later the essay seems to cover the field almost too completely, to be very inadequately documented, and somewhat rhetorical. It clearly belongs to a time when history was still a branch of literature and not a science. It might be suspected that Froude would be the writer's model, and the earlier part of the book gives that impression. Later on it has a slightly more audible echo of Gibbon without Gibbon's glaring faults. It is in fact very well written, very lucid, very easy to read, and full of information, with interesting observations by the way. Already the author is seen to be something of a satirist, though not so pungently as later on. He dispenses praise no less than blame with all the detachment of a judge, and he clearly wishes to be fair. He says that "the testimony of an age against itself is always overdrawn" (p. 73), and is careful to take that into account. The page on which this aphorism occurs is a good specimen of the style and tone:

> We have now concluded our brief survey of the state of pagan morality at Rome during the first century. It is in most respects a dark picture, though some writers have painted it in yet blacker colours. But the dictates alike of feeling and reason forbid us to believe the worst accounts that have reached us. It is no disparagement of the work wrought by Christianity to hesitate before accepting evidence which would argue a radical change in human nature. We should rather rest assured that in the worst times

virtue has never left the earth, and that in its broad features human nature is the same for good and evil as it was 2,000 years ago. The testimony of an age against itself is always overdrawn. Let us correct the fierce invective of Juvenal by the wise warning of Seneca (De Ben. 1.10). 'We must guard against letting blame fall on our own age. This has always been the complaint of our ancestors, that manners have been corrupted, that vice reigns, that human life is deteriorating and falling into every kind of wickedness. We lament in the same strain, and our descendants will do the same after us. In reality, however, those things do not change, but only fluctuate slightly at times like the ebb and flow of the sea; now one vice prevails most, now another, but bad men have always existed, and (alas!) always will.' 'Morality, like everything else,' says Tacitus, 'moves round in a circle' (Tac. Ann. 3. 55). We in the nineteenth century have accustomed ourselves to look for and expect some progress but we must at least try to avoid the temptation to blacken our ancestors that we may make our own improvement seem the greater.

Here we have the Dean already as a scholar, a moralist, a student of human nature, a workmanlike stylist and translator. The first two chapters of the book, on Religion and Philosophy respectively, where one might expect to find the true Inge most plainly, are those in fact which fall most noticeably short of expectation, and taken in conjunction with the rest they would make one think that this young author was destined to be a historian rather than a philosopher or a divine. The Dean's gifts of clear statement, exposition, and analysis are there already, but they want the strength which his lifelong study of mystical theology, his interest in contemporary tendencies in philosophy, his immensely wide reading, and his deep personal religion were to give them. In measuring the Dean's growth in stature both spiritual and intellectual the fact that he was self-taught in theology and philosophy alike must not be forgotten, and when he wrote his Prize Essay that part of his education had not begun. But even if it had never begun on these lines and he had struck out as a historian, there is no question but that he would have distinguished himself. As late as 1925 he wrote: "I have often thought that if I could begin again I should choose to be a historian."[5] His sketches of the development of some line of thought over a period of the past either long or short are amongst his best achievements as a writer, most notable of all the sketch of philosophy and philosophers in the third century of the Christian era in his Gifford Lectures II and III. Long after, in his Presidential Address to the Modern Churchmen's Union in 1928 he said: "If we treat history as the biography of ideas, or of ideals, we are on much firmer ground than when we confine ourselves to a narrative of external events."

The Prize Essay was limited to the first century of our era, but that it was perhaps the author's own introduction to his much more intense study of the two centuries that followed is suggested by the last sentence of the essay itself: "It is only indistinctly that we can trace in the first century the growing influence of that contact between the religious consciousness of the East and the intellectual activity of the West, which was destined to determine the character of mediaeval and modern civilisation."

At the very end of the year 1888 one very important event took place. In April he had resolved to take Holy Orders. His Fellowship at King's was a sufficient title. He was made Deacon by Bishop King of Lincoln, the Visitor of King's College, before Christmas. He had just left Eton and was to take up a Tutorial Fellowship at Hertford College, Oxford, but until he was admitted to it he would still retain his Fellowship at King's.

What had finally brought him to this decision to take Orders he probably could not say himself. It had certainly been the subject of his prayers and the occasion of many good resolutions, but he does not seem to have had any particular ministry in view. It was still quite an accepted thing for a teacher to be a clergyman. At Eton at least a dozen of the masters were in Holy Orders, and it may have seemed natural to one with Inge's background. He did not decide to take Priest's Orders until 1892.

Another and quite different event of 1888 deserves to be mentioned and in some little detail. Although much more trivial than ordination or the publication of a book it has its own interest and significance. Like all good schoolmasters Mr Inge had a favourite pupil, though the favourite pupil probably never knew how much he was favoured or ever gave it a thought.

His name was Calvert—Charles Archibald Calvert: he came to Eton in 1887, so that he had been only five terms at Eton when Mr Inge left. But in the summer term of 1888, when there was a holiday for Queen Victoria's birthday, the young master had taken three boys, Calvert, Oldfield, and Mackay to Burnham Beeches. He said it was the pleasantest day he had spent for a long time, "the weather perfect, the woods in their best loveliness, the boys better than either. I think nothing more charming than Calvert was ever created."

He never forgot it. In March 1890 he recalled that he had had many happy days at Burnham Beeches, "one day perhaps the happiest of all when I took my pupils Calvert, Oldfield and Mackay thither two years ago." In October he observed that Eton tended to become idealised: the reality was less except for one's friends. Even friends change, he found, and young boys tend to become hobbledehoys. "Calvert is so altered that I hardly wished to meet him for fear of destroying the beautiful image which has remained with me for so long." But he need not have been afraid. In March 1891 when he was staying with Dr Warre, the headmaster, "Warre asked Calvert to breakfast hearing that he was a friend of mine. He has grown enormously, being now 6 ft. 2, and is of course no longer the charming little fellow he was, but he has not lost his pretty manners and open honest face. He ought to make a fine man." Fifteen months later "Calvert came to stay with Rawlins. He is nearly 6 ft. 5, but otherwise very like his old self."

This would hardly be worth recording except for one circumstance. On that Royal birthday, when he had taken his three young pupils out for the day, he had been vouchsafed a vision. It was such as had been vouchsafed in the early fifteenth century to the mystic Henry Suso, whom he has made familiar to so many of us. A midwinter visit to Burnham Beeches in 1891 brought it to mind. "I think I shall never forget the day when I took Calvert, Oldfield, and Mackay there in the early summer, and how angelic Calvert looked at the top of a steep bank, his straw hat on the back of his head looking like an aureole, and his eyes dancing like two sunbeams. It was the prettiest sight I ever saw or shall see." This is not the light of common day, nor is it emotion recollected in tranquillity. It is the language of vision, and certainly not the normal language of the man William Ralph Inge; and for that reason it is notable.

Calvert became an officer in the Royal Dragoons, and was awarded the D.S.O. in the South African War. He was a fine shot and rode to hounds within a year of his death which occurred in 1956. He was very much liked by all who knew him.

Inge left Eton at Christmas, 1888. What prompted him to send in his resignation is not very clear. He can hardly have contemplated it when he resolved the previous April to take Orders, for in that case it might be expected that he would wait until it was settled what new work he was to undertake. Probably some fresh fit of depression promoted a sudden decision, but reinforcing it would be the fact more or less realised of his want of success as a schoolmaster and his inability to alter this. His own studies also were leading him outside the range of school interests, and he looked about for more time to read and think. A classical tutorship at Cambridge was an obvious objective, but a Lectureship at Hertford College, Oxford, was suggested to him as a possibility early in October, and on the 17th of November he accepted it. It meant leaving Eton at Christmas, and he wrote to give the Headmaster notice of this. In his diary he describes the Headmaster's answer as kind, but brief. It ran:

Nov. 19. 1888.

My dear Inge

I am very sorry that you are leaving us, but will not question the decision you have made.

I hope that you will find more congenial work, and a sphere fully as useful as that which you might have filled here.

You will take with you the good wishes of

Yours sincerely
Edmond Warre.

It was the right decision, but one which Inge bitterly regretted almost at once, and very frequently for several years. He spent the very day on which he was elected hoping not to be elected, and following on the next day he spent a sleepless night in strong regrets at the step he had taken. On the 13th of December he had a sad day of goodbyes. "Saw all my pupils who were as

nice as they could be. . . . Kind presents from 7 masters."
On the 21st when he was at Lincoln for the Ordination and had
actually left Eton he wrote: "My regrets at having left Eton
rather increase than diminish! For the most inadequate reasons
which I can now hardly even remember, I have surrendered a
career which would certainly have been lucrative and with conscientious care would have been useful and happy. And for
what? Time will only show." Such reactions after a new appointment are not uncommon, but they are often quite irrational.
The career which he pictured for himself at Eton was not within
his grasp, upon any sober reckoning. He would have known
this if he had looked within—or without—for he had never had
many pupils and lamented it. But he might have found in himself reasons for some confidence in what Time would show. He
was cultivating gifts which entitled him to more than a schoolmaster's career, and he must have felt it. But at this period of
his life a profound diffidence did not allow him to admit it.

5

Hertford College

I EXTERNALS

Almost every studious man has been attracted by the prospect of being a Fellow of a College at Oxford or Cambridge. The closely guarded precincts, the walks and pastures, the quiet, the detachment, the freedom from domestic cares, the nearness of congenial company, the great libraries, and for some the existence of the undergraduates, are splendid amenities which cannot be had elsewhere all in one place. And yet on the whole the life is a disappointing one. The dons enjoy themselves for the most part, yet they could hardly be called a happy set of men. Perhaps it is that most studious people, if they were happy, would not be studious. To be sure the climate of the old places of learning in England, Eton and Winchester, Oxford and Cambridge, makes one suspect that the Anglo-Saxons are so unbookish that they will only study when they feel slightly ill. But perhaps it is that happiness is less common than we pretend. In any case it would be difficult to think that the Fellows of a College, taken as a set, are as happy as the schoolmasters at a school of any standing comparable to that of an Oxford or Cambridge College or as the same number of stockbrokers taken almost at random. It would be interesting to enquire from men who had been dons and had then gone to some different life whether they were happier or less happy in the change, but it would be necessary to enquire also from those who remained dons how far they regretted it—or were they perfectly satisfied.

In the old days when a Fellowship was forfeited on marriage, there was of course a fairly constant exodus from College, very often to a College Living. The old Common Room betting books show the great interest that was felt as to the double prospect of a College Living falling vacant and Mr So-and-so getting married. Now the almost universal rule is that no one shall be either eligible or ineligible for election to a Fellowship by reason of his being either married or not married. But it does not seem to have made a great deal of difference. The composition of most Senior Common Rooms changes rapidly. If a Fellowship looks like a kind of nest, it is a nest from which the cuckoo of ambition or boredom or ill-health or what seems the need for the fresh air of real life expels the occupant often enough, and the University only sees him again as a rare and ever rarer visitant.

At Hertford College certain Fellowships which had to be forfeited on marriage were retained for some years after they disappeared from the other Colleges, and it was to one of these Fellowships that Inge was elected. He held it for nearly sixteen years, during which he acquired a great deal of learning in new fields and a reputation as a preacher and an exponent of Christian mysticism. His gifts and his disposition were developed and tested in many ways both by circumstances and by his own interior life, and although these cannot always be kept distinct, the external influences had better be dealt with first. The years at Hertford, though not eventful, are the formative time in the Dean's life.

His work as a tutor consisted in taking the candidates for Honour Moderations in classics. The syllabus covered the traditional curriculum of pure scholarship at an advanced level. He corrected compositions in Latin and Greek which his pupils brought to him weekly, and a piece of unseen translation. He gave occasional essays, and he lectured regularly on some subject required in the examination. This was normally taken in a man's fifth term, and he would then go on to Philosophy and Ancient History (Greats) for his finals. The scholars of Hertford would often not be among the very best in the University and there were not a great number of them, but the average number of Firsts in Honour Mods. each year was two, and in relation to the number of undergraduates at Hertford this would be quite a fair share. One year there were four. It cannot, however, be said that Mr Inge made a great impression on his pupils. The earlier ones thought he had come to do

more for the later ones, and the later ones had just the opposite
idea, nor do the later ones seem to have had much notion that
he was now becoming a distinguished person. The fact is that
achievement in pure scholarship seems to be a natural gift, and
very difficult to impart, especially by one who has not found
much difficulty or needed much teaching himself. The corrections on some of the compositions shown up by Inge's pupils
are jejune.[1] It is possible that he was better remembered by the
undergraduates as a games-player.

As a lecturer he was both diligent and versatile. He began
in the Summer Term of 1889 with a weekly lecture on Critical
and General Questions. This was a Saturday morning lecture,
and he gave it in some form or other almost all the time he was
at Oxford. From 1890 onwards he seldom lectured less than
four times and not infrequently as much as six times a week.
Apart from expounding a prescribed book, rather often Demosthenes, he dealt with the history of the Greek Drama, and also
of Roman Poetry. After 1894 he confined himself mainly to
these two subjects. It is curious to find almost no interest in
either subject in his writings. From 1898 he lectured regularly
on Lucretius, an author whom he often quoted for the rest of
his life. Perhaps the most noticeable item in his programme is
a course given three times a week on the Gospel of St John
which he announced for the Lent term in 1903 and 1904. These
lectures on Lucretius and St John indicate a transference of
interest which was being slowly effected over much of his time
at Oxford. He himself acknowledged a loss of interest in classical
scholarship. By 1903 his lectures on Roman Poetry did not
seem to arouse much enthusiasm in his audience nor in the
lecturer himself; he addressed, or looked as if he addressed, the
pictures on the dais in Hertford Hall and did not mind if they
heard or not. Nevertheless a pupil of his who got a First in
Honour Mods. attended the last time he delivered this course
and liked it and found it useful, and recorded in his diary that
one of the lectures—on Catullus—was the best he had heard.[2]
But everything shows that this classical tutor was replacing his
former studies by much wider and more significant ones,
though no one ever disputed his skill in Greek and Latin
composition, a skill long unexercised but undiminished when

he wrote his beautiful Latin elegy on his little daughter Paula in 1924.

The College in its present form was scarcely fifteen years old when Inge was elected Fellow and Tutor, but it had already attracted some men of distinction to its Fellowships. Prominent amongst the seniors was a great classical teacher J. Y. Sargent, who had in fact examined for the Newcastle at Eton when Inge got it in 1879. Amongst Inge's contemporaries the most notable were the philosopher Hastings Rashdall who presently migrated to New College, where he had been an undergraduate, and H. A. Prichard, later on one of the Professors of Philosophy. A rather younger man was H. H. Williams, subsequently Principal of St Edmund Hall and then Bishop of Carlisle, still happily among us in 1960. In the preface to his Bampton Lectures to all these three Inge expresses his thanks for having read and criticised parts of the work. In Rashdall he found a philosopher who greatly stimulated him, and they remained friends till Rashdall's death in 1924. Williams was also a congenial companion, and they went several tours on the Continent together. In 1894 Lord Hugh Cecil (afterwards Lord Quickswood) joined the College, and those who knew either of them will easily believe that the conversations between Lord Hugh and Inge are said to have been memorable. In a circle of more than two or three Inge did not usually say much, partly because he did not hear much, but what he said was often striking, not infrequently devastating. His deafness was always somewhat troublesome, and he thought it was increasing while he was in Oxford. Nevertheless he attended meetings and discussions; in 1899 he attended many, and only of one of them does he complain in his diary that he could not hear it. He was at one period in considerable request as an after dinner speaker at the Tyndale Society, one of the more serious undergraduate college societies.

Although he did not hold any College office except that of a Tutor, he took his share in College business. In 1894 he was appointed on a Committee of four to enquire into College expenditure, and in 1898 on a small Committee about new buildings. He was a pro-proctor in the proctorial year 1903–4. He interested himself actively at one point in the re-distribution of the Fellowships and circularised a printed memorandum. He records his annoyance once with the Principal, and occasionally found Rashdall "fractious" and Lord Hugh Cecil "obstructive" at College meetings. He experienced once "a state of morbid mental excitement over college business." But on the whole he worked amicably with the team, and the College was tranquil under the chairmanship of Dr Henry Boyd, the Principal, a man whom everyone could respect.

Inge must have spent a good deal of time over his duties as tutor, but in his diary he often reproaches himself for idleness. He had rather curious views about reading, especially as he read so much and so widely all his life. Looking back over 1893 he believed he had "read far too much, thought and written too little." And at the end of the next year he had the same story to tell: "Reading is at present my most vicious habit! Indulged to excess it destroys the sensitiveness of the brain to new impressions and its retentiveness of old ones. . . . Writing will I think provide the discipline which I most need now."

It would be quite wrong, however, to think of the Dean as anything of a bookworm. The diaries reveal a remarkable and in some ways unexpected range of pastimes. He played whist in College, of which he thought there was too much, and billiards with relations and the Principal. Even tiddly-winks gets a mention. And any picture of him would be very incomplete which did not describe his activities out of doors. He played games a great deal, more particularly lawn tennis and cricket, but also real tennis, hockey, croquet, bowls, and golf. He ran and skated. He won tennis tournaments at Oxford frequently, often with his brother or sister. Sophy is said to have been a remarkably good player. His entries about cricket include "Given out lbw wrongly" on 4 August 1888; on 20 July 1889 "I kept wicket—a new experience." In June 1891 he was reading W. G. Grace on "Cricket." On 26 May 1892 he made 53 runs at Radley. His account of this is worth noting. "A most attractive day. Cricket at Radley against the school for Lys' scratch. Though I had not touched a bat for (I think) three years I made 53, including a 6 over the pavilion, and 2 or 3 fours. The whole side only made 127. The unexpectedness of this success made it the more delightful. On the whole it has been the pleasantest day I remember." The *Radleian* from the opposite angle said, 'At first in their innings everything went well with us. But with Inge and his partner our bowling was hit to every quarter of the ground.'

On 1 November 1890 he went to see Horace Hutchinson play golf, and he had some lessons in the game. He took long rides on his tricycle, sometimes with his colleagues. One would have liked to see him and Hastings Rashdall, so different in appearance, each with his own incipient philosophy of religion in his bosom, issuing forth together for a spin in April 1891. It was not till 1896 that he could go about on a bicycle "with tolerable safety and confidence." On 14 October he bicycled in the street for the first time.

He kept a dog as early as 1885, but on 4 September 1894 he wrote, "poor Reaver was killed on Tuesday by order of an ignorant vet. who mistook his epilepsy for rabies. The dog had been a faithful and affectionate friend to me for nine years, and I shall miss him very much." In September 1896 he bought a collie pup from Ormskirk for five guineas. Before the end of his time at Oxford he had somewhat abated his games-playing, but long walks were a great pleasure.

On his holiday tours he was easily aroused to enthusiasm. In 1890 in Guernsey he found himself running, jumping, and singing like a child, and 1894 was a particularly exhilarating year. In the spring he was at Bellagio, "the most lovely place I have ever seen," then at Venice where St Mark's is "the most interesting place I have ever seen," "the Piazza is, I suppose, the finest square in the world." In July he walked from Ambleside to Fairfield, "the best mountain walk that I have ever made."

He was evidently fond of sight-seeing, and the spectacles were varied. One day he went up to London and visited the Royal Academy exhibition which he describes as "very poor."[3] He went on to an exhibition of instruments of torture in Regent Street which he found interesting. Another time he visited Huntley and Palmer's biscuit factory, another time the (then) new Roman Catholic cathedral in Westminster. At Queen Victoria's Diamond Jubilee in 1897 the Principal gave him a ticket for a place on the West Portico of St Paul's Cathedral. The Queen was in her carriage just below the steps. He took the 2.55 a.m. train arriving at Paddington at 4.40, and walked across the Park and all the way to the Cathedral. It was particularly fine weather, what in those days had come to be called "Queen's weather." The Service of Thanksgiving and the Procession he described as "very splendid." He got back to Oxford again the same evening.

In what are now called cultural activities he did not take a great part, but he does not seem to have disliked music as he came to do later. He enjoyed the carols on Christmas Eve at Magdalen in 1890, and again in 1892. Ten days before that he had been to the school concert at Eton and thought it about the nicest concert he had ever heard. One of his early interests was in eugenics, on which he came in time to think strongly and to write extensively. He had attended discussions on it at Eton, and in 1891 shows interest in heredity and population, and the next year in an article on the subject by Arthur Lyttelton. In fact he read anything that he happened to come across that bore upon it. This is worth recording, because it is sometimes said that he owed this interest to his acquaintance with Sir Francis Galton. In fact he first met Mr Galton, as he was then, in July 1899, and under circumstances which had no direct connection with eugenics.

More and more, as time went on, and with much misgiving, he was drawn into the social life of Oxford. He had a home in the Provost's house at Worcester College until almost the end of his time, and when the Provost died in 1903 his mother and sister came to live at 29 Holywell, close to his rooms in Hertford. He went to dine at home fairly often, and stayed at home during the vacation, especially in the winter, but he complains that it was dull. He occasionally looked in for a short time at a dance, and occasionally he says he shirked one. In College he entertained his pupils in small parties which were sometimes not altogether successful; the young men found it hard to think of something to say, but if the company was congenial, things went well. Tennis too brought him into varied company, and croquet also, but he was apt to indulge in fits of impatience, expressed too freely in word and deed,

E   *Dean Inge*

and afterwards deeply regretted. He sometimes thought he must give up games altogether.

Perhaps the most interesting development in his make-up during his time at Oxford was the way in which he began to take notice of young women, of whom one suspects that he was almost unaware until he was past thirty. It is true that he had only been in college at Hertford for just a year when he cal-culated that he might get married in ten years' time and might have seven thousand pounds by then, but he does not seem to have had anything in particular in view. It was in the autumn of 1892 in the University tennis club tournament (a vacation affair) that he had a partner whom he described as "about the prettiest and most lively girl I have ever met, and quite the best lady player I have seen." Three days later they had won the tournament, and he believed he was very nearly in love. Nothing came of this, but at the end of the year he noted that he was getting a little restless at Oxford. "I should like some promotion which would give me a house of my own, and I *think* a wife." He came to notice quite a number of pretty girls throughout the years 1892, 1893, 1894 in the most charming way, they were so nice and so pretty. Of one of them there is a glimpse which is of interest for its own sake. It was at a luncheon party given by Mr and Mrs Lys in November 1894, to which they had invited Mr Blakiston, Mr Inge, and Miss Rogers. All five of them were great characters, but none of them particularly easy. To make up the party there was a girl from Lady Margaret Hall. This is Mr Inge's impression of her: "The lady undergraduate behaved with an odd sort of *camaraderie*, is rather slangy, and not in the least shy or 'feminine,' but I don't know that she is any the worse for that." At Oxford in 1894 this must pass as a pleasingly liberal view of a young lady. And the writer of it *was* liberal. In March 1896 he voted for the proposal that women should be eligible for the B.A. degree, but it was lost by 215 votes to 140.

Unhappily very early in 1897 he proposed to a young woman at Bordighera. She was quite suitable from the social point of view, and after twelve days she accepted him. Before the end of April she had disengaged herself. The rejected lover found consolation in the thought that she had treated him badly, but later he thinks that to cease to love is like being thrust out of heaven. He did not break away entirely. There was an intermittent but not infrequent series of letters and meetings, and it seems clear that the lady kept him on a string. She wrote to him on one occasion that she had lost all her looks and high spirits: but five months later she sent him a new photograph of herself. He, on the other hand, after feeling more than once that he had done with her and was heartily glad of it, would write again and so prolong the friendship—and then much regret it. But in the end it was no more, or not much more, than friendship, though even as late as April 1902 they spent three hours together, and he entered in his diary, "It was very nice, but I don't quite know what either of us is driving at."

The business was not entirely regrettable. It had cost him much. In the middle of 1901 when his colleague Williams got engaged, he could not bear to write to him about it because it recalled his troubles of four years ago, until Haselfoot, another colleague, made him. But he had learned to keep love in its right place, though rather later in life than most men. It coincided with increasing reputation from other interests with which no doubt he had diverted himself. When he made his very successful marriage in 1905, he and his bride, as it happened, took up their residence six doors from his earlier love.

The fits of depression which he often records were a constant affliction during all these years, but they belong more properly to his interior life. But something may be said here of his attitude to money, which often looked rather peculiar. No doubt he had been brought up in a house where there was domestic economy and not merely the science of domestic economy, and where also he found much to give him the idea that it was proper in a clergyman's family not to be sumptuous. The Rector of Crayke would find it necessary to have a carriage and pair to go the twelve miles to York and back, just as the present Rector may think it necessary to have a car, and he might possibly have had wine on the table twice a day. The curate would have at least a pony and cart, and probably another pony or two for his children. A wagonette was available. But in many ways the housekeeping in both houses would be, judged by present standards, remarkably economical. The eldest child, being a good child—and the eldest—learnt the lesson of economy well, and other old-fashioned notions too, as that you could not get married unless you could make some adequate settlement on your wife.

Saving for a very young man is usually difficult. It was in 1889 when he was twenty-nine that Inge was reckoning that he might have £7,000 in ten years' time, but he must have prospered more than he reckoned, for two years later he thought he might have £9,000 by the time he was forty. In 1895 his net surplus for the year was £734, but he wished he could invest it at better interest. In 1899 he seems to have saved nearly £1,000, but this would include a first payment for his Bampton Lectures, probably amounting to £200. As he became more and more distinguished he naturally had many opportunities of earning a great deal of money by writing, and he is said to have made hard bargains with publishers. He could justify himself by saying that he had a wife and five children to provide for over a considerable period, and that the author was the most important element in the production of books and newspapers anyway: and further, he was always very anxious to reach a large circle of readers, and the fact that publishers and editors were willing to pay him well raised a strong presumption that they thought many would be anxious to read what he wrote. Dr Johnson scarcely overstated the case when he said that 'No man, but a blockhead, ever wrote except for money.'

On the expenditure side the Dean was very careful, perhaps over careful. He was very seldom in a vehicle plying for hire, unless when he was offered a lift. Very late in life, when he was paying what was perhaps his last visit to Jesus College, Cambridge, and was well on in his eighties, he was seen by Dr C. H. Dodd, a professorial Fellow, carrying his bag and walking from the station—and what a long way it is! Dr Dodd got him into a taxi at once and conveyed him to College. For a good part of their London days the Dean and Mrs Inge kept no car, and used the public transport service whenever it was at all possible.

He complained often of extortionate charges in College, but what Fellow of a College has not? Nor was it really the bills that he was protesting against, but rather that men should be found to charge too much, and equally that men should be willing to eat too much. When the Founder of Hertford gave a lunch to the Fellows, the diary describes it as "a sumptuous and wasteful entertainment," and when he dined at Drapers' Hall he said it was "an interesting experience, but I cannot think such expenditure morally justified." He was in fact much more indifferent to food and drink, and comfort in general, than people ordinarily are. But if he went to a feast he expected it to be properly done.

The whole question was for him a moral one. In his little work called *Types of Christian Saintliness* (Longmans, 1915, p. 62) he wrote: "A touch of austerity for the sake of austerity—a preference for the simple, unwasteful life, is grievously needed. The new Evangelicalism need not be hostile to Art, it need not be prim, morose, or dowdy: but it should be willing to endure hardness, not in order to keep Church rules—nor to help the poor, but from a conviction that the simple life is the right life for a Christian, who is a pilgrim and a soldier on active service." The author of these words was willing to practise what he preached. He was a Puritan. Waste of time, he said, was the worst kind of extravagance, and waste of money was an urgent matter of conscience. He was serious about them. He may not always have realised that in normal social relations there must sometimes arise situations in which it is necessary to be seen to spend money when it might be saved.

Nor is it possible to tell what a man may contribute in private charity who does not care to spend money on himself. In 1896 he had promised £500 towards a new chapel at Hertford, and in 1902 he offered half his Fellowship for the next four years, "ultimately for the new Chapel, but the buildings fund to have the use of the money." On one occasion he sent £10 to a scholar of the College who was said to be in pecuniary difficulties; it was returned with a warm letter of thanks. A man who is capable of such acts of liberality is capable of more.

6
Hertford College

II INTERIOR LIFE

By interior life I mean the part of the Dean's life which was detached from contact with other people, mainly comprised therefore in his reading, thinking, and writing. In the years at Oxford his reading changed from the classics to the Neo-platonists and Mystics and to anything that might interpret them. His thinking changed from philology to philosophy and theology. His writing, to put it more objectively, changed from school books to Bampton Lectures and the like. At the same time his academic repute changed to public recognition, and a more or less fixed attitude of resignation turned to hopes and conscious aims. This is what I want to trace. Other people will come into the story, but only as influences on the Dean's mind.

Looking back on the past the Dean said that he had very good health. In Oxford he suffered from colds, as most do who reside there, and at times he had bouts of neuralgia lasting even a fortnight or three weeks. In February 1898 he had a day in bed for the first time since he had had the measles, and that was in March 1872. Interiorly, however, he certainly suffered, often severely, from morbid excitement and depression while he was at Hertford. There was sometimes a definite reason for this; on one occasion, as we have seen, it was vexation over College business; but it seems most often to have had little correspondence with his situation or circumstances, and to be what should be called temperamental or nervous or psycho-physical. He was capable of rather enjoying himself and feeling deeply dejected at the same time. The intense regret he felt at leaving Eton did not prevent him entering in his diary on 12 June 1889, that is to say just towards the end of his second term at Hertford, "I wish to record that I have never, so far as I remember, been so well and so uniformly happy as in the last six months: every day this term has been a treat to me."

His deafness was naturally discouraging, especially perhaps in a place where talking and being talked to are the commonest form of entertainment. He was frequently inclined to be despondent about it. He felt the handicap socially, and as damaging to his prospects. He felt isolated. He says sadly in 1892: "People don't seem to want me." The next year he imagined he had no friends even at Nearwell, where in fact he had many kind friends and relations and was really happy. In the Long Vacation of 1897 after playing with the children of a colleague he says: "Thank God for giving me these little friends, when I have so few." The diary, however, does not bear out this complaint of isolation. A scholar must necessarily be much alone, but this one got asked out often enough, and often enough he accepted the invitation. Nor had he much cause to be depressed about his prospects. His progress towards preferment was quite steady, as we shall see. Fairly soon he got an idea that the mere student life is empty and inadequate. He was often thinking that all his colleagues were against him. But his deepest depression was about his own faults. Though 1895 had been a happy year he professes to be aware of "my social defects, intellectual limitations and physical weakness." But his expectations in these respects must have outrun any reasonable standard. He was undersized, so he said, until he left school, but after that he was of average height and capable of physical feats beyond the average at all periods of his life. And his intellectual interests were widening enormously. Yet in summarising the year 1899, even when he acknowledges that the great interest of the year was the Bampton Lectures, he wishes he was dead, and it was not the first time he had wished it.

It is not easy to say whether such depressions as these are a blessing or a curse. They belong very largely to the first half of life, and it cannot be denied that they are very trying. But they may be very stimulating too; the sufferer from depression is often capable of great enthusiasm and energetic action, and Inge certainly was. He could rise to a great elevation of spirit because he could sink into great dejection. He was what he was and he achieved what he achieved just because it was not his nature to go tranquilly along, though by grace he had learned, or rather had retained, a habit of work, and had disciplined his convictions and his misgivings alike into a steady concentration on things as they appeared to him to be. His depressions gradually lifted—his sense of isolation only when he married, his sense of failure when he realised what he wanted to do and that he had the ability to do it.

In 1906, at a very happy period of his life, he commented on all this, no doubt with his own case in view:

> I believe that if we took our tone more from our Lord's own word, and from the proportion observed in His teaching, we should get rid of certain exaggerations which to some appear distressing and to others unreal. I will even go so far as to say that we should sometimes resist, and check by our reason, those fits of intense self-reproach which are a common experience of the devotional life. These feelings move in great rhythms— persons of a nervous and emotional temperament are now exalted to heaven and now thrust down to hell. The recluse especially, of whom it may be said, as of Parnell's 'Hermit' that 'Prayer [is] all his business, all his pleasure praise,' suffers these fluctuations of feeling in their fullest severity. But the man who is leading a normal active life ought not to do so; and the expressions, whether of union or of alienation, which a Suso or a John of the Cross could utter honestly, would certainly not be wholesome, and would probably be unreal, in the mouth of an ordinary good Christian. (*Personal Idealism and Mysticism*, pp. 168, 169.)

It is possible to trace intermittently his progress in philosophy and religion, and it is relevant to start by recalling his careful home training in religion and how some of it stuck to the Dean all his life. His prayers, his good resolutions, his Bible reading and his acceptance of the Church of England were learnt at home, as well as the conviction that a touch of austerity was an indispensable characteristic of the Christian life. At no time could he have been an Evangelical of the traditional type. But he was not the kind of person to accept any forms of thought without subjecting them to close examination, and as soon as he came to think for himself his conclusions led him mainly away from home. He seems not to have interested himself in theology until he had taken his degree, then he was attracted to the liberal side of it. He tells us that *Ecce Homo* and Matthew Arnold influenced him in the direction of honest doubt. The effect was rather distressing. "My father took my heresies philosophically: but my mother could not forgive my defections and I fear never did really forgive me."

It was in his early years at Hertford that he came for the first time to be in touch with good philosophers and theologians—not that Cambridge was deficient in them, but he would be unaware of most of them except as preachers, when he was an undergraduate. It was a time at Oxford when Christian socialism was emerging, and he noted almost directly that Aubrey Moore's philosophy was Christian but led to socialism, and socialism continued to crop up. In October 1893 he speaks one day in his diary of Strong's *Manual of Theology* (which has generally been regarded as a dull but innocuous work) raising religious difficulties, and the next day he thinks liberal churchmanship is untenable and asks if he must attach himself more to the socialistic party of Gore, and the next day again, arising out of Liddon's *Life of Pusey*, he remarks that "the afterwash of Puseyism is Gore's semi-rationalistic socialism." He rejected Christian socialism and all socialisms ever after.

At the same time he was reading modern philosophers. He had not at this period of his life a high opinion of Aristotle and Greek philosophy in general. In 1892 he began to read John Caird and says he understood better the metaphysical objection to materialism. The next year Lotze's *Outlines of a Philosophy of Religion* stimulated comments and led him to maintain objective reality. As he had never had any instruction in theology or philosophy, he could only feel his way tentatively and somewhat hesitatingly towards positions which he might occupy.

It was a piece of good fortune that he took up residence at Hertford the very same term as Hastings Rashdall, two years his senior in age, with similar interests but a rather different education, by profession a philosopher, by pursuit a historian, a convinced liberal in theology, and most valiant for truth. They had much to give one another, for they approached—one might almost say attacked—life with the same ideals, in spite of wide divergence in their philosophical and theological conclusions. A *bon mot* of the time asserted that Rashdall could not believe that Christianity was true but wished it was, while Inge believed it was true and wished it was not. The actual situation, which evoked this witticism deserves a short analysis. Rashdall was strongly, almost exclusively moralist and intellectualist, certainly no mystic. Inge was by temperament mystical and intuitive. Rashdall thought out certain ethical principles by which he claimed that every speculation must be guided and judged. Inge had strong convictions, which came to him by way of what might be called intimations, and he then sought for arguments by which to maintain them. Rashdall's most comprehensive article of belief was in the reality of individual conscious minds or spirits: what Inge stood by was the evidence of the mystical experience in its broad diffusion. Rashdall complains in a letter to Claude Montefiore of 'a tendency on the part of our extreme Liberal Theologians to make Immortality into absorption with the Absolute (which to me means nothing).' Inge on the other hand regarded individual minds as activities and projections of the One mind with which they must be united in order to realise themselves. Rashdall was far better equipped to criticise Inge than Inge was to criticise Rashdall, though this would not, of course, justify the conclusion that he had got hold of more or greater truths. They both loved and wooed ladies called Truth, but they were different ladies.

When they took up residence at Hertford, they had neither of them reached a settled theology or philosophy, but they were tending towards these different positions. Circumstances had brought Rashdall considerably further on his way. Inge had hardly read the Mystics at all, never read Plotinus until 1895, and is only able to declare at last in September 1897: "I have hammered out my philosophy and know exactly what kind of a life I wish to live." But one can see how these tendencies would end in the *bon mot*. Rashdall wished that Christianity was true and was a dutiful Anglican priest, but he could not entertain the notion of an omnipotent God, because God must be bound by certain moral necessities, besides being alongside of and not over other individual thinking minds, nor could strict justice admit of a vicarious redemption from sin. But he seemed to wish that he could break through these necessities, though in fact they were compatible with his Christianity. Inge on the other hand extracted from Plotinus a system which satisfied him. To this system he always attached the doctrine of the Incarnation as completing the system and elevating Christianity above Neoplatonism, but it looked to some of those who heard him and read him as a rather uncomfortable addition, as though, if he were less a Christian, he would not have made it.

In spite of differences Rashdall and Inge respected each other's gifts, and often discussed things in a way which must have been useful. After Rashdall moved to Balliol in 1894, and then to New College in 1895, they would see less of one another, and in his Bampton Lectures Inge went his own way. But they were associated again under various circumstances later on.

Through the years at Hertford, then, Inge was coming to settle his beliefs. He came also, step by step, to see what he wanted to do. At the very end of his first year at Oxford as a classical tutor he remarked in his diary (29 December 1889) that he should like to do some theology. Two years later he resolves "to abandon minute classical research and to 'run myself' as a teacher and preacher, the goal a headmastership or high office in the church." He ran himself most successfully as a teacher and preacher, as the event showed, but if he pictured himself as a headmaster or even a bishop his ambition must have been somewhat thick-sighted. In the Christmas vacation, 1892–93, he got through a good deal of Moral Philosophy and Theology and found it useful to write reviews of the books he had read. In the August following he realised that he would never get a headmastership, but soon there was to come into view a much more definite objective. On 1 February 1894 he writes: "I mean to resume my studies in 2nd and 3rd century literature and history—for a book or Bamptons."

It was a decision of far-reaching importance if he had known it, and the signs of this appeared at once. For on the next day he says he had found a religious philosopher who completely satisfied him. So he described Marcus Aurelius, and five days later he did "a good day's work on Renan's *Marc Aurèle*." By the end of the year he saw before him "a possible career as a man of letters." Characteristically he remarks that the prospect was grey, but he was thankful it was not black. In the middle of January 1895 he was perplexed, almost in despair. "If only I could find a good subject to write about—and ideas!" But it is darkest before the dawn. The very next day it occurred to him: "I must read Plotinus sometime." When he did so, it was to mean a very great deal to him, more perhaps than anything else he ever read outside the New Testament, more perhaps than that at times.

So we picture him studying the second and third centuries and interested in the Neoplatonists. But these studies now widened and narrowed at the same time. They widened because they came to embrace mysticism in many centuries, they narrowed because they concentrated on Christian mysticism. In 1895 he read small bits of Plotinus here and there. In April 1896 he resolved "to try to keep my mind on this subject—Christian mysticism, and write down all ideas that occur." In August the *Expositor* published an article of his on the Mystical Element in St Paul's Theology. The next year he became really set on the business. "Hoc age, you half-alive dreamer," he writes for his own good, "live in the present, though not for the present," and he shows some signs of Plotinian influence. Finally, in the middle of the Long Vacation, he comes to a settled purpose: "I am determined to make my reputation by this work on Christian mysticism, and also to make myself a good essay writer and preacher." It was no vain resolve. The first fruits of it were seen in a paper on 'The Permanent Influence of Neoplatonism on Christianity' finished in November 1897.

On 29 April 1898 he sent in his application to be Bampton Lecturer for 1899. No doubt he would have made some enquiries as to whether there were likely to be other more acceptable candidates, and had reason to think there were not, for he was much alarmed to hear four days later that the Bishop of Colombo (Copleston) had offered to preach them. "Now I am ship-wrecked." A week elapsed, and the Heads of Houses proceeded to an election. Mr Inge was successful with ten votes against three for the Bishop. He delivered the lectures in St Mary's Church on eight Sundays between 26 February and 4 June. The vacation intervened between the third and fourth, and this enabled him to go on a Hellenic cruise, from which he only arrived back on the day before the fourth lecture. He remarks that the last lecture was well received and there was a large congregation. Six weeks later he sent the MS. to the publisher (Methuen), and the volume was out at the end of October under the plain title *Christian Mysticism*.

The year after the delivery of the Bampton Lectures he seems to have diminished his quota of writing, and he spent a good deal of his time and interest upon the College. It does not appear that there was any official Chaplain at Hertford at this time, but on 1 March 1900 he inaugurated a College Church Society with a successful meeting at which Rashdall read a paper on 'Apostolical Succession.' In May he had a lunch to talk over the Church Society, and there were two good meetings during the summer term, and others in the following year. In the year after that it was still successful. He read a paper on 'Physicians of Souls and Bodies' himself. He also held services of preparation for Holy Communion which met with some support. Of outside activities a paper on the 'Theologia Germanica' at Holy Trinity, Sloane Street, on 4 March 1900, shows that his reputation as an authority on Christian Mysticism had reached London. In Oxford also he now came in for some recognition. In July 1901 he gave three lectures on the Logos doctrine to about eighty clerics, no doubt at a Vacation Course. In October he was appointed "Catechist" at Exeter College, entailing some special preaching. The next year in December he regarded it as "a gratifying compliment" that he was nominated by Dr Sanday as Chairman of the Oxford Committee of the Christian Evidence Society. This month was in fact an important one for him. He was asked by Canon Hensley Henson, the Rector of St Margaret's, Westminster, to preach a Lenten course at St Margaret's. Canon Henson was spending a Sunday in Oxford, and on the Monday Inge wrote as follows in his diary:

"Henson strongly advised me to give up my classical teaching and devote myself entirely to theology. He thought I might exercise a real influence and hope to get one of the London canonries. This is what I should like better than anything else; and the idea of giving up my teaching grows upon me. I am never well at Oxford: I take no further interest in classics, and I feel myself that with freedom to take infinite pains I have it in me to write and preach as well as any of my contemporaries." Canon Henson with that great gift of his had cleared his friend's mind and crystallised his ambitions. A fortnight later a practical question reinforced some of what he had said. "The Dean of Wells asks me to conduct a Quiet Day for the clergy of the diocese at the beginning of October. Wrote to accept; but these demands upon my time are getting too much for me: I shall have to let classics drop." But his ambitions also took on a new and less emulous look, as he summed up the year 1902. "In spite of my increasing ear trouble I have received enough recognition to feel that my life may be worth something to my generation."

7
Hertford College

III AUTHORSHIP

The Dean's life was not of the sort which people generally have in mind when they speak of an eventful life, but the publication of the Bampton Lectures in 1899 was an event of importance to the lecturer and to English Christianity. Though Charles Bigg had given the lectures on 'The Christian Platonists of Alexandria' in 1886 which his successor in 1899 described as "known all over Europe," and had followed them up in 1895 with a good account of *Neo-Platonism* (S.P.C.K.), the subject of *Christian Mysticism* was not a familiar one. It is true to say that in the first two decades of the twentieth century a great group of people who aspired to a little culture and a little Christianity were reading the English mystics and talking however inaccurately about mysticism, and that they owed this interest entirely to Inge's Bamptons. The author had performed an immensely difficult and worthwhile task. He had read and digested and extracted and ordered a body of ancient authors, all strange and many of them obscure, and had created a demand for their works. He speaks, for instance, of "the beautiful but little known *Revelations* of Juliana of Norwich"; they were widely known a very few years after. The Lectures themselves were re-issued in a cheaper edition in 1912.

The author seems to apologise in the Preface for adopting an historical method, when his purpose was to present "a philosophy and a rule of life," but he did well in guiding people back to his sources. The most impressive thing about the book is its almost entirely religious character. There is very little of art or politics or sociology or even dogmatic theology in it; it is all about God, and man in relation to God. Science is only touched upon because science has its own view of the

world. The book has also one really great external advantage.
It gets easier as it proceeds, and in this respect it is unlike a
great many of the Bampton Lectures and other works of the
same class which are apt to erect a great scaffolding, but somehow the superstructure topples down at the last, and the truth
eludes the lecturer and his audience. This was perhaps true of
N. P. Williams's *Ideas of the Fall and of Original Sin* and of
Sanday's attempts to write the Life of Christ, good as they
both were. But Inge was a very judicious writer. He had a
very good idea of what could be dealt with successfully, and
where the natural boundaries of the subject lay. He allows in
his Bamptons, for example, that "the function of evil in the
economy of the universe is an inscrutable mystery" (p. 120)
and that "the reciprocal action of spirit and matter is the one
great mystery which to all appearance must remain impenetrable
to the finite intelligence" (p. 258). He often comes to a point
where he says an author or a theme he has referred to does
not belong to the subject under discussion, or cannot be
profitably discussed. This, I think, is characteristic of all his
writings, and is already seen here in the first of his major
works.

The book is very largely descriptive, and a great number of
authors are dealt with, most often by way of quotation. Where
the quotations are brief and numerous, they are apt to dazzle,
but the comments on them are to the point and put them in
their place precisely. A philosophy of mysticism hardly emerges
quite clearly, but what mysticism is not is told in great variety,
and likewise what it must have to show, if it is to be mysticism
at all. At the end, when the lecturer tries to sum up his own
convictions, he does not succeed completely, though much of
what he says is moving. He believed that the world at the time
when he was delivering the Lectures was in need of this particular approach to religion, and there is much to make one
think he was right. The one unaltered basis of his own religion
was that the experience of the presence of God was vouched
for in quite different times, places, and religions in the same
terms, and he thought this afforded an unassailable position,
which could hold out when the old seats of authority, the
Church and the Bible, were so fiercely assailed. He thought,

too, that there might be an approach to the scientific mind by the presentation of the spiritual world which the mystic believes to be the reality that makes this world significant. This theme underlay almost all his subsequent teaching and preaching, and almost half a century later at the age of eighty-eight he expounded it again at about the same length with great lucidity and riper conviction in *Mysticism in Religion*, a most extraordinary performance.

Not the least valuable contribution to learning and religion made by *Christian Mysticism* was that it compelled the author to put his knowledge and his opinions into order. He says in the Preface (p. vii): "Until I began to prepare the Lectures, about a year and a half before they were delivered, my study of the mystical writers had been directed solely by my own intellectual and spiritual needs." He began the writing presumably in the Long Vacation of 1897, and he must by then have had in his mind the fruits of wide and varied reading. To control it and present it, as he did, suggests a severe discipline, but it was a profitable one. He mastered the ordering of a book as a whole, the ordering of the different parts of it on an appropriate scale, the marshalling of details in a significant succession, and a style which left no doubt of the meaning and perpetually arrested attention.

Three years after the publication of the Bamptons in 1892 he played a great part in the appearance of a book of some importance. The project of a symposium by some Oxford dons of liberal views had been mooted. On 14 February in the previous year the essayists met at the house of Dr A. J. Carlyle, then well known as a philosophical historian and a theologian of independent mind. Inge noted that there were "amusing divergences and dissatisfactions with each other's heresies." The book *Contentio Veritatis* does not suggest that these were altogether resolved at subsequent meetings, but certainly no impasse was reached. In October Inge was looking over the proofs. The volume was published on 25 March 1902. "My book, *Contentio Veritatis*, came out to-day," he wrote in his diary. It is clear in what sense he called it "my book"; he had been responsible for dealing with the publisher and seeing it through the press. He had in general a very practical turn,

F   *Dean Inge*

where publishing was concerned, so that he probably fell imperceptibly into being the leader in this particular publication.

Of the contributors to the volume, described on the title page as 'Six Oxford Tutors,' Inge alone contributed more than one essay. The second of these, on 'The Sacraments,' though not lacking in definite statement, seems to reveal the author as sometimes in two minds. The first on 'The Person of Christ' shows him to great advantage. In it he was able to use his great gift for the historical exposition of theological ideas, and here perhaps he shows it more clearly, because more succinctly, than anywhere in the Bampton Lectures. The doctrine of development, the place of dogma in religion, miracles, the unique character of the Incarnation are discussed. Wide reading leading up to decided opinions distinguishes the essay, as it distinguished all his writing from this time onward. If there was a defect it lay in the way that a somewhat miscellaneous character was given to the essay, but that gave it also a kind of charm which theology often wants.

This was the second item in the book, and the first was by Hastings Rashdall on 'The Ultimate Basis of Theism.' The two essays afford an instructive contrast in the handling of themes which to some extent overlap. Rashdall, as was to be expected, shows himself much more strictly a metaphysician and a moralist. He keeps to his line of thought very steadily and his argument gains weight by accumulation. It lacks variety. It is impressive, but it is not very lively, which Inge's pages not infrequently contrive to be. An extract from each essay will show Inge's qualities reaching maturity, yet lacking somewhat in Rashdall's stronger gifts. Both passages are on the subject of miracles, which in 1902 was rather more perplexing than today.

On pp. 57, 58 (Rashdall):

It forms no part of my task, as I have said, to apply these considerations to the criticism of the Gospel narratives, but I will allow myself one concluding remark to prevent misunderstanding on the one hand or on the other. I believe that it will be found that a sober, historical criticism, based upon the principles here suggested, will leave us in a modified form the beliefs about Christ's Person which are most cherished among ordinary

Christians—notably (1) the general fact that much of his time was spent in the healing of physical disease by means of extraordinary spiritual capacities; (2) that after his death there occurred to his disciples visions of Himself which were not mere subjective delusions, and which confirm—for them and for us—the fact of his continued life and love for his followers. Belief in miracles, in the sense which is here in question, may not be wholly without spiritual value now. But we may be quite confident that for minds which have once appreciated the principles of historical criticism, or minds affected by the diffused scepticism which has sprung from historical criticism, neither religious faith in general, nor any doctrine of primary religious importance, will ever depend mainly upon the evidence of abnormal events recorded to have happened in the remote past. Criticism must be wholly free; though when it is seen that faith is independent of miracles, it may become less destructive on one side and less desperately apologetic on the other. Belief in God will rest in the long run upon the instinctive rejection of materialism by the common-sense of mankind, confirmed by the reflective analysis of the philosopher. Belief in his goodness will rest upon the testimony of the moral consciousness. For minds which dare not explain away or minimize the presence of evil in human life, belief in Immortality will be a corollary of that goodness.

On pp. 90, 91 (Inge):

Religion, when it confines itself strictly to its own province, never speaks in the past tense. It is concerned only with what is, not with what was. History as history is not its business. And abstract science, which concerns itself with the relations which prevail between phenomena, without reference to ultimate truth, is not its business either. Events or aspects of events, which relate *only* to the past, may be left to historians. Phenomena, or aspects of phenomena, which relate *only* to the material world, may be left to men of science. Errors in history, or errors in science, do not save or damn. Errors in religion are always due to what Plato calls "the lie in the soul"; but a man may believe in "Brute the Trojan," or in the philosopher's stone, without being a knave. Religion is a very practical matter: its object, as an intellectual faculty, is to see things as they are, not to discover how they came to be. This is not said to disparage the past, or to suggest that it is unimportant. The glacial age is extremely important to the engineer, seeing that it hollowed out the valleys through which he has to lay his road or railway; but a man may be a very good engineer and at the same time a very bad geologist. In the same way a religious genius may be a very bad historian, and know nothing of science. These subjects are not his business, and he is not really interested in them. When the theologian puts historical propositions into his creed, he does so because he is convinced that there are important truths, in the spiritual order, which are dependent on, or inseparable from, those events in the past. Let us then (to return to the particular topic which we are now considering) ask ourselves, What is the truth, in the spiritual order, which it is intended to protect by the doctrines of the virgin birth, resurrection, and ascension? The answer is plain: it is the identification of the man Christ Jesus with the Word of God.

A man's achievement in any particular intellectual field is very often enhanced by other interests which seem only indirectly connected with it or scarcely relevant at all. Such interests subsidiary to theology or philosophy might be in aesthetics or politics or history or mathematics or in natural science. The Dean does not seem to show any inclination for mathematics except where he thought certain statistics supported some contention he was maintaining; it is safe to say that he would not have cared to be a statistician. For history he had a natural talent of a high order and he cultivated it. He had the Englishman's special interest in politics, but he did not go in for political science except of his own making. He excelled in arresting comments upon society, many of which were just and some most unpopular. In natural science he had had no serious teaching, but his education and his own studies were designed to train his mind to distinguish sense and nonsense, and he was able to acquaint himself with the main direction in which the scientists were prosecuting their researches and to take their findings into account. Quite early on he felt it important to act on the supposition that we live in a world where miracles do not happen. He might have disallowed the notion that this was equivalent to saying that they never had happened.

In aesthetic experience he must on the whole be judged deficient. Scenery delighted him more than art. Aesthetics was one of the few things perhaps about which he did not think much. Even in literature his strong sense of style was not aesthetic. Writing is for him a tool with which to express his thoughts. It is everywhere most lucid, and that it could not be without craftsmanship, but the craftsmanship nowhere obtrudes itself, not so much because the writer was artful enough to conceal his art, but because the thoughts he wished to express were themselves clear as crystal, and where the matter tended to grow difficult he stopped. The whole effect of his writing does give a certain aesthetic pleasure to the reader, it is so neat and economical. But it is not beautiful writing nor even ornamental, though it must not be left unnoticed that it has beautiful quotations in it; but these are introduced not for their beauty, but for their testimony. As they often testify to the mystical experience in the various forms in which poets have met with it, or to the Platonic element which is strong in most of our great poets, the extracts often comprise some of the most famous lines in English. But this did not prevent the writer from putting in very commonplace verses, if they served his purpose. Of foreign poets Dante and Goethe were often requisitioned: the Greek and Roman classics here and there, of whom Lucretius seems most congenial. As a curiosity of taste and an indication perhaps of dejection it may be mentioned that in September 1893 Inge copied out and learnt by heart parts of Fitzgerald's *Omar Khayyam*. This suggests the formation of a commonplace book, and his writings as a whole give the impression that he had such a book and knew most of it by heart. Such a book does in fact exist, with 1,716 numbered extracts in it, inserted between 1886 and 1947. He was a better judge of prose than of verse, partly because it was an art in which he was a master, but also because the best prose is that which tells the most, and in proportion as it does so is the more acceptable to one who valued what he read for what it told him.

It was clear by the end of 1902 that Hertford College would not keep Inge much longer, and this became more certain still when his father died at Worcester College in May 1903. There had been a bond between them ever since long ago at Crayke; they had not only studied the classics together but enjoyed them, and this common interest had continued. Nor was there any tension between them over religious questions as there was between mother and son. The usual situation was in some respects reversed. Mrs Inge was a bracing influence as well as a loving mother; the gentle old Provost was a companion and a refuge. It is perhaps unusual therefore but not altogether surprising to find that the effect of losing his father was to make Inge wish to have a wife, and the path was perhaps a little easier, since he inherited from his father a property worth some £5,000. His ambition also was more clearly defined by the request in June of the same year that he should edit St John's Gospel for the International Critical Commentary series, a striking indication of the high standing he had now reached in the world of theology. He turned the offer down, however, after carefully considering it. "Too big a job; wd absorb all my leisure for about 4 years: Johannine problem probably insoluble, and I think unimportant: I should probably arrive at conclusions which wd not help my prospects: above all, I am not cut out for a commentator, and rather despise the breed, tho' St John is of course well worth spending years over. My literary ambitions lie in quite a different direction and, if they are to be realised, I must lose no time in beginning."

A useful piece of self-knowledge.

8

1904

Church life in London was very different at the beginning of the twentieth century from what it was to become fifty years later, and it always was very different in the East End from what it was in the West. The work of the clergy in East End parishes was astonishingly vigorous for many years from about 1870, mostly on Anglo-Catholic lines, though very successful evangelical churches and chapels also existed. But the work of the Church in the West End was more astonishing still, if rather less obviously Christian, and rather more at the mercy of fashion.

The area described as the 'East End' suggested to most minds a continuous and extensive built-up area stretching some miles east and north from Liverpool Street, and down to the river. 'The West End' was less easily defined. Its hard core always was in Mayfair, which meant most of the area bounded by Oxford Street, Regent Street, Piccadilly, and Park Lane. But fashion claimed extensions vaguely to the north, certainly to the south as far as Pall Mall, and from Knightsbridge nearly to Victoria, and in the second half of the nineteenth century this block tended to stretch further and further towards the west until it wavered and was stayed at Queen's Gate. It is interesting to think now of so many very large houses occupied by single families. It is interesting, too, to recollect in passing that in 1900 Smith Square, Westminster, was a slum, and the church of St Martin-in-the-Fields had a minute congregation.

The progress of fashion was reflected in the rise of fashionable churches, which exhibited their own particular brand of Christianity. The congregation in these churches was large, and consisted mainly of people who lived close by. They avoided having their carriages out on Sunday unless they were old or infirm. They rented their seats. They wore their Sunday clothes. They did not resent sitting through Mattins, Sermon, Litany, and

Ante-communion. They sat through most of it literally: they
seldom knelt; they assumed an attitude of devotion. They gave
not ungenerously to the collection, and on Hospital Sunday
there was a keen competition amongst several churches to send
in the largest collection. It sometimes exceeded £1,000. After
church on Sunday, if they were not far off, the worshippers
went and walked in Hyde Park for a space. This 'Sunday
parade' was a recognised institution. In the week quite a number of people would attend a 'missionary meeting': not so
many, but a goodly few, would go to a prayer meeting in a
private house. The incumbent and his wife were asked out to
formal and rather sumptuous dinner parties and were expected
to make afternoon calls. They would give dinner parties themselves, if they could manage it, but this was not necessary.
George Howard Wilkinson, a really holy man, who did a great
work at St Peter's, Eaton Square, before he went as Bishop to
Truro, made it a rule to dine out three times a week. He said
afterwards that if he had his time over again he would dine out
six times a week. The curates usually came to supper with their
vicar on Sunday. They were generally not much in the picture,
mainly for the reason that the best of the newly ordained were
at that time taking their title in the East End. Dr Winnington-
Ingram, who became Bishop of London in 1904, wielded an
enormous personal influence in every part of his diocese, but
his heart was in the East End and he never really succumbed
to the seductions of the West.

All this has disappeared. It was disappearing before Queen
Victoria died, and two generations later it looks not very
Christian. But a great deal of piety and sense of decency went
with it, and good works of a rather fumbling nature too. While
it lasted it presented the Church as an institution quite as powerfully as the Roman Church, though in an utterly different way.
It did not sow the seeds, but it did prepare the soil, for the
abdication of the ruling class, for Christian socialism, and the
welfare state. Those who exercised this peculiar ministry must
be commended. They preached Christian virtue, and they built
churches; unfortunately they forgot to endow them, when it
might have been possible to do so. They had what does now
seem rather an odd notion, that, if a man could not persuade

people to rent his pews and provide him with his livelihood, he must do something about it for himself. A great many incumbents had private means; a few of them still had proprietary chapels. At one of these which lasted well into the twentieth century, St George's Chapel, Albemarle Street, Evensong on Sunday was at 9 p.m., and the congregation were expected to be in evening dress.

It was a piece of very good fortune for the future Dean that his appointment to new work and his engagement to his wife occurred at the same time. Of course the two events were not wholly unconnected, but when he went about to find a means of escape from Hertford the opportunity of marrying was not his motive, at least not a conscious motive; on the other hand he was falling in love before he had secured a new appointment, and the appointment clinched the resolve to propose to Miss Kitty Spooner, and fortunately she accepted him.

In 1904 he was much in demand as a preacher. He preached in Westminster Abbey in February, at Lincoln's Inn in March, at St Paul's in April. London was becoming the natural place for him to migrate to. But at first he was not successful. He failed to get the Gresham Lectureship in Divinity, and after entertaining some expectations of the Rectorship of St Michael, Cornhill, he missed it. "I am now more disappointed than I like to own. I am getting very sick of life in College rooms, and this appointment would have suited me exactly in every way." But his record, striking as it was, did not give any certain ground for thinking that *he* would suit *it*. Although the residents are so few, there is work to be done in the City, where there have always been quite a large number of people who will attend a midday service once a week, or oftener, if it is the kind they like. But the City is a hearty place, and not very intellectual. It might cross someone's mind that Inge's gifts were better suited to the West End, and it did cross the mind of the Rector of St Margaret's, Westminster. He wrote to his friend on 7 September 1904:

Dear Inge,
    The living of All Saints, Ennismore Gardens will shortly be vacant, and as patron, I must find a Rector. There is a good

church in the Italian style, excellently appointed: and the ceremonial tradition is moderately 'High Church.' The congregation,
almost exclusively parochial, is aristocratic: there are no poor
save a few hangers on (coachmen and stableboys etc.) belonging
to the well-to-do residents. Thus the 'parochial work' is limited
to what may be described as 'friendly and sick visiting': and the
principal work is that of preaching. There is also a certain amount
of preparing candidates (mostly young ladies, whose brothers are
confirmed at school) for confirmation, and this is really important
as giving the Rector an opportunity of wielding spiritual influence
over a wider sphere than he can know. There is a good Rectory
quietly placed in a quiet street, and the income (mainly derived
from seat-rents) averages about £1,350 per annum. The contributions to the parochial expenses average (so the Rector assures me)
about £100 yearly at most. If you cared to take such a position
as this in London, and did not dislike the notion of parochial
work such as I have described, it would be a great personal
satisfaction to me to offer you the living. The present Rector—
Canon Ravenscroft Stewart—will not resign until Christmas, so
that we must maintain secrecy as to arrangement for the nonce.

Believe me,
Affect^{ly} yours
H. Hensley Henson.

The living was in fact not a Rectory; Canon Stewart was the
vicar. The letter reached its destination on 10 September, and
Inge wrote to accept the offer the next day. He reflected that
he would have "seven months in which to prepare for this great
change." And for another great change, too, as it happened.
Within a fortnight he was engaged to Kitty Spooner.

They were connected by marriage, for Ralph's uncle George
Inge had married Kitty's great aunt, so they both used to stay
at Walton near Stafford, where "Uncle George" was Rector. It
was a family living. Ralph began one of his visits on 16 September 1903, and Kitty arrived the next day, and made a favourable
impression on him. "She is a very bright clever girl, rather
mature for her years, which I guess to be about 21–2." He
entered no further remark on her in his diary, but five days
later, when he left, she drove him to the station. It is said that
she wrote home at first to say that Ralph Inge, who was staying
at Walton, was a very odd man, but a day or two later that he

was a delightful talker and they had got on famously. They do not seem to have met again till the following February when he went to stay with Archdeacon Spooner, Kitty's father, at Canterbury and to preach in the Cathedral. He describes the two daughters of the house "Kitty, whom I met at Walton, and Ruth, six years younger, a clever musician." The next day Kitty showed him round the Archbishop's house. It was only a week-end visit: he left the next day with the reflection, "If Kitty Spooner were rather older, or I rather younger, I should try my luck." In May Kitty and her mother came to stay with Dr William Archibald Spooner, "uncle Archie," newly installed in the Warden's lodgings at New College. It was Eights week and Ralph Inge took them to the races. In June at a reception at All Souls he had a talk with Kitty "whom I like immensely, but I am not in love." But was that really so? At any rate fate so contrived that, when in September he received and accepted Henson's offer of the living, he was on a nine days' visit to Walton, and Kitty was there too. And so it was only four days after that he began "to feel much harassed and perplexed about my relations with Kitty. *Ought* I to think of marrying her at my age, etc.? And am I, or can I be, properly in love with her? Of course if I go to London, it would be an unmixed gain to me to have such a helper as she would be." The next day there was a picnic on Cannock Chase, and he "had a long and confidential talk with dear Kitty. . . . I am beginning to love that dear girl: her brightness and cleverness are only the outside of a most beautiful character." The next day they had a most delightful walk. Two days later he left Walton in a state of some misgiving. But "it has been a very happy week, whatever comes of it." Two days later again he proposed to Kitty by letter, and she wrote back and accepted him. They had made no mistake: it turned out most wonderfully well. The course of true love could hardly run smoother. He hastened at once to Canterbury.

The last three months of the year 1904 were occupied with visits and preparations for departure from Oxford. Kitty came to stay with her future mother-in-law and Sophy at 29 Holywell, and then went on to New College for a week with her uncle and aunt in the Warden's lodgings. There were many acquaintances for her to make. The new Provost of Worcester, Mr Daniel, showed them over the Provost's lodgings which had been Ralph's home for so long. There was a corresponding visit to Canterbury for Christmas and the New Year when Ralph stayed partly with the Spooners and partly at the Old Palace with the Archbishop and Mrs Davidson. The Archbishop discussed his new work with him.

The new work of course occupied his thoughts and time very considerably. On 10 October he went to see Canon Stewart, and his account of what he gleaned during the visit is worth transcribing.

> To London to see Canon Stewart. A rubicund man about 60, looks like a bon vivant, but shrewd and kindly. Six sons, one daughter. *The house*—fine drawing room—dining room adequate— study v. poor—a dingy room at back might hold books—about seven bedrooms, none large—accom. for five servants—basement good. No bathroom or el. light. *The Church*—I like it very much. Apse profusely gilded—frescos newly done on walls. Seats 1,300. *Answers to questions. Curates*, paid by parish except £100. Senior, Cassidy, has got a living; junior Graham, weak in body and mind, he should only be kept for a short time to preserve continuity. Not easy to get good curates. *Ceremonial*—E.P. coloured stoles. Sermons, people are used to written sermons—they don't like strangers. Best congregations in morning. No special services for servants: the chief way of getting hold of them is in confirmation classes. *School*—complications at present. *The Choir*—not much information. *Offertories* nearly £2,000. Main objects—E. London, Bishop of London's fund, Hospital Sunday. *Register* of communicants to be kept if possible. *Poor-relief* in hands of Vicar; trustworthy Mission woman. *Collecting* at present done for £20 by an ex-churchwarden, but Rector thinks Verger would do it for £10. £50 out of Poor Fund for Mission Room. *The living*—Pew Rents £900, Endowment £116, Fees £70, Easter offerings £250: outgoings: curate's fund £100: Rates and Taxes £120. Collection P.R. £20 (see above) Payment to Parish Expenses [Compulsory] £15 to general Churchwardens' fund. *A Refuge*, said to be unnecessary—question of closing it and transferring support to larger refuge in Pimlico. Also a *Clothing Club*, said to be rather demoralising—advised to close it. Parish nearly empty in late summer, and half empty Jan.–March. Weekend habit has not hurt them much, tho' neighbouring parishes complain.

On the whole this was an encouraging report. As so often happens in such cases the estimate of the income was somewhat optimistic, and Canon Stewart's excellent record might perhaps be a little disquieting. He was leaving All Saints to be Archdeacon of Bristol after a happy ministry of more than twenty years. When he came the next year to stay a night with the Inges, his successor reported of him: "The Archdeacon is a charming guest. K. and I were delighted with him, and well understand why he was beloved in the parish." He would not be an altogether easy man to follow.

Inge attended the services at the church on the first Sunday in December, and at the very end of the year he came up from Canterbury for the day with Kitty and her father and met Sophy at the Rectory, which was at 34 Rutland Gate, close to the church. Otherwise he was mainly occupied with bidding farewell to Oxford and Hertford College. The undergraduates presented him with a beautiful chimney clock. He carefully summed up his work in retrospect and in prospect at the close of the year:

> So ends my last year of work at Oxford. My 15 years there have not been a complete failure, though I have gradually lost interest in the work of classical teaching, to do which I was brought to Oxford, and though I have not done nearly enough in a pastoral way for my pupils. On the University my influence has been slight, but it has been growing lately, and so far as it went, it has been of a sterling sort. I am closing that page in my career with predominant feelings of great thankfulness. Of course I have not made many friends—I have not tried enough to please people and show them the more amiable side of my character. My want of cheerfulness in society has probably been the main cause why I have been asked out so little: but I think I am improving in this respect. Now I am about to launch my crazy little skiff on unknown waters. I expect to make many blunders, but not to fail entirely, unless ill-luck or ill-health is added to my handicap. I must try hard to be a better Christian, for my own sake and that of the parish, and not least for darling Kitty whose love is a great and wonderful blessing which God has given me. Deo gratias.

9

London 1905–1907

Dr Johnson, our great authority on London, once claimed as one of its advantages that 'a man cannot know modes of life as well in Minorca as in London,' and that might be true for Johnson who had been in a variety of situations in London. But Minorca is probably not without its many arresting modes of life, and on the other hand a Londoner does not ordinarily know much outside his own circle. The innumerable streets of small houses in the East End were built with a particular mode of life in view, and this is equally true of the handsome squares in Knightsbridge and Brompton. When the new Vicar of Ennismore Gardens gave up College life for a London parish, he was exchanging one very stylised mode of life for another. Outside the circumference of these circles there was probably the same variety to be seen in modes of life at Oxford and in London, but of course on a very different scale. This is commented on by Inge himself on the first page of the Letter which forms the Introduction to his *All Saints' Sermons* (1907).

It is not easy to say what it is that makes London different from other places. One who comes to live here after living in the country is conscious, after a short time, that the great world is showing itself in a new and probably truer perspective : that sectional interests take a less prominent place in the picture of it, and that the working of the social machine has become in some ways more intelligible. The existence side by side of different social sets, each with its own standard and scale of values; the mixture of freedom with what seems at times a strange bondage to fashion, prescribing even the exact phrase to be used in appraising men and things : the combination of genial tolerance and hardness which characterises life in great centres—all these make up a world very unlike the society of an University town.

In the first four months of 1905 Inge was fully occupied in settling into his living and getting married. On 2 February he was instituted and inducted into the living by the Bishop of Kensington (F. E. Ridgeway), "who gave a very kind and nice address, and the service was really impressive." He assumed his parochial duties at once. He spoke the next day to the All Saints' Communicants' Guild. On Sunday the 5th he read himself in at the morning service and preached in the evening. He moved into the Vicarage, where all was "chaos," on the following Saturday. Soon he was launched upon confirmation class, school managers' meetings, calling, dining out, as well as his weekly sermon.

The work did not at first go very well. The congregation diminished rather quickly. It was scarcely to be expected that it would be otherwise. In London the impact of the parish as such is not very strongly felt. People attach themselves to the minister they care for, and fifty years ago that generally meant to the preacher they cared for. Canon Stewart had had a successful ministry, but those who liked him and his sermons would probably find Mr Inge rather remote and his sermons rather difficult. And so it turned out. By the middle of March the vicar was in a state of acute depression and regret at having abandoned Oxford, and this was intensified a month later at Easter. On Easter Day itself he recorded:

> Miserable congregations and offertories. I am very much depressed about my prospects here. Ever since I came the congregations have been going from bad to worse. And it was for this that I gave up the secure happy congenial life at Oxford! No more ruinous and insensate sacrifice of a career was ever made. I have spoilt my life most dismally. How could I have supposed that a smart West End parish would care for me or my preaching? What have we in common? May God have mercy upon me, and provide some way of retreat from this terrible mistake, incomparably the worst blunder of my life.

And on the next Sunday: "Congregation and offertories much worse even than last Sunday." He could not know and could not believe that he was in the process of largely replacing one congregation by another; and some of the existing congregation did like his sermons too.

Nor had he been without other successes. On the night of

5 April he travelled up to Aberdeen, and stayed with Bishop Douglas, and on the 7th he received the Honorary Degree of Doctor of Divinity and had "a very flattering reception." Of those who received Honorary Degrees with him Thomas Hardy is the best remembered. In Lent he delivered the St Margaret's Lectures which Hensley Henson had invited him to give. The day after he delivered the last of them he was discussing with the Vice-Chancellor of Cambridge[1] the proposal that he should give a course of lectures in Cambridge with undergraduates mainly in view. His comment on the discussion was, "I think this plan of lectures is a great opportunity, if only I can rise to it. I wish I had more time to give to the work." He found the time and he did rise to it, but no doubt he was getting very busy. He wrote to an old Hertford pupil, Norman Whatley, to congratulate him on a First in Classical Moderations: "Hearty congratulations on your First. I thought you would be near it, but was not very sanguine. You must come and see me here when you are in London, for alas! I shall very seldom be able to run over to Oxford. The work here is much heavier than I expected." This was in April 1905.

It was on the last day of this month that he felt so utterly depressed about his prospects. But it was only three days to his wedding day, and that was to make all the difference, not only in the years to come, but at once. He went down to Canterbury on the previous morning, 2 May, and was accommodated at the Old Palace, where the Archbishop was in residence. In the afternoon the best man, Arthur Benson, arrived at the Palace, and numerous relations went to the Spooners and other houses. There was a display of the presents in the King's School gymnasium, and in the evening a large dinner party, including Mrs Inge and Sophy, the Walter Hows, the New College Spooners, and Benson. When Inge and Benson returned to the Old Palace they were joined by the Archbishop's chaplain, and had a long conversation about Liberal Catholicism and kindred subjects. Inge saw the Archbishop for five minutes. He spent the next morning in the garden, and in the early afternoon the Archbishop performed the marriage in the Cathedral in the presence of a very large congregation and gave "a most beautiful and happy little address." More and more relations came, and a

Kitty

contingent from Hertford College, as well as all the staff from
All Saints. Before five o'clock the bride and bridegroom were
on their way to London. They stayed the night at Rutland Gate
and travelled the next day to Grasmere where they spent a
fortnight with perfect weather all the time. "Each day is much
the same—Letters and work in the morning and walk in the
afternoon." The honeymoon ended with two days at Walton,
where they had been courting eight months before, and they
reached Rutland Gate again on the evening of 19 May. It was
rather a mixed home-coming for the vicar: "Found the house
in capital order, pictures hung, flowers, etc. Simms" (the
curate) "came in for a few minutes after we arrived. In rather
low spirits about the whole business. I ought of course to have
remained at Oxford and devoted myself to theological work.
Then a Professorship and a literary reputation, and honours,
would have been certain, almost, and in any case my life would
have been free from trouble and anxiety. But there is no going
back, and I must try to make the best of it, and make my dear
little wife happy."

They entered together upon the duties of the parish and the
London 'season.' They accompanied the Communicants' Guild
on an outing to St Albans. The parish lumber sale was held. The
choristers were entertained, and then the choir men. There were
many social engagements. The vicar was a little critical of the
company he was invited to meet, and the parties were not
always wholly to his liking. They dined on one occasion with
an Honourable Lady. "A party of 5 in a doll's house, dinner
very badly served. The other 2 guests a young German who
wanted to talk to me about Immortality, and a middle aged lady
with black hair, who smoked." But there were pleasant diversions too. Relations came to stay, and there were visits to
Oxford and Cambridge and Canterbury, and two or three days
off at Lord's. Once at least the vicar played tennis in Ennismore
Gardens. He said it was his first game for years and he enjoyed it.

By the end of July all this kind of thing died down. They
were able to take a holiday from 30 July to 9 September, and
even after that to go little expeditions together to the Museums
and Kew and as far as Eton. There were very few parishioners
to call on, no social events, no parish functions till the end of

the month. But then things began to look up, and on the first Sunday in November the vicar was able to record "a much more encouraging Sunday, 96 communicants, good offertories, and a large congregation in the evening."

One rather troublesome business arose. Inge was pressed by several friends at Cambridge to allow himself to be a candidate for the Norrisian Professorship of Divinity vacant by the selection of Dr Chase for the Bishopric of Ely. He was in several minds about it. He hankered after the academic life, forgetting perhaps with what determination he had recently quitted it, but he naturally felt some misgiving about leaving All Saints after so short an incumbency, and his wife understandably enough did not fancy a fresh home-making so soon. He did what is seldom wise; he let it be known that he would accept the Professorship if he were elected, but would not offer himself as a candidate. The electors, who were the Heads of the Colleges, chose F. C. Burkitt, a Fellow of Trinity, a layman and already much in repute as an orientalist. Burkitt fully deserved a Professorship and the Norrisian was by custom the only one open to a layman. It was no reflection on Inge that under the circumstances Burkitt was preferred.

It was in fact a piece of good fortune for him. Later on people used sometimes to speak as though his time at Ennismore Gardens was a failure, but this it was not. The congregations came to be large; even on a week-day when the rector gave an address on Marcus Aurelius the church was full. His preaching was effective, too. On 1 July 1906 he preached on Holy Communion "with the gratifying result that we had 86 at the celebration instead of about 40." He and Kitty were asked out perpetually, and he began to make friends with many of the people he met. He reckoned those two years the happiest he had had, and perhaps for a long time after none was happier. He got very useful experiences, too, which he had not met with before; a long negotiation over the schools, which involved difficulties with the Parish of Brompton, but ended successfully; taking the chair at a meeting: dismissing a female pew-opener, "a very unpleasant job": dealing with an illegal marriage at the church. And he found himself much interested in London life, and he was not at all insensible to its beauties. He immensely admired Battersea Park (and well he might fifty years ago), and he thought it worth noting down that he watched the sunset one evening in August from the east end of the Serpentine, and it was one of the finest he ever saw.

His churchmanship at this time was somewhat undecided. It was quite natural that he should be considerably influenced by Hensley Henson. On the other hand he could not altogether resist the glamour which then attached itself to Gore. He had been in a difficult situation during the whole of his clerical life so far, reacting steadily against the Tractarianism in which he had been brought up, but finding the Evangelicals impossibly rigid in their interpretation of the Bible. He was decidedly a liberal, and the Anglo-Catholic successors of the Tractarians were the only organised body which represented liberal views of the Bible. In London he came into contact with the group which Gore led. Its chief activity at this time was in promoting the Christian Social Union, and in February 1906 he "attended a big meeting of C.S.U. at Church House. Heard Scott Holland, Gore, Talbot, Barnett, Fry, and a labour leader—Rogers." These were the big guns, though. This was not his first contact with the movement. Already in the previous November he "took the chair at the Inaugural Meeting of the Kensington Group of C.S.U. G. K. Chesterton gave an address, clever, but thin and padded, on Society." It is not altogether easy to know why he was asked to chair this meeting, and why, when asked, he accepted. In the event he abandoned the C.S.U. entirely.

He did, however, take a great interest in Birrell's Education Bill of 1906, and felt himself in strong disagreement with what he believed to be the clerical view. Here he was in opposition to Gore, but this did not make their relations less cordial. He stayed with Gore at Birmingham in July 1906 for a conference about the Christian doctrine of sin. It was a distinguished gathering. Rashdall, Dean Strong, Headlam, Tennant, Burn, Rendel Harris were there. "Not a bad discussion, but no particular results. . . . Gore is a very good host," was Inge's impression.

The coming Education Bill was much canvassed in Church circles, and the first stage of agitations and negotiations about it continued until 19 December 1906, when the House of Lords finally rejected the measure. Briefly the situation was that the education of the nation was still largely given in schools which were managed by members of the Church of England, but it was seen that the State must in future satisfy far the greater part of the ever extending need for schools and teachers, and the Government with a huge Liberal majority naturally wished to embody the Liberal principles of the day in the new measures which it was bound to put forward. They pressed for a large measure of State control. A tremendous struggle ensued, which mainly turned on what facilities for denominational teaching would be accepted by the Government. The feeling against the Church of England was much stronger among the Nonconformists then than it is now. Such an Act as that of 1944 would have been regarded by all parties as a sacrifice of principle. An 'agreed syllabus' would have found very few supporters. Inge attended a number of meetings, not to agitate for one thing or another, but to inform himself. He heard part of the debates in the House of Lords. He preached two sermons at All Saints on the question. He confided to his diary at the time his disagreement with those who were thought to express the views of the Church of England:

> I find myself quite out of accord with the majority of the Bishops and others, who speak for the Church. I cannot give up the idea of a national Christianity, and think even a mutilated teaching, given to all by the regular teachers, far better than the unlimited sectarianism of allowing each parent to choose his own religion for his child. Yet this solution, which expresses the dissidence of dissent, in its extremest form, is the policy advocated by the 'Catholic' party in the Church.

In its main outline the present system is an application of Inge's views to the problem, though he would be against the right to withdraw a child from the daily act of worship.

The six lectures which he had been asked to give in Cambridge were delivered in January and February 1906 and published on 19 June under the title *Truth and Falsehood in Religion*. They had been attended by a large audience, never less than two hundred and fifty, mostly undergraduates. One of those who heard them wrote some months later and said he could not

express what he owed to the lectures; he had given up thoughts
of ordination, but after hearing them he had determined to be
ordained, and was ordained deacon at Trinity. This was F. W.
Dwelly who afterwards did such a remarkable work as Dean
of Liverpool. The success of the lectures is not surprising.
They are on the most important aspects of the Christian religion,
full of striking assertions and penetrating analyses in a workmanlike style, and seldom far away from the practical problems
of everyday life, as they present themselves to men who are
capable of thinking about religion and are actually doing so.
There is a certain amount in them which belongs to their own
period, when miracles were much debated and the difficulties
they seem to raise were thought to be solved either by Pragmatism or by Modernism. This is all largely forgotten now,
though the essence of it, the elevation of the Will above the
Intellect, is found fifty years later to be still widely maintained
in different terms. Inge would have none of such modernism,
and opposed the philosophy of Pragmatism. But here he had
not philosophers in view. In the lecture on 'Fact and Fancy'
(pp. 91–123) he came to the border of philosophy more than
once and then turned back, not so much because of his audience,
but because of his own mind, which was always ready to admit
"ragged edges"[2] and knowledge not yet made perfect.

The book marks a definite stage in the Dean's career. In it
he perfected his style, cultivated but not academic, sometimes
forthright, but with an element of subtler criticism, full of
general knowledge without being simply popular, and full of
specialised knowledge without being technical, sometimes very
serious—but not always, on occasion immensely eloquent,
though not intended to be rhetorical. His views of the world,
too, now fell into the pattern from which they never deviated
much. There is a spiritual world, he would say, which has its
own existence, but can only be known by us through the world
about us. But what this present world can teach us of the
spiritual world must be spiritually discerned. No mechanical
interpretations by the light of scripture or the teaching of the
Church will lead us to the truth, though they are the means to
truth when rightly employed by the spirit. In all this his mind
owed much to St Paul and Plato and Plotinus, but the Gospels

were the foundation on which he built. He was sure that they gave an unmistakable and consistent impression when taken as a whole, and therefore the detailed criticism of them, then being so vigorously undertaken, was not very important. Later on after a more intensive study of Plotinus he viewed the spiritual world at successive levels and related it more closely to the potentialities of human personality, but he never conveyed more naturally and persuasively than in *Truth and Falsehood in Religion* the relevance of the spiritual world to our present condition. There is very little asperity in the book, and less pessimism. A certain amount of anticipation was natural in addressing an unusually youthful audience. One of these anticipations is of interest, for it accounts for a situation in history which is constantly recurring and is recurring now, and according to his view arises out of the permanent conflict between the intellect and the emotions. He is maintaining the thesis that "Christianity has nothing to fear from science unless we refuse to learn from it," and he says :

> One of the struggles of the future will be between this religion of science, which, though ethical in its ends, is purely intellectual in its methods, and the organised religion of 'the Churches,' which is swayed principally by the emotions. The conflict will divide the political world also into two camps, for there is hardly a burning question in politics that is not answered differently by the intellect and by the emotions. (*Truth and Falsehood in Religion*, p. 160.)

Strangely enough, when the book was published, he felt very much disturbed about it. He begged his mother not to read it. He feared it would get him into trouble about miracles, and heartily wished he had kept clear of the subject altogether. Sixteen days after it appeared he called on John Murray, the publisher, to discuss the advisability of suppressing the first edition. But he found that Murray

> does not think it likely to give serious offence, so I shall allow the sale to proceed, and shall put myself right, if necessary, in the preface to the second edition, which will probably be required, as Murray has only printed 1,000 copies. Just before I started, a message came from the Archbishop and Mrs Davidson, approving of the book, and advising me not to stop the sale.

So all was well. All was well on the next day, too, 5 July 1906, when Kitty had her first child, a fine boy, weighing close upon 8 lb. He was christened William Craufurd on the first of August. William Temple, the Archbishop to be, was one of his godparents.

Meanwhile the parish work grew and prospered. Archdeacon Stewart had not given quite the right impression when he said there were no poor in the parish. There were some five thousand in the angle between Knightsbridge and Brompton Road, many more in fact than there are now. But there were still two curates, whose duties mainly lay among the poor and the numerous servants who lived in the parish. Not that the vicar was unmindful of them. He went with Kitty to see the house-keeper at the Hyde Park Hotel about a class for the maids there. They gave two tea-parties for them, a dozen or more turned up each time, and a class was formed to be taken by one of the curates. Something of the same kind was attempted for the employees at Harrod's, though with less success. It would be taken for granted that the incumbent's real concern was with the Sunday morning congregation. In the church life of such a parish as All Saints the segregation of rich and poor was quite unconscious but quite complete, and whether this was ever complained of or not no complaints reached the ears of the rich. It was not very surprising, however, that, as Mr Stewart had noted, curates were not easy to get. Their work was difficult, and did not attract much attention. They seldom preached on Sunday morning; Inge soon found out that he must not let them do it often.

In 1906 the new baby determined the character of the summer holiday, which was spent partly at Canterbury and then for ten days on a farm at Sandling. Inge returned home each Sunday to take the duty. In not deserting the parish in the off-season he no doubt had in view his forthcoming absence on a visit to America to deliver the Paddock Lectures at the General Seminary in New York, and to give addresses at Harvard and Princeton, which entailed being away from London from 25 September to 10 November. Kitty went with him, and they regarded it as a holiday, in fact Inge called it that in his diary, which at this point is unusually full. One gets the impression that the Paddock Lectures were only incidental to the tour of the eastern States, and one of the students at the General Seminary has said that they saw much less of the lecturer than they had hoped. He came once or twice to dinner where he sat with the Professors and did not come into close contact with the junior members. For the most part they did not find what he said very interesting, and it is possible he did not find it so himself, for after delivering the last of them he wrote, "They have not been at all good, mainly old work—dished up and too disconnected. But I could not help it, having nothing else to say, and no time for research." By the terms of their foundation the Paddock Lectures must be printed, and they were published in June 1907, no doubt altered in many places and improved. Already on the boat coming back to England he was working upon them.

But as a holiday the trip was a great success in spite of a very strenuous programme. They arrived at New York on 3 October. The *Oceanic* had done the passage from Queenstown (Cobh) in five days and seventeen hours, "a remarkable record," and after being introduced to Mr Pierpont Morgan on the quay they were taken off to stay in Long Island with American friends called McBee. After five days of luxury sight-seeing they left with great regret to stay at the General Seminary with Dean Robbins of whom Inge formed a very favourable impression. Robbins was in fact a most outstanding character. Inge enjoyed his company, and almost as much that of two junior lecturers who lived with him, Hunt and Gumph. Gumph was afterwards well known as Rector of Holy Trinity, Baltimore. The Paddock Lectures were delivered on 8, 10, 12, 15, 17, 19 October, with the week-end in the middle at Pittsfield, Mass., with the Bishop of Nebraska, "in a beautiful house in the middle of an old-world tree-shaded town—a most grateful change from New York."

Between the fourth and fifth Paddock Lecture Mr McBee showed his guest round Washington, and they lunched with President Roosevelt at the White House.

Met Mrs R. who is charming, Montagu, governor of Virginia, Kirk, just back from Philippines, and others. The President talked mainly about the Philippines, also about Panama, and a little about Cuba, speaking freely with no reserve, and with great energy and vigorous common-sense. A very remarkable man, and a very good ruler for this country—a gentleman, a straight and honest man, a sincere Christian, and quite fearless. After lunch he and McBee and Montagu discussed the negro problem, with especial reference to the President's coming message to Congress in which lynching is to be condemned.

Between the fifth and last Paddock Lecture there was time for a visit to Princeton, when Inge lectured to a large number of students on "the development of the religious consciousness." He notes with a mark of exclamation that he received $100. He admired the University buildings.

The day after the lectures were finished he and Kitty left for Washington to stay with Dr McKim, the Rector of Epiphany Church. Inge preached the next morning at the church, and on the following day showed Kitty some of the sights. In the afternoon they went to the Virginia Seminary near Alexandria, and enjoyed their "first and only glimpse of the South." Two days later they arrived in the early morning at Buffalo, where Bishop Walker with whom they had crossed the Atlantic met them. They stayed three nights with him, and visited the Niagara Falls, which Inge found quite as grand as he had pictured them, "desecrated rather than spoiled by the power-houses." He spoke to the Buffalo Clergy about the Education Bill and the affairs of the Church of England in general. The fourth night was spent in the train for Boston to stay with the Dean of the Episcopal Theological School at Harvard and he gave three lectures on the Logos-doctrine there.

On the first of November they returned to New York and boarded the SS. *Celtic*. It sailed the next day at daybreak, and berthed at Liverpool on the evening of the 10th. They reached Euston at midnight and drove straight to Rutland Gate. "Very glad to be back, though our holiday has been a great success."

It was no doubt a success in that it was very enjoyable, and the various lectures had been well attended. Inge had met many Americans, many Americans had met Inge, and more had seen him. But he had probably not added much to the reputation which had preceded him. What he had done was to go a further stage in putting his own ideas into order and confirming the conviction which runs through all his theology that "Platonism cannot be torn out of Christianity without destroying it." "Even to this day," he said, "I doubt whether anyone can be an orthodox theologian without being a Platonist. Our creeds are the formulae of victorious Platonism."[3] The Lectures have the appearance of being based upon a number of studies which he now shaped into something of a unity and brought to some definite conclusion. What he "dished up" was the substance of numerous occasional papers in which he had had the opportunity of exploring and testing his own thinking over what he had read and noted. The result is that we have in *Personal Idealism and Mysticism*, as the book was called, an exposition of what the author himself believed to be the essentials of the Christian Faith. It is an important work as revealing his particular turn of mind. He says in the Preface to the Third Edition, written seventeen years after the book originally appeared, that he did not find anything that he wished to alter, and further that "the book discusses the relation of current philosophical controversies to Christology, a subject to which I have referred only incidentally in my later writings." The book may be read as a personal view, and approached in that way, it has a peculiar interest. Inge tended after this towards a more definitely philosophical treatment of his themes, with a special element of psychology. But this was not really his line, and in his later years with powers redirected but undiminished he reverted largely to the historical and prophetical interpretation of the world and the age. Of his *theology*, as he worked it out and finally settled it for himself, the Paddock Lectures are the true and adequate foundation.

The year 1907 also saw the publication of the Lectures which he had delivered in St Margaret's Church, Westminster, in Lent 1905. They were a supplement to the Bampton Lectures under the title *Studies in English Mystics*. In the preface he said: "They cover part of the same ground as my Bampton Lectures of 1899: but the selected writers are discussed more fully, and the Introductory Lecture embodies the results of further study since the Oxford course was written." The selected authors are Julian of Norwich, Walter Hylton, William Law, Wordsworth,

Browning, and the anonymous writer of the *Aucren Riwle*, who may be Bishop Poore of Salisbury who began the building of Salisbury Cathedral in 1220. After fifty years this is said to be the volume of Inge's works which is now most in demand, and that is not to be wondered at. Although the Bampton Lectures did a great deal to make these mystical authors known, this volume followed it up. It is no less serious, but rather easier reading, and more in touch with flesh and blood, and the first lecture on the Psychology of Mysticism connects mysticism with a wider range of experiences. It explains how the life of devotion has its mystical state, but so also has the intellectual life its mystical state, so also the poet's worship of nature, so also the sympathetic study of human character, so also the active life, and the routine of the daily round. All this is illustrated from the different authors, and the last lecture (on Browning) ends with a fine claim for the mystic and his religion. Incidentally Inge displays himself as a literary critic who has useful things to say.

He had only returned from America five days when a new prospect loomed up. St John Parry of Trinity College, Cambridge, sent him "a kind note," giving information about the mode of election to the Lady Margaret Professorship. It had become vacant by the nomination of Dr A. F. Kirkpatrick to the Deanery of Ely. In view of his fitness for academic life it was very unlikely that Inge would not be a candidate for the post. He may have had some hesitations, for he was happy where he was, and he would not care to miss a second professorship after being passed over for the Norrisian. But he was sure to be an applicant in the end, and on 21 January 1907 he sent in his letter to the Vice-Chancellor at Cambridge, stating the general line of study he would propose to follow if he were elected to the Professorship. He had had two months since Parry's letter in which to estimate his chance of election. On 1 February he had a letter from the Vice-Chancellor, saying he had been chosen as one of the four candidates for the Professorship who were to appear before the electors, without any details as to who the others were or how many applicants there had been. This seemingly good news was received in characteristic fashion. "K. and I hardly know what to wish for

—in spite of the honour of being elected, we should be very sorry indeed to leave this happy home." There was a further misgiving. On receiving advanced copies of his Paddock Lectures he wished they had been kept back till the Cambridge election: "I don't think they will improve my chances!"

However, he went through with it, and was encouraged on 15 February by a visit from F. J. Foakes-Jackson, a Fellow of Jesus, suggesting a Fellowship at that College, if he were elected to the Professorship. There was at that time an interest in theology at Jesus and a good number of men reading for holy orders. Foakes-Jackson's visit naturally made Inge think his chance of getting the Professorship very good, and he was right. But once more there was a set-back. The Master of Magdalene wrote to say that many of the Electors were doubtful about voting for him on account of his attitude with regard to miracles. "I wrote a letter for him to show to them explaining (in part) my views about the Virgin Birth and the Resurrection." Three days later, in accordance with the regulations governing the appointment, he delivered a Praelection on the Spirit in St John's Gospel in the presence of thirty-eight Doctors and Bachelors of Divinity, and then came straight home. The election by the graduates in Divinity was at 11 a.m. the next day. The telegram which arrived at Rutland Gate to announce the result was addressed to Professor Inge.

10

Cambridge Again

Margaret Beaufort, Duchess of Richmond and later of Derby, deserves to be remembered. 'The Lady Margaret' is a sweet name for a sweet lady, one of the most attractive figures in the early years of the Renaissance in England, learned, able, patient and wise. No more sensitive face and hands were ever portrayed in bronze than those of her effigy in Westminster Abbey.

The first forty years of her life were stormy and perilous. She had a distant claim to the throne, being great-granddaughter of John of Gaunt, and this was vaguely strengthened by her early marriage to Edmund Tudor whose father had married King Henry V's widow. By him she was the mother of a son Henry, who by strange vicissitudes and long endurance got to be King of England. But many princes had to disappear before his turn came; some died young, some died in battle, some were brought to the block. The record is a gloomy one. Richard II, grandson of Edward III and his rightful heir, was deposed by his cousin Henry IV. His grandson Henry VI was deposed by his cousin Edward IV. His son was murdered, by Richard III so it was said, and Richard III was killed in battle with Henry Tudor, the Lady Margaret's son, who assumed the crown because there was no one left to dispute it with him. Through the latter part of this age of confusion the Lady Margaret lived in enforced retirement, vigilant and much sought in counsel. She was condemned to death in the reign of Edward IV, but begged off by her third husband, John Stanley, Earl of Derby. Henry was an exile in Brittany at the same time. His mother was prominent in the movement which brought him home to take the crown from Richard.

But once he was on the throne, she turned her thoughts from politics to learning, perhaps perceiving that here England was much behind Europe. She took for her adviser John Fisher, a Cambridge scholar, who did a great deal to promote the study of Greek in England. In 1502 he persuaded Lady Margaret to establish Readers in Divinity, one at Oxford and one at Cambridge. They were to read and presumably to comment on what they read most mornings in term except during Lent, when it was expected they would be preaching. They were to be chosen by the graduates in Divinity at the University. They were not to take any fees, and the Foundress provided an endowment of the annual value of £27 13s. 4d. in the hands of Westminster Abbey to be divided between them. King James I augmented the Cambridge Reader's stipend by annexing to it the Rectory of Terrington in Norfolk. These were the first Professorships (as we call them now) to be established in England. Lady Margaret was a pioneer in this, as she was also in her patronage of printing. She very substantially supported Caxton and Wynkyn de Worde. Wynkyn de Worde printed Hilton's *Scale of Perfection* at her command. Fisher was her guide in all this forward-looking munificence. She had had a mind to leave her wealth, which was not small, to Westminster Abbey. Fisher saw that the future was with the Universities and not with the monasteries. Aided by him she completed the foundation of Christ's College, Cambridge, in 1505, and in 1508 she founded the splendid College of St John the Evangelist. In the next year Henry VII died, and she only survived him a short time.

There was an interval of seven months between Inge's appointment to the Lady Margaret Professorship on 26 February 1907 and the beginning of the Michaelmas Term at Cambridge when he had to take up his duties, but in this interval there was much to be done. Two days after his election he wrote a letter to his parishioners announcing his forthcoming departure. Three days after that, on 4 February, he was in Cambridge and looking at Brook House in Trumpington Street as being possibly a house he might like to take, and after considering some others he did rent it in the end, and it was where he lived until he returned to London. It attracted him at once, but at once also Rutland Gate, "our first happy home," became more dear than ever before. "The wrench of leaving will be terrible." And there was the question of a successor at All Saints. He was leaving "a full church and flourishing finances," and Hensley

Henson who was still at St Margaret's, Westminster, and as such the patron, told Inge he did not want to move anyone in London, but to bring in an intellectual man, not a mere windbag, from the country. The Revd. J. H. F. Peile, Fellow and Chaplain of University College, Oxford, was appointed. He was at the moment making a great success of his Bampton Lectures, and was offered the living early in May. Inge was glad, and had him to preach in the middle of June, when "he preached excellently and made a very good impression." A lady parishioner reported, after he had begun his ministry, that he was even shyer than Mr Inge. He did not stay long, however, for he was made Archdeacon of Warwick in April 1910.

Inge's departure from London was genuinely regretted by his congregation, and this found expression in a great number of letters and invitations. He had secured a large following as a preacher, and as a farewell gift he published his *All Saints' Sermons* dedicated to the parishioners and congregation, the memorial, he said, of a short ministry, and "a token of your unfailing kindness to me and mine." In the Farewell Letter which he prefixed to the volume he wrote: "The time may come, I suppose, when I shall look back upon my brief ministry here as a short episode in a life spent mainly at the Universities. At present, however, it seems to me that I am closing a chapter that has been too full of new and happy experiences to be called an episode." He had at any rate come to have a real love for life in London, and Kitty had the feeling even more strongly. By the time he retired from the Deanery of St Paul's he had actually spent about one year more of his life at Oxford and Cambridge than in London, but it was not as a don or Professor but as a great citizen of London that he was famous.

The move to Brook House took place at the beginning of September. Kitty left Rutland Gate on 1 August, and the vicar on 21 August, though he continued to officiate at All Saints on Sundays till the end of September. They took up residence in Cambridge on 2 September, and on 1 October the Professor was formally admitted to his Professorship. He was elected a Fellow of Jesus College, and he dined there as Fellow for the first time on 20 October. Already he had got to know the other divinity Professors and had arranged to lecture on Faith in the

Michaelmas Term and on the Theology of St John's Gospel in the Lent or Easter Term. He was specially impressed by Burkitt, his successful rival for the Norrisian Professorship in 1906. Foakes-Jackson had told him in April that they wanted him to *philosophise*, and he was glad of that. In May he noted that his congregation one Sunday morning at All Saints was not good. "It is curious how difficult I find it to preach popular sermons since my thoughts have been running on Cambridge lectures and problems of philosophy." One of the great secrets of his power was that he spoke and wrote out of a full mind, and of course it all depended what his mind was full of at the time. The book on Faith which he published while he was Professor, though he thought it the best of his theological works, had only a moderate sale. It was a little too professorial to be popular, though none of his books after about 1905 had a small sale. Its full title was *Faith and its Psychology*.

He retained the Professorship for four years. It was customary for the Professors of Divinity to lecture in two out of the three terms in each year. Inge does not seem to have given any inaugural lecture, but at the opening of his first lecture on Faith at the Divinity Schools the large hall was three-quarters full and seventy undergraduates gave in their names to continue to attend. In the Easter Term sixty were present at the first lecture on the Theology of St John. Later on the Professor complained that his lectures on philosophy were not well attended. "I must try and find out what the undergraduates like, and give it to them." Altogether he gave three courses on St John, three on Elements of the Philosophy of Religion, and one on the Development of Thought in St Paul's Epistles. He did not repeat the course on Faith. All the divinity Professors gave notice every term that they would be at home on Tuesdays from 6–7 p.m. to see any students who liked to call. In Inge's case this developed into an informal class, a kind of seminar as it would now be called.

His most notable lectures were in fact not given in Cambridge at all, but at the Passmore Edwards Settlement in Tavistock Place, the Jowett Lectures, as the course was called. "About fifty people attended the first lecture, a few superior artisans, but mostly intelligentsia." The book on Faith (Duckworth,

1909) was an expansion of these lectures. From the contents it may be conjectured that the expansion was towards a more academic treatment. It was a plea for the application of both the Will and the Intellect to religion. The argument is carefully built up, and as it runs in some degree counter to Mysticism it is worth setting out: Faith gives value to beauty, truth, and goodness, and makes possible an immediate experience of God. But Faith is apt to stop short and remain static in an infallible Church or an infallible Book or in the life of Christ on earth only. Then, when infallibles are rejected, Modernism makes an attempt to separate Faith from Fact. But this will not do. We must apply our reason to the objects of our faith, on the assumption that both Faith and Reason are dealing with realities. *Faith* is a serious, somewhat difficult, but practical book. At the end we know better what Faith does than what it is.

Another of Inge's publications, while he was Lady Margaret Professor, deserves notice, though it is of a slighter kind. In January 1911 he gave four devotional addresses in the Chapel of Corpus Christi College to the Annual Meeting of Public School Masters and College Tutors, commonly called 'The Dons and Beaks.' This is a somewhat notable gathering of its kind; Inge had attended it himself in 1886 and 1888, but the meeting of 1911 was specially remembered for his addresses, which were published under the title *Speculum Animae*. The audience, consisting mostly of fairly pious and fairly intelligent people, were well able to appreciate their preacher as he enforced the claims of "experiential" religion, but beside this and because of it the claims of duty also. The addresses are mystical in outlook, but also slightly mysterious. They were greatly admired when they were delivered, and many have made a constant companion of this small volume.

It is astonishing to find how carefully and at what length such books as these were reviewed in the daily press, not only in London but also in the provinces and in Scotland. *Faith* would now hardly be noticed except in the Church papers and some of the few monthly and quarterly journals that survive. The fact that it secured so much attention is partly a tribute to the author's eminence, already greater than any serious writer on religion can claim fifty years later, but it also points to a changed emphasis in journalism. The reviews were most respectful on the whole. The *Church Times* took the opportunity to urge its own theological standpoint without damaging the book. The *Cambridge Review* in an article which confined itself to the philosophy of the argument was dissatisfied, perhaps with some reason, perhaps only because a prophet is without honour in his own country.

Inge gave many other sermons, lectures, and addresses in London and all over the country, which he did not publish, but the preparation of them and the travelling they entailed must have made his days very full. He seems to have had to reduce his general reading a great deal. Even in the vacation he had many engagements. He was writing in the Reviews, and writing and speaking frequently on the Education Bill and also on eugenics, a subject he had now been interested in for more than twenty years, though he did not join the Eugenics Society till 1908. In 1910 he found Bernard Shaw "flippant and immoral" in an address to the Society. Inge always took the matter very seriously, especially in regard to the transmission of ability and the menace of overpopulation.

He was a trenchant writer, and he sometimes got himself into trouble. Later on he became less sensitive to criticism, and occasionally enjoyed it, having acquired what *The Times* described as 'the formidable graces of a first-rate controversialist,'[1] but at this period it was not so. He noted in his diary on 2 March 1909 that the *Cambridge Review* and *Punch* were making fun of him "for saying in London that the upper classes in this country are the finest type, or near it, that have flourished since the old Greeks." Sometimes his opponents made him angry, and he had need of all the self-control he could muster. "I find that Leighton Pullan and others have gone on attacking me in the *Guardian*: but I am determined not to read their nonsense that I may not be provoked into replying to it." This was at the end of August 1910, over his article 'Towards Educational Peace' in the *Nineteenth Century*. He blamed himself also, perhaps too severely, for feelings that were only human. "Injustice makes me too angry. I made resolutions again and again not to think of the *Guardian* attacks, and broke them in a few hours, in a most humiliating way. I have also got a foolish idea into my head that I should like the vacant deanery of Lincoln, and watch for every post as if there were the smallest likelihood of the offer being made. In both these ways I am being made painfully conscious of my moral weakness and silliness. My beloved Plotinus would save me from all such perturbations, if I could *live* his philosophy as well as study it." In this last sentence there is the age-long *cri-de-cœur* of the philosopher. It is very different from the casual thought of 1895, "I must read Plotinus sometime," different too to what he was to write in summing up the year 1908: "My wish now is to write a modernised defence of Plotinus' philosophy of religion, which I think would make a good book for the Gifford lectures, if I am ever invited to give them." He was invited to give them nine years later.

Life at a University where the vacations fill more of the year than term time does not want for its domesticities and diversions. Brook House turned out well. It is something of a mansion built or perhaps modernised about 1850. The façade is of a basement and three floors above, with four windows in a line. Its depth is considerable, so that Kitty on the day of her arrival wrote of "the *large* hall," "the *huge* dining room," "the drawing room more lovely than I can describe." The house is now the office of the Oxford and Cambridge Schools Examination Board, and the rooms are certainly very large and light, though the particular loveliness has departed. The Inges had chosen their wall-papers in the King's Road, Chelsea, and it seems that the little Craufurd's nurseries on the top floor had a touch of greenery-yallery about them: "his nurseries are really looking lovely," Kitty thought, "with his yellow and white Morris curtains in his day nursery, and his yellow and green cork carpet and green walls with the frieze of puppies and goslings walking round in procession." The garden was an added joy. It ran back a distance of some 200 feet to Tennis Court Road, with a big lawn, fruit trees beyond, and Downing Park as a background. Alas for Brook House! Just half a century later this and the adjacent gardens have been acquired by Addenbrooke's Hospital and covered with needful extensions of its work.

When they arrived in Cambridge Craufurd was fourteen

months old, and rather less than three months later, on
21 November 1907 the second boy, Edward, was born, and
on 17 March 1910 a third child appeared, to be called either
Barbara or Catharine. Ultimately Catharine prevailed, the name
of her mother, her mother's mother and a gifted cousin.[2] At
the Census of 1911 there were six servants in Brook House,
but this would include a nurse and nursery maid. The Professor
expressed some dismay at the prospect of an increase in his
family each time it occurred, and did not show a great deal of
interest when a new baby arrived, but he played with them as
soon as they came to an age when they could play.

Towards the end of his time at Cambridge, on 6 June 1910,
Inge completed the first fifty years of his life. Some picture of
him seems called for. He was still a very young looking man
and remarkably active. On 18 April 1910 he walked eighteen
miles by himself during a solitary stay in Dorset "for reading
and thinking." He still played tennis occasionally and said he
found that for three sets he could play nearly as well as ever.
He had given up playing cricket, but when the Master of Jesus
had a party to celebrate his eightieth birthday, there was mixed
cricket and the Professor joined in: "I, alas, disgraced myself
by getting bowled for O by a perfectly simple ball and by fielding
badly. Cricket is plainly not a game to take up again lightly
after 15 years' desuetude!"

But apart from definite physical recreation he was quite tire-
less in travel on business or pleasure. In 1910 he made something
like eighty journeys by train. He and Kitty sometimes went a
tour which sounds very restless from their description, but was
evidently full of zest. His diary shows that he could write a
travel story effectively; the interest that he felt in anything new
makes his descriptions very good reading, as for example in the
following passage, which is also marked by a measure of
prophetic insight. It is from the diary for 28 July 1910.

> Motored to Torquay, where we saw the Dreadnought with the
> King on board, and Graham White flying over the harbour and
> ships. This was a very wonderful sight: the grace, ease, and
> rapidity of the aeroplane were remarkable. But I had an uneasy
> feeling that if this invention is ever perfected, the day of ironclads,
> and perhaps of British naval supremacy, will be over. It was clear

that Graham White could have destroyed the Dreadnought by dropping bombs, and it is doubtful if her existing guns could have brought him down.

Small things were found well worth recording too. He went to see an old Hertford pupil near Exeter:

He is chaplain to Sir Thomas Acland, and lives in a doll's house in Killerton Park. He is rather an odd fellow with two hobbies. He keeps a cage of lizards, who require fires in his sitting room in the hottest weather; and he is writing articles on eschatological beliefs in the 1st century.

Almost every year the family went to a country place in the summer, and Inge took the clerical duty for three weeks or so. More than once they went to Charlie's attractive Rectory at Holmwood. In 1910 they went to Newington near Sittingbourne in Kent for the whole of August. The diary presents us with a pleasing picture of The Professor in the Country:

Aug. 31. Our month at Newington has been a great success in every way. We have made real friends with the Lockes and Webbs; I have had several excellent games of tennis; the children have been well and happy; Craufurd has made rapid progress with his alphabet, and has even achieved two or three letters, to his two grannies, and to Miller our cook, who was married on the 27th. They have also learned a number of things belonging to country life, which they could not have seen at Cambridge. There are a number of pretty walks round Newington, with public paths through woods and hop-fields. Lastly we got through a good deal of reading, Lecky Hist. of 18th Century Vol. I; and the Creevey papers, and I have got on with Plotinus, and with sermons, addresses etc.

He had good reason to get on with sermons and addresses. In the course of the year he delivered fifty of them at least, some on occasions of considerable importance. This is excluding his professorial lectures in the Divinity School.

If they could be happy in the country, the Inges could also be very happy in London. Already at Christmas 1907 in his usual way the new Professor found himself wondering why he ever left his London parish, though he had not much doubt really that he was right. There were no further expressions of regret, but a year later when he went to stay with the Davsons, old parishioners, "it was a joy to be in London again." In 1910 he visited London eighteen times for a variety of engagements, clerical and social. He would easily be drawn into the social life of London once more, if he should ever find himself living there again.

Cambridge of course had its diversions too. The social round there was somewhat different from that in Knightsbridge. At Cambridge the University people seemed to spend an amazing amount of time in one another's houses, lunching, dining, and making afternoon calls. And the Inges, perhaps more than others, seemed to have relations and friends for visits long and short. There must sometimes have been thirteen or fourteen people sleeping in Brook House. It was taken for granted, too, that the visitors must be entertained. May Hinckley, a sort of relation, stayed ten days or more in July 1910, and her host thought it worth remarking that "she likes being with us, even when there is nothing going-on." But few guests stayed without a dinner party being got up to meet them, and other entertainments.

There was much congenial company, and the Inges were often invited to meet distinguished visitors to Cambridge; it may be conjectured that the visitors sometimes asked if they would have any opportunity of seeing Dr Inge, whose abilities and wit were now widely known. The Professor of course dined frequently at Jesus and at other High Tables, and sometimes the ladies were invited to a great function, as for example to a huge dinner to mark the centenary of Darwin's birth. Inge rather often did not think much of the speeches. At the Universities the conversation is normally better than the speech-making, or used to be before academic interests became so highly specialised as not to be easily shared or communicated, whereby conversation suffered. But in the first decade of this century the dons for the most part spoke the same language and possessed a great deal of their knowledge in common. Inge found Cambridge more self-centred than Oxford, where he thought the non-University element helped a good deal to make things socially pleasant. "Still there are many agreeable and cultivated people. Kitty is most intimate with the Howard Marshes, who are more London than Cambridge." Something of what was in his mind here may perhaps be found in the following entry in the diary: "The Donaldsons, like the Howard Marshes, give *shorter* dinners than some hosts here. Just so in London, we noticed that the length of the dinners tended to vary inversely with the social position of the host and hostess."

So Ralph Inge at the end of half a century of life could look back with satisfaction on his progress and position. He was comfortably settled in a post he could fill with some distinction, he was blissfully happy in his marriage and hopeful about his children. Although he sometimes failed to hear, his deafness did not trouble him, as it once had done. His religion satisfied him, and he knew where he stood. He was writing with vigour and speaking with facility, and doing both a great deal. Only with that discontent which infects the world he fancied himself at times as the Dean of a cathedral in the provinces.

On 18 April 1911 he received the offer of the Deanery of St Paul's. The Prime Minister, Mr Asquith, wrote in his own hand as follows:

Confidential 17 Ap. 1911

Dear Dr Inge,

I have the pleasure of proposing to you with the King's approval, that you should be appointed to the Deanery of St Paul's, in succession to Dr Gregory, who is about to retire.

I need not enlarge on the responsibilities of the position, which is in some respects unique in the Church. It is, I think of the utmost importance that it should be held in these days by one who can restore the traditions of scholarship and culture associated with the Deanery in the past, and at the same [time] maintain the services of the Cathedral at the standard of sober beauty which Dean Gregory has done so much to establish.

It has been arranged that the late Dean (who is now in his 92nd year) shall retain the Deanery as his residence during the remainder of his life—a deduction bearing some relation to its hypothetical rent being made from his retiring allowance.

Believe me to be

Very faithfully yours

H. H. Asquith.

Inge's reaction to this offer is described in the following passage, the very first which he printed (with omissions) in his *Diary of a Dean*:

April 18. By the second post arrived a letter of the utmost importance. Asquith tells me that he has the King's consent to offer me the Deanery of St Paul's, vacant by the resignation of Dean Gregory. I showed the letter to Kitty, and at first we could hardly realise it. We had often joked about the Deanery, because Dr Morrison & Henson had told me that I would be in the running for it when it became vacant; but we did not believe anything of the sort. I wrote to the PM to say that I felt rather overwhelmed by so unexpected an honour, and that I hoped he would allow me time to consult the Archbishop of Canterbury to-morrow before making up my mind. Then we telegraphed to Canterbury to ask them to take us for one night.

April 19. We went together to Canterbury. The Archbishop is away in Cornwall, and left no address at Canterbury; so the letter which I wrote to him yesterday will have been sent on first to Lambeth, and he will not get it till to-morrow, Thursday. But before I reached Canterbury I had really made up my mind to accept. If the Prime Minister singles out a man who has never stirred a finger for preferment, who has no friends in high place, who is not even a political supporter, it means that he deliberately thinks that this man is the right man for the post, and it is rather a fine thing that he should do simply what he thinks best for the Church. He may be grievously mistaken in his estimate of me, but that is his affair. I have no right to refuse to go where I am sent. I am not elated, though when I remember all the humiliations of those four years at Eton, 1884–8, I cannot help feeling rather pleased that fortune has made me such ample amends. The work will of course be less congenial to me than the quiet leisured existence here, with its ample opportunities for reading, writing, and thinking; I shall encounter great difficulties, and, what I have not yet had to face, bitter hostility and envy. But it is not such an alarming jump as from my little rooms at Hertford to 34 Rutland Gate and the utterly unknown work of a parish priest; besides, my confidence in myself has risen a good deal since 1904. So—may God help me in this new and great work!

I found Kitty's parents ready to accept either decision, but both were in favour of my accepting. My father-in-law said plainly:

If you have no better reason for refusing than that you would rather live at Cambridge it is your duty to accept.

In the meantime his mother, to whom he had communicated the news, wrote him an affectionate letter, characteristic of her great piety and her great good sense:

29 Holywell
Ap. 19, 1911.

My dearest dearest Ralph,

Thank you for letting me share this momentous question, & thank you for letting me have dear Sophy's sympathy and prayers to strengthen my own. You will not expect us to have opinions or wishes to give you: only our most loving prayers: and I may, I think, venture to say that I have a most happy confidence that you will be led to a right decision & that I shall feel no disappointment whichever way it ends. I am quite sure that there will be very much indeed to make the prospect far from attractive, & even distasteful to you: & this makes one less afraid of any lure of ambition affecting your choice. So, my own dear son, let your 'own mind,' under the guidance of the Master whom you desire to serve, 'tell your more than seven watchmen that sit above in a high tower.'[3]

As I write these words I am reminded of R. W. Church, who repeats them to himself sadly when he had accepted the Deanery, full of overwhelming distress at the task before him, & thinking he had 'made a mistake'! So, don't let your 'own mind' decide without the utmost endeavour to gain a true equilibrium. R. W. C.'s thinking he had 'made a mistake' is a lesson not to be forgotten. For I should think there never was a greater man than he in a great office. Perhaps his self-distrust all helped to mature his wonderful vision and sympathy and strength.

Your very loving Mother
S. M. I.

So the acceptance of the offer was sent, and on Monday, 24 April, the appointment was made public in the press. Asquith's conduct of his ecclesiastical patronage has been consistently praised and justly, but on this occasion some surprise was expressed that earlier in the year he had appointed Scott Holland, who was a considerable public character, to be Regius Professor of Divinity at Oxford and now appointed a don to the publicity of the Deanery of St Paul's. But he was perfectly right. The professorship at Oxford after the quiet and long tenure of Dr Ince needed someone more ebullient, and that is what Scott Holland eminently was. London needed a scholar.

Once the matter was settled Inge began to have mixed feelings about it:

> *April 25.* A veritable deluge of letters—all very friendly and complimentary. My own feelings are mixed. I am very proud of the honour done me, and hopeful that I may be not unworthy of it; but it means living always in the public eye, and few opportunities of thinking out my philosophy. It is doubtful whether 'Plotinus' will now ever see the light, and if it does, he will not be nearly so good as if I had written him in the *umbratilis vita* of Brook House. And it is sad to think of leaving this beautiful house and garden, now looking its very best in the fresh green of spring and the pure white blossoms of the fruit trees.

It was clearly not so much leaving Cambridge as leaving their Cambridge home which they both felt so regrettable. What happens to be a dark and sunless Deanery was a poor exchange for Brook House. And so Kitty records in her diary on the day the offer arrived: "W R I said at last: 'I feel that if I refused such an honour when it has come so unsought for or wished for, that I should feel a poorer man all my life after,' & then he looked round our lovely little garden and said: 'O bother the man, why could he not have left us alone for another 4 years?' " His brother Charles made the same point with St Paul's in mind when he wrote: 'I know you and Kitty will be feeling rather sad at the thought that there is not a blade of grass (as far as I know) within "pramming."'

When the appointment was made public four or five hundred letters and telegrams poured in. Two of these may be given here, for what they tell of the new Dean and what might be expected of him. One is from his old colleague and fellow philosopher Hastings Rashdall, now Canon of Hereford as well as a Fellow of New College; the other from Dr Spooner, the Warden of New College, his wife's uncle.

Rashdall wrote as follows:

My dear Inge,

My very heartiest congratulations on your great preferment. Your appointment is the most definite encouragement that liberal theology has yet received from the dispensers of Patronage. I hope you may live to do even more than you have done to deserve the abuse of the 'Church Times' and the gratitude of those who wish to be helped to a reasonable faith.

I have only seen an extract of what you have been saying lately about Eschatology. My present state of mind is that I heartily wish that you or anyone else could show that there are no genuine eschatological sayings of our Lord, but I am afraid that the undertaking is historically impossible. That Schweitzer's view is enormously exaggerated I do not doubt.

The Deanery of St Paul's is an enormously attractive post, and yet if I were in your present shoes I am not sure that I would have given up for the Deanery.

Ever yours,

H. Rashdall.

From the Warden of New College came this:

26 April 1911
New College,
Oxford.

My dear Ralph,

I am very sorry to seem remiss in sending you my congratulations on your appointment as Dean of St Paul's. I returned home only on Saturday from Trengwainton & the West & have spent all my time in bed ever since except for a brief interval yesterday when I went up to London to make arrangements for the appointment of a New Headmaster of Winchester.[4] Can you recommend me one?

I am very glad of yr appointment on both public and private grounds. I have read your last Cambridge addresses[5] through again with much interest & feel, as I did when I listened to them, that you are able to take up a confident and strong position, strong in faith and confident in criticism, which should enable you to be of real help to a halting and doubting age. Your studies in mysticism help you in this way. And if there is a fresh crisis in Education, as there seems likely to be, there your counsel should be of use, and not to our side only. So in every way I rejoice & congratulate you & Kitty with you very heartily.

Yours affectionately,

W. A. Spooner.

Many of the letters of congratulation were, of course, from people in Cambridge. Their chief friends had been the Howard Marshes at the Master's Lodge at Downing close by, and "the whole Morgan family" at the Jesus College Lodge. But they had a large circle of less intimate friends, since they were so willing to go out and hope to enjoy themselves, and their own house was so much frequented by senior and junior members of the University. As a Professor Inge probably had ultimately more influence on his colleagues in the Theology school than on the undergraduates. But this does not mean that he was indifferent to the undergraduates. On the contrary he showed a notable tenderness for them in his remark quoted above, "I must try and find out what the undergraduates like and give it to them." Many professors would think this an uncalled-for concession. Men who dropped off from his lectures probably judged them 'no use for the tripos,' a reflection on their own intelligence rather than on the lectures. Inge had certainly changed his Hertford College style. He was stimulating, he was decided, and he was unusual. The *Cambridge Review*'s appreciation was just to him if not to his colleagues in saying, 'He has provided the University with the sort of teaching which has been long demanded and seldom provided by the Divinity Professors.'

He did not delay his departure: "*May 23.* I gave back the papers done by my Lecture Class, and signed their books. This is the end of my work as Lady Margaret Professor. *May 24.* My last day at Cambridge. The house and garden look more alluring than ever, alas! *May 26.* The *Installation Ceremony* took place." Mr Asquith's letter had been dated 17 April.

PART TWO

The Deanery
1911–1934

11

Settling In

The building of a church normally creates two activities, one the use of it by a congregation, the other the measures necessary for maintaining the fabric. Matters of law, finance, and religion are involved. Some persons in each parish become bound by law to perform certain duties. One or more of the parishioners become responsible for collecting and husbanding the endowments of the church and usually for augmenting them. Someone is responsible for the performance of Divine Service and the spread of Christian doctrine and the Christian way of life. In an ordinary church all these duties are performed by the parish priest and the churchwardens, usually two in number, assisted or hindered, as the case may be, by a parochial church council (the P.C.C.).

But there are churches in England, most of them cathedrals, which are organised differently. They are mostly very large churches, and they are mostly not parish churches. They are *collegiate* churches, where the government is entrusted to several priests, the chief of whom is called the Dean or Provost, the others Canons, and collectively they are the Dean and Chapter. More often than not they are now five in number, and these five form the College. Attached to the foundation there are on the one hand clergy, organist, choir men, choristers, and vergers who contribute to the beauty and dignity of the services; and on the other hand the surveyor of the fabric with the clerk of the works and his staff, who are concerned only with the beauty and security of the building. The Dean and Chapter have also a Chapter Clerk, who is an official of importance, and a Chapter Office where the Receiver General, under this or some other name, sees to the accounts and the administration with the assistance of the appropriate staff. In the background (occasionally in the foreground) there are wives.

In any collegiate church this general pattern can be discerned, just as a general pattern can be discerned in an Oxford or Cambridge College. But there are differences of detail, mainly arising from differences of origin, as there are at Oxford and Cambridge. Westminster Abbey was for its first five centuries a large monastery under royal patronage. Twenty years after it was dissolved it was refounded as a collegiate church, chiefly for the reason that something had to be done about it. St Paul's, on the other hand, has been a collegiate church and a cathedral from the seventh century. Its clergy have never been monks, but secular priests, though of course till the reformation they were in most periods celibate. A collegiate church, unless exempted, is subject to the laws which govern things ecclesiastical, to the Acts of Uniformity for example, and also to its own statutes. The statutes of the cathedrals often came down from the Middle Ages, but they were mostly reformed between 1930 and 1940. They are reinforced and may be replaced by custom. But whatever the instruments of government, they will work, if the Dean and Chapter mean them to, and they will not work, if the Dean and Chapter do not mean them to. The collegiate system makes the administration cumbrous, but the alternative would be to leave the authority in the hands of a single priest. In practice the Dean's position greatly varies. At Westminster he enjoys many prerogatives of importance. At St Paul's it has been asserted that the Dean is no more than the Senior Canon, and chairman of the Chapter meetings, enjoying certain appropriate marks of respect. Dean Inge was told that the Dean of St Paul's is like a mouse watched by four cats.

The Dean and Chapter are in many ways in much the same position as the Directors of a Company, but they are probably less united, and Chapter meetings are probably less harmonious than Board meetings. There are many reasons for this. The Directors in practice at any rate recruit their own colleagues. A cathedral Chapter has the vacancies in its membership filled by the Bishop or not infrequently by the Prime Minister acting for the Sovereign; they cannot choose someone who will suit them. The first appointment made after Dr Inge became Dean of St Paul's was regarded by him as thoroughly bad, though he came entirely to revise his opinion. And secondly, the Directors of a company always have profit and loss in mind,

not only as a matter of prestige for the company, but almost
always of greater or smaller income for themselves, and this is
a steadying thought. Until not much more than a century ago
this same consideration affected Deans and Canons also; after
paying expenses the surplus revenue year by year was distri-
buted among them; it was called the dividend. Unfortunately
they had not to consider the interests of any shareholders or any
congregation. The inclination was towards underspending on
the fabric and the services. But now that the stipends are fixed
by statute, although many cathedrals are greatly in want of
funds, finance is not the chief interest. It is shared with many
other interests historical, biblical, evangelical, ecclesiastical,
prelatical, and on any of these a member of the Chapter may
come to think strongly, and an able man often does. But he has
no sure curb to his particular convictions, and no sure test of
the relative importance of his notions. They will neither raise
nor lower dividends. They do matter, but unfortunately they
matter most to him. Chapter meetings are therefore apt to be
heated when they should be cool. But it must be allowed the
Chapters are at their best when some great thing has to be
decided.

As soon as the appointment to the Deanery was made public
Dr Inge went into the details of the change with his usual energy
and speed. He ordered his "decanal costume" on 27 April, and
on 4 May he took a room at the Thackeray Hotel, Bloomsbury,
and settled to take 11 Bedford Square on a yearly tenancy, from
Michaelmas, rent £200. He described it in a letter as "a most
beautiful old mansion, half as big again as 34 Rutland Gate."
He had also purchased himself a first-class season ticket to
Cambridge; it was one of his rare fits of feeling rich. He set
about making the acquaintance of the Cathedral Body.

The Prime Minister in offering the post had explained that
the official house would not be available, a most unusual and
anomalous situation in connection with a Deanery. In those
days there was an arrangement, now happily done away with,
by which an aged incumbent might get leave to retire and take
by way of annual pension a sum not exceeding one-third of the
value of the living. Dean Gregory, if anyone, certainly deserved

I   *Dean Inge*

to have this arrangement made for him. He had served the Cathedral most devotedly and vigorously as Canon and then as Dean for forty-three years. But the arrangement was varied in his favour, without much authority, so as to entitle him to spend the rest of his life in the Deanery. This was a merited kindness, for he was ninety-one years of age and had lived in the house more than twenty years, but it seems strange that no alternative accommodation was provided for his successor. Many might think that 11 Bedford Square was a better house in several respects. For the children the Dean thought it definitely preferable to the Deanery. But it was not really suitable and was a mile from the Cathedral.

Mrs Inge, as the Dean's wife must now be called, remained at Brook House with the children, though in July she was measuring the rooms at Bedford Square for carpets and so forth. It was fortunate that they had not got possession at midsummer, for on 2 August Dean Gregory died. It was not, however, until the night of 22 December that the new Dean and his wife slept in the Deanery for the first time. Although the house was in good condition, the old Dean's daughters had first to vacate it, and then it had to be redecorated and the electric light installed. The Dean found the workmen dilatory: meanwhile he oscillated between the Thackeray Hotel and the Precincts, where he was often offered a bed, with not infrequent though brief visits to Cambridge. The Duke of Bedford's agent kindly released him from his obligation in regard to 11 Bedford Square.

In the end Dean Inge's entry into his office, if not altogether propitious, turned out happily enough, and the task which Mr Asquith had especially commended to him, that of "restoring the tradition of scholarship and culture associated with the Deanery in the past" was congenial. But the Dean was less fitted to carry out the further behest "to maintain the services of the Cathedral at the standard of sober beauty which Dean Gregory had done so much to establish."

Here he was at a disadvantage. The Cathedral services which have been to many a Dean such a solace and a support, were to him little short of an abomination. Five years before, on 7 January 1906, he had preached in St Paul's for the Feast of the Epiphany, and Mrs Inge records in her diary that "the service was fully choral much to W. R. I.'s disgust and dismay—it took just upon 3 hours." Less than two months before he accepted the offer to succeed Gregory Canon Simpson had asked him to preach in St Paul's, "for which," he wrote, "I tried to appear grateful, though I dislike preaching there, and have no love for the place or the services." And familiarity never bred affection. His first Sunday was far from promising. "*May 28.* Spent nearly the whole day in church 8–9; 10.30–1.15; 3.15–4.45; 7–8.30. I have never before had work to do which wounded my conscience, but these services seem to me a criminal waste of time. I have held different views at different times about the character and nature of the Creator of the Universe; but never at any time have I thought it at all probable that he is the kind of person who enjoys being serenaded! However, I believe I can, without giving offence, pursue my theological studies in my stall. But for this, I really could not reconcile it with my conscience to spend about 22 hours a week in so futile a manner." But he found he could not have recourse to the relief he had hoped for. "*June 7.* I am getting more and more depressed by the intolerable boredom and waste of time of the services. I find it won't do to read books—the congregation would not notice, but the choir, who are more important, would. The noise gets on my nerves and interferes with consecutive thought—I am conscious of growing irritation and dislike of the Cathedral." It was not dislike merely of St Paul's Cathedral. A month after his installation he attended the Coronation of George V in Westminster Abbey. He had a poor view of the ceremonies from the seat which was allotted to him, and he complained of this in his diary, and added: "I prudently brought in a book, but the boredom of the six hours in the Abbey was extreme."

He never got rid of this feeling, but he remained in spite of it a very frequent attendant at the services in the Cathedral, though he succumbed to the practice of reading in his stall, and it was common knowledge that he did so. It might be thought that he did not care for going to church at all; but this was not the case. He very much liked a country church. Going to church at Crayke was probably his indelible notion of a satisfying service. His feeling for Crayke was strong. As he sat by his mother's bedside, when she was believed to be dying in 1915, and thought of her and himself, he found that "the happiest and dearest memories are those of the old Crayke life."

The Dean was also at a disadvantage in his new position through want of sympathy with his colleagues' Churchmanship. He never belonged to any definite party in the Church. But brought up as he was, he retained a sense of duty as an essential part of religious practice, and took it for granted that private prayer and the study of the Bible and adherence to the Church must be chief among those duties, not for orthodoxy's sake but because the stuff that religion is made of was to be found there. As time went on he fortified prayer with mysticism, he made his own selective use of the Bible, and he ministered as a faithful Anglican while finding in his pen the instrument of a wider influence. At the same time he would have nothing to do with Anglo-Catholicism which he characterised as sacerdotalism and superstition.

But the Canons of St Paul's, and the Bishop of London too, were Anglo-Catholics and the more recent tradition of St Paul's was all in that direction. They attached great value to the Choral Celebration of the Holy Communion on Sundays and great Holy Days, which the Dean disliked. They mainly appointed High Churchmen to the numerous livings of which the Dean and Chapter were patrons. They had actually passed a resolution which the Dean thought "disgraceful" not to appoint to a living anyone who took 'the North end' when celebrating the Communion. In their teaching they defended Christianity on lines which in the Dean's view could only damage Christianity. It must also be admitted that he was capable of being annoyed by 'high church' ways, as most Englishmen are, for reasons which scarcely come to consciousness.

There was in him too a more widespread impatience. He was convinced that he was a Liberal, and that all the opinions he had formed were liberal. He certainly had the equipment of knowledge and the powers of mind that justified confidence in his own opinions. He felt entitled therefore to think those who disagreed with him illiberal, and (a favourite word with him) obscurantist. He did not much suspect that other elements in his make-up besides brain and knowledge contributed to the formation of his opinions. It was the mixture of intellect and intuition which made him so outstanding, but it made him somewhat incalculable at times and not always easy to work with.

On the other hand he came to St Paul's with some great advantages. Just what the Prime Minister had in mind, when he brought to his notice the names of Colet, Donne, Tillotson, Milman, Mansel, and Church, is not very clear. The name of Inge was already almost as well known as theirs, and his writing and speaking held in high esteem by many. He was already in the public eye, and was soon to be remarkably familiar to the public. His outward appearance assisted here. It did somewhat belie his nature, but it was arresting. This is how he struck a writer in the *British Weekly* in November 1912: 'In appearance Dr Inge might well belong to the class of mystic ascetics. His thin, pale face, hollow cheeks, spare figure and dreamy remote expression give him something of the air of a hermit.' This of course is journalism, but to inspire such a description was an asset, and almost more so because the suggestion as to the character that underlay this outward appearance was very wide of the mark. The Dean was something of a Puritan, but he was no ascetic and had no use for hermits.

In fact he was extremely energetic in going about and being seen and heard. He more readily than ever accepted invitations to preach and lecture, often at great distance from London; he attended all sorts of gatherings, social, theological, and philanthropic, and often took the chair; he visited the livings in the gift of St Paul's most conscientiously for the induction of a new vicar or to preach. Naturally he was invited to many public functions, some of which he did not much care for; he was going once more to many dinner parties which, when he came to the Deanery, were still accepted as an enjoyable form of private entertainment, and he generally did enjoy himself.

The greatest advantage of all perhaps was that he was married to Mrs Inge. A more successful marriage would be hard to imagine. She loved her husband and she greatly admired him.

She made it easy for him to go into London society, and she shielded him from it too. She made it easy for him to overcome his shrinking temperament, and often turned to cheerfulness a diffidence in him which seemed like want of interest and sometimes was. He was not infrequently rather unforthcoming; she was wonderfully uninhibited and could make things go, even when the conditions were not very promising. Her husband thoroughly appreciated this, and could never be too thankful for her love. They did not always see much of one another, but they had at intervals beautiful holidays together. Some of their friends thought she spoilt him, but if so she did it with a certain amount of discretion, of which two examples may serve. The first is the account she gives of a party for the vergers and others at the Deanery, about forty in all. "When I began to explain to W. R. I. what we intended to do, the only remark he vouchsafed was, 'I should have thought a little quiet conversation first, and then music, would be much more suitable—a great mistake to force grown up people to play games.' Of course I bit his head off, but he did not mind!" The party seems in fact to have been a great success. The Dean described it, too, "After a substantial dinner, childish games . . . Kitty and Ruth of course were splendid at making things go." The other occasion is noticeable because it concerns the Dean's writings. In May 1914 he had a long article in the *Church Family Newspaper* defending Dr Sanday against Bishop Gore. "His pen," his wife wrote, "is sharper than a two-edged sword—so in 2 places I made him alter. Of course he is right and true—but I do not want him to frighten his timid friends, or exasperate the other side." She was also, like a good clergyman's wife, invited by him to give her opinion of his sermons. He was very ready to criticise them himself, but this was evidently not final. On one occasion after he had preached in Canterbury Cathedral his wife says, "When he came back, he came to my room with a deprecating look on his face, as he always has when he waits to hear whether I approved or not!" In what she called "the most scathing and brilliant of all his Essays" (in *Outspoken Essays*), she says: "his comments on the American Nation he must tone down before it is published."

Mrs Inge enjoyed the social life of London, the visiting, the

shops, and the good works into which she was most willingly
drawn, but it was an over-full life. She was urged on by a great
fund of energy and a genuine and practical religion, but
undoubtedly she overtaxed her strength, and there was the
added care of the children, of whom before she got into the
Deanery she had had four in a little more than five years. Even
at Cambridge she had often to stay in bed the whole morning,
and in London she soon had longer periods out of action. At
the end of 1913 on New Year's Eve she examined herself:
"Last night as I tried to recollect my thoughts—I prayed to
God that I might have more strength to recollect myself and
Him. My life seems too much like a breathless race. I long to
know if I am doing right, yet I feel I shall go to the grave with
only the feeling of panting haste to keep up with each day as
it comes, and that surely is wrong. We were meant to *think*,
above all things think and so understand God's love for us,
and learn from the writings of the good and great how to keep
near Him. I mean to try and be quieter if I can."

A truly just appreciation and a wise resolution, and just a
year later she wrote: "There is no happier woman on all the
earth than I." Yet to keep up with her husband and her children
and the Cathedral and friends and acquaintances and very
numerous relations and the servants (who changed rather
frequently) was strenuous, sprinting work. And while she
engaged in these reflections her husband was writing in his
diary: "My darling Kitty is the most wonderful wife a man
ever had. If no other blessing had ever been granted me, the
one sovereign boon of her love would outweigh everything."

From the practical point of view it was an advantage that
neither he nor she had any wish to make a display of affluence
or to compete in the business of entertaining. They gave successful dinner parties themselves from time to time. The Dean
sometimes thought a dinner he was invited to over-sumptuous,
and he soon got accustomed to and occasionally rather bored
with the traditional City dinners. He notes in his diary with
approval a well-served or well-managed meal, but almost never
mentions anything in particular that he had to eat. Mrs Inge
had the art or instinct of taking things as they came, yet a
specially grand dinner with the Dean of Westminster and Mrs

Ryle in Jerusalem Chamber called forth from her a heartfelt reaction: "Very magnificent. My heart failed me, if I thought that was how we ought to live." But it was not because they could not have lived so if they wished. The Dean was soon earning from one source or another a very large income.

So Dr Inge entered on his duties in some ways uncommonly well equipped, in some ways handicapped. The effect was what might be expected. The man who presided over St Paul's was presently one of the most famous of its Deans, but he presided over it with a certain detachment and a certain friction. Undoubtedly also there was a want of organisation of ordinary business which multiplied the Dean's own business and corre-spondence unnecessarily. Apart from Canon Alexander the Canons were not really men of affairs, and the Dean withdrew from some activities where he was prevented from being useful, judging perhaps rightly that he could find better employment. But this is not to say that he had no aptitude for business. He certainly had, when he was permitted to exercise it, nor would it be true to suggest, though it often is suggested, that he was on bad terms with his colleagues. They did not well understand him, and he was disappointed after the first impression had been readjusted, but they maintained a friendly intercourse partly through Mrs Inge's efforts. At the least they got used to one another. The Dean was sensible on the matter. When Canon Simpson had absented himself from the Chapter Meetings over a long period, and the other Canons wished to try and remove him by legal action or an appeal to the Bishop as Visitor, the Dean restrained them and expressed the opinion that it would be useless to attempt it and he would not if he could. After a few years he was able to write in his diary: "Canon Simpson is staying with us for a few days. We both like him more and more in spite of his cranks." He records an odd tenderness for Canon Newbolt. On St Paul's Day 1915 "the Archdeacon told me that Newbolt's feelings would not be hurt if I cut the choral celebration and processional litany, so I did so to my great relief." After Newbolt died years later he was surprised to be told that 'he was very fond of his Dean.' It is sad to say that in contrast with this the Bishop of London and the Dean of St Paul's drifted further and further apart, inevitable perhaps when we consider the different intellect, temperament, and outlook of these two indisputably distinguished men.

In one way the Dean improved his accomplishments. By chance or by necessity he found himself on several occasions speaking from notes or even extempore. He was sometimes called upon to speak after dinner with no notice before he arrived; he sometimes found he had to preach without having reckoned on having to do it; on one occasion he went to preach at Cambridge, and found he had brought the wrong sermon. He had been Dean less than a year when he discovered in regard to after dinner speaking that he was improving in what he described as "this difficult but necessary part of my duties." At any rate he often ceased to prepare very completely, and yet could speak effectively.

But this is to anticipate. The present chapter shall close with some account of the delivery and publication of the lectures which earned for their author the title of 'the gloomy Dean.' They were delivered at Sion College to the Women's Diocesan Association on 10, 17 and 24 November, and 1 December 1911 and published under the title *The Church and the Age*. His subject had been proposed to him, 'The Co-operation of the Church with the Spirit of the Age.' He approached it, he said, with a slight feeling of irritation. He was in fact against the Church co-operating with the Spirit of the Age. He felt obliged to ask his audience what the terms really implied, and in the first lecture he laid about him considerably on progress, and democracy, and other popular notions. He was not hopeful about them nor about the prospects for this country "To anyone who is able to view the situation without prejudice or passion, the outlook is disquieting in the extreme," he said, and much more in justification of this disquiet. He did not know that reporters were present, and on the next day the *Daily Mail* called him 'the gloomy Dean.' In his second lecture he defended himself.

Since I gave my first lecture, which I imagined to be a quiet little talk to a few London ladies, several of them my friends, I seem to have emerged into a publicity which I neither expected nor desired. I have found myself dubbed "the gloomy dean," in contrast with certain more popular ecclesiastics, who, because they can always conscientiously shout with the largest crowd, are naturally cheerful deans.

Well, you who heard me last week know that I was only telling you (1) not to use catchwords till you are quite sure what you mean by them; (2) not to worship "the idols of the market place" till you are quite sure what they are made of.

The title which you chose for me put me on the defensive. I am in the middle of proving to you that the Spirit of the Ages is a much better Spirit to co-operate with than the Spirits of this particular age.

He did not withdraw what he had said, and made a special stand about democracy in the Preface to the lectures, when they were published:

I see no reason to retract or apologise for what I have said about democracy, though it will be seen that my remarks on that subject were not intended to take a prominent place in these addresses. . . . I called democracy a superstition and a fetish: and I repeat that it is plainly both. The so-called "will of the people" is merely the whim of the majority. I cannot agree with Lord Morley that "the poorest and most numerous class is the People": it is simply the poorest and most numerous class.

He rebutted the charge of pessimism: he called it "ridiculous."

No Christian can be a pessimist. Christianity is a system of radical optimism, inasmuch as it asserts the ultimate correspondence of value and existence, or, to put the same thing in less technical language, it asserts that all will be well, some day and somehow.

But he did not think the day was close.

As I have argued, we may reasonably expect great improvement in the constitution of human society, and, which is far more important, in human nature. . . . But the process of improvement will (so far as we can presage) be so slow as to be hardly perceptible, unless indeed we discover how to breed goodness and ability as race-horses are bred for swiftness and cart-horses for strength. I confess that any hopefulness for the future of civilisation is based on the reasonable expectation that humanity is still only beginning its course.

These extracts, though they do not justify the *Daily Mail* reporter in his estimate, enable one to understand his mistake and even to forgive him, especially as 'the gloomy Dean' became almost a title of affection, as time went on. It is said that one of his children, having spilt a great splash of ink on the carpet, was heard speculating as to what the gloomy Dean would say. As late as August 1959 a correspondent in the *Daily Telegraph* was writing to say how pleasant it would be to come across a public house called 'The Two Gaitskells' or even 'The Gloomy Dean'!

There was a large and quite enthusiastic audience at the last lecture, and *The Church and the Age* in book form, though rather provocative, is in some places brilliant, and it expounds notions which the Dean never much modified. It is not gloomy, if you are prepared to be religious—the overwhelming superiority of religion to all other human activities is the theme of it all.

As a characteristic passage his summing up of the Church of England may be cited:

> Our own Church is a characteristically insular institution, which evades all classification. In its present shape it was the product of a political compromise, which was so framed as to include Catholics who would renounce the Pope, and Puritans who were not anarchists on principle. It is officially Protestant, and dislikes the name. It has framed tests of Catholicity which separate it from the non-Episcopalian Churches, and which are scornfully rejected by all other Catholics. It has been, in a word, the Church of the honestest and most illogical nation on the face of the earth.

Meanwhile the family life had been brightened by the birth of a daughter on 24 October. Appropriately enough she received the name of Paula.

12

Peace and War

1911–1918

There is more salt in the Thames estuary than in the brine baths
of Droitwich, and undoubtedly there are more brains in London
than in Oxford, but the salt shows up more in Droitwich and
brains show up more in Oxford. In London, to say the truth,
the University, splendid though it is, makes little impact on the
citizens at large except for the diversely coloured scarves which
the students wear all over the place with such a gay effect.
Brains there are at London University in plenty, but the chief
activity of London brains is in the council chamber, at the Bar,
in a great number of royal, and some very unroyal, societies,
and in much of what is done by way of hobby or diversion.
Such activity has not much conscious intention of adding to
the stock of learning: it is exercise rather than productive work:
a strong intellect will have exercise, and it chooses what kind
of exercise in the same way as a man decides what game to take
up, according to his aptitudes and whom he can find to play
with. In London people mostly earn their living by their wits;
brains are not exactly what they need for the purpose; in
London brains are for recreation: and it is notable that to be
at the English Bar, where brains really do come in, is one of
the finest games in the world, especially if you get good partners
and good opponents. But there are many other intellectual
resources too. At the end of the seventeenth century all the
brains in the country began to drift towards London, and they
made the eighteenth century what it was. Then they began to
drift back to Oxford and Cambridge and (strange to say) into
many a country rectory. London in the nineteenth century was
mainly social and commercial. But in the twentieth century the
tradition has turned again, and London has become once more
the magnet of the intellect.

The Dean naturally enough was invited into almost every intellectual circle in London; and he very soon found himself deeply involved. Any engagement that meant thinking and writing seemed attractive at a distance of time, and often, though not always, enjoyable in fulfilment. His days fell into a pattern only modified and not abandoned even in the holidays, a pattern of work all the morning, a meeting in the afternoon, another meeting or a dinner party in the evening. The most notable occurrence came to be a quiet day.

A plain chronicle of such a routine could only give a very incomplete idea of the Dean's life, and what it can give is to be found in the *Diary of a Dean* which he published in 1949, a book which presents a picture of London Society, useful to the historian of the period, but far from self-revealing. It does not do justice to the Dean's mind or account for his extensive and peculiar fame. Another method, that of looking at his tenure of the Deanery as a whole, might more clearly reveal his mind and account for his success with the public. But there seems to be one definite point at which a break occurs in this period. It is signalised by the publication of the second series of *Outspoken Essays* which contained with other items his 'Confessio Fidei.' This confession of faith was written on and off in 1921 and 1922. It crowns the first ten years at St Paul's, a decade marked by three years of peace, four years of war, and again three years of peace. The period is notable in the Dean's career for the delivery of his Gifford Lectures on Plotinus, for the many outward marks of distinction conferred upon him, and for the way in which he acquired wider and more secular interests, without any abandonment of divinity, but possibly at the expense of further philosophical achievement.

The activities into which the Dean allowed himself to be drawn were numerous and varied. He had been installed less than five months when he was made Warden of the Society of Sacred Study, a reputable but somewhat flagging affair. Six weeks later he took the chair as Warden of the Clergy Home Mission Union; at its meetings a large group of evangelicals heard papers read. On this occasion he read a paper in which characteristically (he tells us) he "took occasion to criticise all parties in the Church." Three months later again he took the chair at the Sociological Society, where a paper was read on 'Eugenics and National Insurance.' In the same month (February 1912) he attended the first meeting of the Clerical and Medical Committee; one of its activities was to investigate the claims of Christian Science. It was remarkable how often he was at the first meeting of a newly formed body, and it certainly looks as if his support was considered valuable in securing a good start. So early in March he read a paper on 'The Mystical Experience' at the inaugural meeting of the Religious Thought Society. He had been at a number of meetings concerned with the foundation of this society and was its acknowledged head. He took a great interest in it. In the middle of the same year he dined with a Norwegian guest at the inaugural banquet of the First International Congress of Eugenics, and early in 1913 he went on a deputation with members of the Eugenics Society to Mr Trevelyan at the Board of Education. In the middle of that year he was at the first meeting of the Birth Rate Commission appointed by Convocation. It met frequently, and on 19 March 1915 it was he who presented its report to Convocation. In June 1914 we find him at the London Society for the Study of Religion, a most distinguished body in which Claude Montefiore and Baron Friedrich von Hügel were prominent; it still flourishes. In November 1914 he spoke at the first meeting of the National Council for the prevention of Venereal Disease. By this time the 1914 War had begun, and his activities were restricted, but he seems to have established himself as one who would contribute richly to discussions on religion and on various matters where sociology and science met.

But his literary gifts also found recognition. He was elected at the end of 1913 to the Academic Committee of the Royal Society of Literature, a distinction then highly thought of. In January 1914 he took the Chair at a meeting of the English Association. In July he attended a preliminary meeting of the Shakespeare Tercentenary Committee.

On the whole he may be said to have liked meetings, but it would probably be fair to say that he liked discussing what one ought to think better than what one ought to do. He was impatient when people did not think what he thought, but he was apt to be really angry when they did what he considered wrong or mistaken. He was an *ex officio* member of Convocation, but he very soon got rather tired of that. He found it tedious and it wasted his time, and he despaired of rescuing it from the Anglo-Catholics. He first attended it on 4 July 1911, and came in for a discussion on Prayer Book revision. In his diary he sums up the situation acutely from the point of view of a revisionist:

> The revisionists have a strong majority, nearly the whole of the official element being in favour of revision. The anti-revisionists are mainly the extreme sacerdotalists who are nominated as Proctors by the parochial clergy. Their motive in obstructing seems to be partly fear that the licence which now prevails might be curtailed if the limits of ritual were prescribed, and partly the hope that their superior organisation may some day give them an overwhelming majority, which they might use to destroy the Reformation settlement and remodel the Prayer Book according to their own ideas. They are agitating for a 'reform' of Convocation which would reduce the official element to impotence. They are supported by a few stupid Evangelicals, who only see that some concessions are likely to be made to the 'Catholic' party, and by the Dean of Canterbury, who is certainly not stupid, but who seems to me to be in a false position.

This in fact *was* the situation, though others might have expressed it in different terms and with an altered array of epithets. His capacity for acute analysis made the Dean dislike most assemblies of the clergy.

In February 1913 he wrote: "I am cutting Convocation this time: I am more and more disgusted with that Assembly: and I don't think the obscurantists can do much mischief in the session." But his want of sympathy made him less influential than he could have been. His opposition at the Convocation of May 1918 suggests this: he did not consider the other man's point of view. "I spoke in opposition to a wild-cat socialistic resolution by Canon Garbett and W. Temple. The opportunist House paid no attention to the unanswerable economic arguments which I brought forward, and voted the resolution by about three to one. It was a melancholy and humiliating scene."

This debate merits some description, because it displays the

Dean in a situation in which he not uncommonly found himself. The wild-cat resolution was in the following terms: That this House, convinced that the demands of labour for a national minimum wage, for State provision against unemployment, and for a recognition of the status of the workers in the industries in which they are engaged, are in accordance with the principles of Christianity, calls upon the Church both to support these demands, and at the same time to further all efforts now being made to promote closer fellowship and co-operation between employers and employed in the service they are both rendering to the whole community.

It is noticeable that it was proposed and seconded by two men, both of whom were later Archbishops. Canon Garbett, then Vicar of Portsea, spoke solely from the experience of a successful parish priest in an industrial area: he said he was not a member of the Labour Party. William Temple, who was enjoying his brief incumbency of St James's, Piccadilly, spoke from the academic point of view and said he had joined the Labour Party 'last week.' Between them they marshalled the still familiar arguments effectively. The Archdeacon of Monmouth (Dr C. A. H. Green) proposed an amendment that for the word *support* should be substituted *urge the High Court of Parliament to a serious and impartial consideration of*. He said it was no business of Convocation to tell Parliament what Acts they should pass. The Dean of Canterbury agreed, and was followed by Canon Jones.[1] The Dean of St Paul's then made a speech of some length, in which he dealt more closely with the economic effects of a minimum wage and of insurance against unemployment. He did not concern himself so much as previous speakers with what was right but with what he felt sure would actually happen; he expected harm from these expedients. But he ended on a different consideration, one often urged by him, and one well calculated to raise any debate to a high level. The *Chronicle of Convocation* (1 May 1918) reports him as saying that 'he did not speak only of what they all believed in their hearts, that the only true, absolute values were those which increased by sharing, those values of which one man's gain was not another man's loss, but he spoke of the application of the Christian standards of value to questions of Labour and Wages. . . . If

they could accept the Christian standard of values the nation
would be rich in human values beyond the dreams of avarice.'

More speakers followed, and the Archdeacon of Monmouth's
amendment was defeated by 45 votes to 19. Other less drastic
amendments were accepted, and the original resolution in a
revised form was carried. The modifications would meet with
the Dean's approval, though he would still feel bound to vote
against the motion. He had not directly influenced the outcome
of the debate, though he had made to it a contribution all his
own.

The Dean's diary gives a strong impression that he was much
more comfortable and probably more influential in informal
gatherings when the discussion was fortuitous than in gatherings specially constituted to promote a particular policy or
cause. He was very fond of a small clerical society of ten
members called the Brotherhood; they dined monthly at one
another's houses. It had a history behind it and still exists.
There was no business and no papers were read. William
Temple, when he discovered this, at once resigned his membership. The talk sometimes developed into discussion on current
events or controversies, sometimes it was only gossip, but it
was an assemblage of minds and personalities which must have
been stimulating. The Dean found the same stimulus at some
of the other dinner parties too. It was a time when leading
politicians and leading Churchmen in London saw a good deal
more of one another than they do now. The governing class
was still a reality, although not spoken of as such. The men at
the top in politics, in the law, in the Church, met constantly in
one another's homes as well as in their clubs, with a certain
admixture of authors, artists, and physicians. Among such
people the Dean of St Paul's was soon very much in request.
He was something of a novelty to them: this was a new world
to him. Here he respected opinion and made many enquiries.
He found new sources of information on politics and science.
He soon remarked that it was "very interesting to be in the
midst of things." On the other hand his isolation in the Church
largely threw him back on his own resources in theology, and
he had the strength of mind to fortify and adjust his convictions and work out his own salvation, not without much

thought, but without much fear or trembling. Consequently one of the most striking qualities in his writing on religion is its independence.

It is very noticeable how the war of 1914 seems to have taken the governing class by surprise. In the months that preceded it they were far more engrossed in controversy over Ireland and with the suffragette agitation. As the suffragettes directed their attentions very considerably to St Paul's, it was their activities which most disturbed the Dean. He was in quite violent opposition to them before ever they came to the Cathedral; in fact this was what brought them there, for in November 1913 he joined in a correspondence in *The Times* against what he calls in his diary "this feminist outbreak," and there were severe reprisals a fortnight later. On Sunday, 7 December, "we were in fear of a great Suffragette disturbance, the women being wild about Pankhurst's imprisonment, and incensed against me for my letters in *The Times*. But though about 40 hussies were present (paid, I believe, 10/- a head by a society to which the Bishops of Lincoln and Kensington and Canon Simpson subscribe) they contented themselves with singing some nonsense for about a minute and a half between the two Advent Collects. They did not molest me during my sermon, in fact they nearly all went out during the Introit." By the following March things were worse: "We are having a very anxious time with the female anarchists whose blasphemous interruptions of our services are of almost weekly occurrence." These scenes continued through the summer, and in the middle of July they were still troubling him. Only on 27 July he wrote: "We seem to be in for a terrible European War." It is the first mention of the prospect of war in his diary; then on 4 August, "The Germans having invaded Belgium, England declared war."

The Dean was greatly agitated throughout this war, which was also true of the nation as a whole. So great a war and so near, and to be engaged in it, was what the British had had no experience of for nearly a hundred years. One can see that it was a great deal more trying than the 1939 war in spite of the comparatively light bombing. This was mainly because in 1940 the Germans had already lost a decisive battle (in the air), whereas in the former war they suffered no significant reverse till 1918. From 1914 to 1918 without intermission men went about clutching at straws, asking anyone who might know or might guess what the issue was to be. The Dean had frequent opportunities of meeting people who might know, and in his diary he records what generals and politicians said in greater detail than anything else. The generals were optimistic: but the news was generally bad.

The nation started on the wrong foot with the slogan 'Business as usual'; it led to that feeling of 'doing nothing about it' which is so bad for the nerves in war-time; the Dean had this feeling already in the second week of the war, and he certainly fell into extremes of anxiety and depression, and in the views he expressed in print or committed to his diary seems not specially interested in who was to win the war but in what could be saved from the ruin which he thought must fall upon all the combatants. Within three weeks of the opening of hostilities he foresaw that a bad time for civilisation was coming, and at the end of September 1914 he summarised his feelings and anticipations in a remarkable passage in his diary. After protesting against German brutality he continued:

> The vindictive hatred of the Germans towards ourselves is such that even worse atrocities may be expected if they ever land on our coasts. Meanwhile, there is the constant danger of bombs dropped from aeroplanes; for this method of murder is very popular with the modern Huns. I cannot feel hopeful about the issue of the war, for the enemy have siege-guns which make any fortress untenable in a day or two; and they have endless numbers, while the French army seems not to be up to its nominal strength. I never thought to have lived to see such a return to barbarism. Civilisation is in danger of dissolution; and democracy and freedom, in the Old World, may be crushed for an indefinite period. Whatever may be the issue of a campaign in which we have Russia to help us, France and England must emerge from the struggle with the rank of second-rate powers. Our day of political pride is over. A great race we are and shall remain; a great power we have been and are no longer. I am haunted with the thought of possible danger to my dear ones; and of course the comfortable independence to which I looked forward, for myself and them after me, is now very problematical. But I

believe above all the feeling that after all these years Corsica has vanquished Galilee, and military despotism is about to triumph on freedom, fills me with wretchedness. Neither religion nor philosophy gives me any comfort.

The course of the war did nothing to relieve these brooding fears, and on 15 April 1915 he ceased to write the diary which he had kept up at greater or less length since 1888. He resumed it in 1917 with reflections "on the terrible misfortunes which have befallen the civilised world during the $2\frac{1}{2}$ years which have passed since the war broke out." By February 1917 he had ceased to read the newspapers, which only made him miserable, and on 7 February he had to write, "I am suffering from the worst fit of depression that I have had since I was at Oxford, and even before that. I put it down to submarines, taxes, and the rotten state of the Church of England: but possibly there may be some subjective cause as well. At any rate I am feeling profoundly dejected." Only seven weeks before the end of the war he felt he had "no message now, except to prepare for the worst."

But after all life must be lived, and he had in fact been busy about many things. Opportunities for war service did not offer themselves so freely as in the later war, and social amenities were only gradually reduced. There was still much preaching and travelling. Most of the Committees he was on still met, and the business of the Cathedral was not diminished. Although the Dean's diary was suspended Mrs Inge still kept hers, and it throws light, though not of course full light, on the period of twenty months between 15 April 1915 and 31 December 1916. In the *Diary of a Dean* (p. 34) it is stated that the volume of Mrs Inge's diary which might have helped to make up for the Dean's silence was lost, but if so it has been recovered. It presents a remarkable record of coming and going at the Deanery, occasional air raids, which did not cause much alarm, a growing shortage of meat, darkened streets and rising prices (coal actually 35s. a ton). But there is a great deal of entertaining, though by May 1916 Mrs Inge entered a protest against 'a huge and luxuriant feast of every delicacy' which she attended with fourteen other ladies. The Dean's depression is sometimes mentioned, and there is often bad news which usually turns out not so bad after all and good news which is often contradicted. But Mrs Inge did not share her husband's apprehensions. The chief event for her is the birth of Richard on 6 December 1915. When she had first known that this was to be she had hoped it might be twin boys, whereas the Dean had written in his diary, "Alas! I am afraid we are to have an addition to our family." Richard turned out a great delight to both his parents.

Another event of importance and a great pleasure to them both was the friendship they formed with Lord Haldane and his sister. They made particular friends at a dinner party in October 1915, and in September 1916 in the course of their summer holiday the Inges made a visit to the Haldanes at Cloan, not far from Gleneagles. Lord Haldane told Mrs Inge at the end of their five days' stay, 'I have only known three men in my life who were able to follow and understand all I wanted to say, and they were Balfour and Asquith, strangely enough, and your husband. Grey has always been a faithful and true friend to me, but there are things that he does not know and understand.' Lord Haldane and the Dean shared philosophic interests and walks and talks which were a great bond. The Dean inscribed his volumes on Plotinus to his friend. Lord Haldane came in for much obloquy and abuse during the war on account of his supposed German sympathies, but as War Minister in the years 1905–12 he had re-shaped the British Army with the coming conflict with Germany in view. He lent the Inges his memorandum on his aims and work at the Ministry. Eventually public opinion was enlightened, and his services came to be understood.

The publication of his Gifford Lectures was for the Dean personally the leading event of these war years. An official invitation to give the lectures for 1917–18 at St Andrew's reached him on 20 March 1917, and he gladly accepted it. The subject was inevitably Plotinus, and the opportunity of giving the lectures was timely, for the long awaited book on Plotinus, the *magnum opus* at which he had toiled for so many years, could provide the material; and without any considerable adjustment could be given lecture form. It was now nearly twenty-four years since he wrote in his diary: "I must read Plotinus sometime." In the intervening period he had read and studied him long and deeply and had mastered the tenets of his philosophy, and he had got from him convictions which supported his own spiritual life. About 1901 he had begun to write what he meant should be his great contribution to philosophy, and to religion too, since he found in Plotinus a deeply spiritual mind. When he furnished his study in the Deanery, he arranged a Plotinus table with the necessary books and papers on it and hoped to do a little at it every day. In this he was disappointed. Of his first complete month in the Deanery (January 1912) he has to report, "I have not opened poor Plotinus." Still, he did get on slowly, and with growing appreciation of his author. The work in book form had apparently not got very far at the end of 1913, for he was then making copious notes which (he says) "I think will be useful in my book, if it ever appears," and the last words in his diary for that year are, "But I *must* produce my Plotinus—it has dragged on ineffectively much too long." In the following April and May he gave three lectures on Plotinus at the Royal Institution in Albemarle Street, and spoke about him elsewhere in June. The war coming in August 1914 was a discouragement, but by the end of the year 1916 he could say that the book was nearly finished, and early in February 1917 that all but the last chapter was ready for the press. The first part was in the hands of the publishers by the middle of that month. The lectures were delivered according to custom in two series, in October and November 1917 and in the same months of the next year. They were published under the title *The Philosophy of Plotinus* in the second week of December 1918.

It is no necessary part of biography to offer a criticism or a summary of an author's books except in so far as they record his acts or reveal his character. But there are parts of Inge's *Plotinus* which are self-revealing, and characteristics in it which display the man. It is laid out on quite simple, massive lines to the extent of 150,000 words or more. After an introductory chapter which tells you what the author has in mind as his aims, there is one of those pieces of a kind of history in which the Dean excelled, an account of the thought of Athens and Alexandria in the third century with special attention to its debt to Plato. Then the forerunners of Plotinus are dealt with individually. At the sixth lecture (out of twenty-two in all) the main part of the work begins and the philosophy of Plotinus himself is introduced. First the World of Sense is discussed, then the Soul and its immortality, then the Spiritual World, then the Absolute; these are the levels of the spirit's ascent in Plotinian thought. Lectures XX and XXI are on special aspects of Ethics, Religion, and Aesthetics, and the book ends with some Concluding Reflections. Thus the whole ground is covered. This would make it another major philosophical work; it would not be more if it were not for the discipleship which is so manifest in the author's attitude to Plotinus the master, as expressed in many places, but most in the first and last chapters. Some extracts will display the extent to which we have here philosophy without philosophical detachment. The very same thing might be seen in Plotinus himself. In his *Enneads* he too is a mystic, a theologian and an enthusiast. He energised these strains in Inge, who was an optimist in the same exclusive sense:

> My study of Plotinus has therefore been, of necessity, a novel as well as an intellectual discipline. And I have not found that he fails his disciples in good fortune or in evil. Like Wordsworth, he is an author whom a man may take up in trouble and perplexity, with the certainty of finding strength and consolation. He dwells in a region where the provoking of all men and the strife of tongues cannot annoy us; his citadel is impregnable even when the slings and arrows of fortune are discharged against ourselves or our country. For he insists that spiritual goods alone are real. . . . I have found him, I say, a wise and inspiring spiritual guide; and if I have also found his philosophy intellectually satisfying, it is partly because a religious philosophy must satisfy religious needs as well as speculative difficulties. (Vol. I, p. 9. Second edition.)

> When after much labour, the student has become familiar with the mannerisms of the author, he has his reward. The sustained elevation of thought, the intense honesty of the man, who never shirks a difficulty or writes an insincere word; the deep seriousness which makes him disdain all ornament and fine writing, but frequently moves him to real eloquence by the grandeur of his intellectual visions; the beauty of holiness which pervades even

the abstruse parts of the dialectic, produce a profound impression
on those who have given themselves time to surmount the initial
difficulties of reading the Enneads. (I, p. 16.)

His philosophy will not permit him to doubt for a moment
that a noble life cannot possibly be extinguished by death, that
the cause of justice and righteousness cannot possibly suffer final
defeat, and that no earth-born cloud can long prevent the beams
which stream from the eternal fount of light from illuminating
the dark places of this lower world. He bids us, as his master
Plato had done, to 'flee hence to our dear country.' But this
flight is no shirking of our duties: it is, as he puts it, 'a being
made like to God'; and this we can achieve without any running
away; for the spiritual world is all about and within us, 'there is
not much between us and it.' And when we have in heart and
mind reached our dear country, all earthly troubles fade into
insignificance. So it may be that others besides myself will find in
this prophet of a sad time a helper in public and private sorrows,
and that they will say of Plotinus what he said of his master
Ammonius, 'This is the man I was looking for.' (I, p. 23.)

These words were spoken in October 1917. In his diary for
7 July 1917, he had written:

I have been reading the first Ennead of Plotinus in Mackenna's
new translation, and was uplifted for the time by the wonderful
elevation of thought and detachment from the changes and
chances of mortal life; but I cannot sustain myself on this level:
the world is a much worse place than I ever thought it.

The Introductory Chapter or Lecture can hardly have been
written before the book was nearing completion, and it was
certainly from internal evidence written in war-time. It may be
assigned perhaps to the earlier part of 1917. It is a worthy
opening to the lectures. The last Chapter of Concluding
Reflections strikes an even more personal note, but is perhaps
not quite worthy of the close, though it contains some good
things and some fine things. The first part of it is concerned
with the war:

I now lay down my pen amid more tragic scenes. Civilisation lies
prostrate, as a maniac after burning her house and murdering her
children is bleeding to death from self-inflicted wounds, her

wealth and credit destroyed, her hopes of reasonable and orderly progress shattered. The parallel between the decay of our social order, the beginning of which I think we are now witnessing, and the economic ruin of the Roman empire in the third, fourth, and fifth centuries seems now even closer than when I wrote my introductory lecture. (II, p. 221.)

He must have been writing these words about July 1918, for he was busy with the proofs and making the index in August. It was an unexpected and rather untimely circumstance that he delivered them three days after the war was ended by the Armistice of 11 November. The second part of the lecture was a noble summary of what Neoplatonism has to say to us.

The *Plotinus* was a more complete survey of the philosopher's teaching than had yet appeared in England, though Thomas Whittaker's book *The Neo-Platonists* (1902) is called by Inge, "an admirable survey of the subject." In the last thirty years more has been learnt about third-century philosophers than Inge could know.

His special contribution was, as might be expected, in his exposition of the mysticism which is fundamental in Plotinian doctrine, but this will be dealt with in a later chapter.

The lectures were not very well attended, nor were his lectures on Plotinus at the Royal Institution. But the book, published just a month after the Armistice, had a wide circulation. It went into second and third editions in 1923 and 1929. The Dean criticised himself in his diary: "I am not quite satisfied with the book. Owing to the tinkering manner of its composition, it contains too many repetitions, and abrupt transitions due to interpolation of paragraphs." But this would be more obvious to the writer than to the reader. On the whole there is a broader sympathy than is sometimes to be found in his writing, and the epigrams are more gnomic and deeper. The reading is immensely wide, but it is not just a reading up of the subject. It displays judicious borrowing and obvious relish. The references to the writings of Plato always seem to be made with pleasure, respect, and understanding. "The famous myths may be unlike anything else in Greek literature: but they would be much stranger in any other," is a flash of original criticism. (I, p. 72.) One of the Dean's contentions is that Christianity is the heir to Hellenism and for that reason and as a result it is the religion of the West, and his own religion too. Plato is ultimately to be thanked for this: "We cannot preserve Platonism without Christianity nor Christianity without Platonism, nor civilisation without both." (II, p. 227.) This perhaps, though not the height or depth of the mystery, is the conclusion of the whole matter.

The important article which the Dean wrote for Hastings's *Dictionary of Religion and Ethics* may be mentioned here, as showing the extent of his researches. As befits an encyclopedia they deal largely with facts and avoid speculation. They are intended to provide food for thought rather than thoughts, and no doubt performed that service for the author himself. He wrote on 'Alexandrian Theology' (published in 1908), on 'Ecstasy' (1911), 'Logos' (1913), 'Neo-Platonism' (1917), and more briefly on 'Synderesis'[2] (1921). All this is solid work.

The Inges got back to London from St Andrews on 19 November, and the process of recovery from the war began. The Dean was not greatly exhilarated by the cessation of the fighting. "The situation is so perilous that only thoughtless people can be lighthearted over our victory, complete as it is."

On the domestic side the Deanery had first to be reinstated as a home. As the war went on London had become more dismal and the air-raids more threatening. For the summer holidays of 1917 what the Dean called "the little doll's house at Bourn" was rented. This was "The Mulberries," about ten miles to the west of Cambridge, discovered because the village policeman was father to Ella, the nurse. It proved so satisfactory that it was kept on and was where Mrs Inge and the three younger children lived until the end of the war, though she was away on frequent visits. The two elder boys also spent a good part of their holidays there. The Dean found himself often at the Deanery alone. He wrote to his wife in September 1917: "I must own to feel lonely without you and the children. I don't think I could live alone in this dark house. The children seem to humanise it, and it needs humanising. I suppose the girls begin their queer school experiment to-day." Catharine and Paula were to go to the village school at Bourn, where temporarily they picked up "a rich provincial dialect."[3]

On 6 December 1918, "the Bourn party returned looking very well." Catharine was now eight years and eight months old, Paula seven years and one month, and it was Richard's third birthday. Craufurd, nearly twelve and a half, and Edward, just eleven, were brought by their mother from their schools at Oxford on the 17th, and so the whole family were reunited.

At the end of the year the Dean, as usual, summed up in his diary; this time he wrote:

> So ends a strange year, in which the country, after being in danger of destruction by a foreign power, had a sudden and unexpected deliverance. . . .
>
> My home life has been happy, though I hate London more than ever, and feel the futility of my position as a dignitary of the Church of England. But there is no escape; I must make what leisure I can and use it as well as I can. My big book is now off my hands, and I must consider what to study next.

London was to grow more agreeable again, and opportunities of escape which offered themselves were refused. He was perhaps feeling a little sore at the moment, because efforts were made to get him nominated Provost of Eton when Dr Warre vacated that genial post in May 1918. He was led to think his appointment likely and fancied he would welcome it, but the Provost of King's, Dr Montague James, was available, and the choice inevitably fell on him.

13

'Outspoken Essays'

Medicine among the ancient Greeks got just as far as one would expect among a people richly endowed with the scientific spirit but less far advanced in scientific method. Dr Charles Singer, writing of it in the *Oxford Classical Dictionary*, says that 'the general line of treatment—surgery excepted—was not very unlike that of an intelligent and rather conservative English country practitioner of about a century and a half ago.' (Art., 'Medicine,' 1949.) The similarity is not surprising, for the English doctor had probably used Hippocrates and Galen as his textbooks when he was a student; Bath in his time was probably devoted to much the same kind of treatments as were tried at the great temple of Aesculapius at Epidaurus, and Bath and Epidaurus both offered the same kind of amenities to beguile the patients. A great many of the names used in medicine by the old Greek and Roman physicians are the same today: some of the most famous, like 'humours' and 'temperaments,' have drifted away from medicine, but they serve in other contexts. One expression still heard among us, but more frequent in the eighteenth century, preserves a Greek word and a notion much cherished by the Greeks—'the Grand Climacteric.' The notion was that every seventh year of a human life was physiologically important and rather dangerous, because it brought with it some noticeable change. Perhaps this corresponded with reality about as much as the idea often expressed nowadays that the material of which the body is composed is entirely replaced every seven years; at any rate it was generally agreed that the sixty-third year, the end of the ninth period of seven years, had a particular significance; and so it was the Grand Climacteric; *Climacter* is the Greek for the rung of a ladder; and this marked the highest rung of the ladder of life. In his sixty-third year a man was at the height of his power, mentally at his best and not physically handicapped. After that change must mean loss, and after sixty-three it was held that one need not necessarily look for a cause of death other than the failure of the vital powers.

Most people would say that there is something in this, though nature seems inclined just now to let us climb another rung. In any case there are obviously many exceptions. Painters often show no decline till a much later age: mathematicians on the other hand are normally precocious. G. H. Hardy gave the warning that 'no mathematician should ever allow himself to forget that mathematics, more than any other art or science, is a young man's game.' But if there is a climacteric, perhaps sixty-three is about right for its culmination.

The late Dean of St Paul's played tennis on his sixty-second birthday. He published the *Outspoken Essays*, Second Series, in his sixty-third year. He entered upon his great fame largely in consequence of this and the earlier volume. He wrote steadily for another thirty years, producing besides innumerable essays and articles and shorter books three solid works of some 90,000 words or more. But he never surpassed or even equalled the first sixty pages of that Second Series, in which he reviewed his own beliefs and convictions under the title 'Confessio Fidei.' Perhaps he felt that the moment for this review had come. He was just about to clutch the highest rung. He affords a classic instance of the Grand Climacteric.

After the appearance of *Plotinus*, the Dean, to whom writing had long been a necessity, did not know what to be at. Already more than a year before, at the end of September 1917, he had felt able to say that his ideas for his next book were beginning to take shape. "It is to be a discussion of the present conditions and future prospects of religion and social organisation, showing the importance of machinery and the necessity of accepting the Christian standard of values. I shall find great interest in studying books on political science. I am already beginning this work." He was making notes from such books at St Andrews in November, when he was there to deliver his first series of lectures.

Meanwhile he satisfied himself with reviews and a certain number of more substantial articles. In March 1918 he found himself "rather at a loose end," waiting for proofs of *Plotinus*, but it was not that alone which made him uneasy, for in April he confessed that his ideas for his next book were not shaping themselves well. "The fact is, I am in despair about the future of the country, and of the Church." But the proofs soon came in and occupied his mind, and the end of the war brought various distractions; the projected work on politics was laid aside. But he could not forego the making of books, and before June 1919 he had an arrangement with Longmans to put together some of his longer articles and make a volume of them. It appeared under the title *Outspoken Essays* on 22 October 1919, less than a year after *Plotinus*. *Outspoken Essays*, Second Series, appeared on 12 October 1922. These two volumes mark a distinct stage in the Dean's career as an author, and demand a special study independently of the other events in his life at this period.

The title was no doubt a telling one. It characterised the *Essays* and it characterised the Dean. As early as November 1912, the *Church Family Newspaper* had remarked that 'instead of the gloomy Dean he will soon be known as the outspoken Dean,' and certainly he often courted either epithet. But he spoke out in a sort of innocent way, as though telling the truth could never do anyone any harm. He was indeed a Mr Valiant-for-Truth, but he seemed not to know how powerfully he was armed. He was surprised when his bombshells exploded with such a clatter, though he got used to it in the end, as one gets used to any noise. The effect of this was to multiply his readers, but somewhat diminish his influence. The explosives wounded when they got home, else were apt to be admired as fireworks.

But in any case he was not speaking out all the time or anything like most of the time. He was expounding the serious views on serious subjects of a very well-informed mind trained by long discipline to think intently, and the result was unsurpassed in its own domain of the essay. For these were essays; they had not the weight of their author's bigger books, but as a vehicle for notable ideas intended to travel far and wide they could not be improved upon.

The First Series consists of eleven items. Of these the first, 'Our Present Discontents,' was written last, and in fact immediately before the manuscript was sent to the publisher. It is in some degree an introduction to the rest. The remainder of the book consists of four articles contributed to the *Edinburgh Review*, four to the *Quarterly Review*, and two to the *Hibbert Journal*, between the years 1908 and 1919. Some of the articles are theological, some political, and there is an obvious distinction between the two kinds corresponding closely to the division into earlier and later work, that is to say, into articles written before the 1914 war and those written during the war. The four theological essays (V–VIII) form the earlier group. They are 'Bishop Gore and the Church of England' (1908), 'Roman Catholic Modernism' (1909), 'Cardinal Newman' (1912), and 'St Paul' (1914). As their titles indicate they are strictly ecclesiastical. The last is most truly an essay, since it is an attempt, not to maintain a thesis, but to see how far our fairly extensive knowledge of the Apostle Paul can yield a life-like figure of him, and of what stature that figure is. The other three articles are more polemical: one is aimed at Anglo-Catholicism, one at the particular mode of reconciling fact and faith which the Roman Catholic Modernists, Loisy and Tyrrell, strove to commend and justify; one at anti-intellectualism. It is easy to see that, as far as religion goes, St Paul is Inge's man, and Gore, Loisy, and Newman are not. The boy of twelve who wrote a life of St Paul was father to the man who could write the following appreciation (p. 213):

The dominant impression that he [St Paul] makes upon us is that he was cast in a heroic mould. He is serenely indifferent to criticism and calumny; no power on earth can turn him from his purpose. He has made once for all a complete sacrifice of all earthly joys and all earthly ties; he has broken (he the devout Jewish Catholic) with his Church and braved her thunders; he has faced the opprobrium of being called traitor, heretic, and apostate; he has 'withstood to the face' the Palestinian apostles who were chosen by Jesus and held His commission; he has set his face to achieve, almost single-handed, the conquest of the Roman Empire, a thing never dreamed of by the Jerusalem Church: he is absolutely indifferent whether his mission will cost him his life, or only involve a continuation of almost intolerable hardship. It is this indomitable courage, complete self-sacrifice, and single-minded devotion to a magnificently audacious but not impracticable idea, which constitute the greatness of St Paul's character.

Here is enthusiasm justifying itself and eloquence in its right place.

Attached to this group of ecclesiastical essays, but not quite closely, is 'Institutionalism and Mysticism' (IX), a short paper delivered at the Congregational Hall, Farringdon Street, in March 1914. It is far less occupied with mysticism than with institutionalism as exemplified in the Roman Church, which in that particular form is said to be altogether alien to the Gospel. The contention is not quite convincingly urged, but then it was addressed to an audience who probably did not need much convincing.

The rest of the essays in this volume are in order of composition: 'Patriotism' (1915), 'The Birth Rate' (1916), 'The Indictment against Christianity' (1917), 'Survival and Immortality' (1917), 'The Future of the English Race' (1919), and 'Our Present Discontents.'[1] They are with one exception political and largely secular. The exception is 'Survival and Immortality,' which is religious and philosophical and owes a great deal to Plotinus. It was written in April and May 1917, specially for the *Hibbert Journal*, when *Plotinus* looked like nearing completion and was in the forefront of the Dean's mind. The remaining five essays are much less concerned with religion, and that is true even of 'The Indictment of Christianity,' where there is only one definite point against Christianity. The seeds of the Dean's pacifism are in it, however.

There can be no disputing a trend towards secular interests in the Dean after 1914, and this arose naturally out of the war. The topics of these later essays are what the war might raise apart from the primary question, Who will win? His war-time writing has consequently the special value of not being simply dependent on the war-time situation. It is based on the lessons to be learnt from past history, and the permanent features of human society. But to write them he must draw upon stores of learning new as well as old. New problems, political and economic, had sent him to fresh sources of information. He was a better historian and sociologist at the end of the war than at the beginning, and was (as we have seen) reading with a purpose towards a volume where this width of reading could be methodically employed. But in these occasional essays he was throwing off his thoughts and setting down his views on particular questions as they confronted him. That the Dean's work will be read by posterity, like Donne or Hooker or Hobbes, is a reasonable conjecture, but it may also be conjectured that he will be read mainly for his theology and not for his politics. He wrote no fiction, and as a political writer and satirist he is rather (perhaps not much) behind Swift, and even Swift is mainly read for his fictions. A great deal of political writing wears out. Although it is good reading the essay on 'The Birth Rate,' for example, is already superseded, because the statistics would now be handled differently. The disasters which always look like accompanying attempts at Democracy are always being averted by the wonderful power of society to heal its own wounds and recuperate. The Dean did not suspect this until very late in life,[2] because Great Britain had not needed during the industrial revolution to display this power of recuperation to any great extent. His forebodings are sometimes awry. But his gift of describing and analysing a political situation and bringing history and human nature to bear on it, a gift hitherto only partially developed, now blossomed; and it bore fruit too, if not quite of the kind that was expected.

A good example of his anticipations, based on historical consideration, is in 'The Future of the English Race' (pp. 98, 99):

> The old aristocracy showed a tendency to decay even when they were unduly favoured by legislation, and a little more pressure will drive them to voluntary sterility and extermination. Even more to be regretted is the doom of the professional aristocracy, a caste almost peculiar to our country. These families can often show longer, and usually much better pedigrees than the peerage; the persistence of marked ability in them, for several generations, is the delight of the eugenist. They are perhaps the best specimens of humanity to be found in any country of the world. Yet they have no prospects except to be gradually harassed out of existence, like the *curiales* of the later Roman Empire. The power will apparently be grasped by a new highly privileged class, the aristocracy of labour. This class, being intelligent, energetic,

and intensely selfish, may retain its domination for a considerable time. It is a matter of course that, having won its privilege of exploiting the community, it will use all its efforts to preserve that privilege and to prevent others from sharing it. In other words, it will become an exclusive and strongly conservative class, on a broader basis than the territorial and commercial aristocracies which preceded it.

A certain knowledge of human nature applied to political economy produces the following passage in 'The Indictment against Christianity' (pp. 261, 262); a noted economist of the day, J. A. Hobson, had attempted to estimate the 'human costs' of labour; the Dean is commenting on this:

> Creative work involving ingenuity and artistic qualities is not 'costly' at all, unless the hours of labour, or the nervous strain, exceed the powers of the worker. More monotonous work is not costly to the worker if the day's labour is fairly short, or if some variety can be introduced. The human cost is greatly increased if the worker thinks that his labour is useless, or that it will only benefit those who do not deserve the enjoyment of its fruits. Work which only produces frivolous luxuries is and ought to be unwelcome to the producer, even if he is well paid. It must also be emphasized that worry and anxiety take the heart out of a man more than anything else. Security of employment greatly reduces 'the human cost' of labour. These considerations are comparatively new in political economy.

There is something of a period flavour about these two extracts, the first from the pen of a diehard resigned to his fate, the second from a belated Ruskinite; yet both extracts are alive. The Dean had not really much knowledge of 'the working man's' thoughts or way of life. His picture of him was an idealised picture very much damaged. He admired his supposed pacifism: he hated, and worse still he sometimes despised, his apparent ignorance. But on the whole his liberalism kept him straight.

The *Outspoken Essays* was an immediate success. Less than two months after its appearance Longmans was printing a fourth impression, making nine thousand copies in all, and in January 1920 a fifth impression was called for.

This popularity is not in the least surprising. To begin with, the style of *Outspoken Essays* is so very lucid and lively, within the capacity of anyone who was accustomed to read any serious book or magazine. And then the topics dealt with are those which were exciting wide interest at the time. Each essay dealt with something which many people were thinking about, but did not know what to think. Dr Inge told them what he thought in no uncertain terms without the least doubt that it was what they ought to think too, and his thoughts were many and multifarious, studded with paradox, and fortified with common sense. He laid out his material in a pattern which it was easy to trace, and without much digression or too many illustrations drove home his point and came to a conclusion. He did not merely let the reader see his mind at work: he freely disclosed his feelings. He was determined not to be dull, and he never was. The exercise of gifts such as these might have made no more than a very good light-weight writer, but he ran no risk of this. There was underneath his accomplishments an earnestness and an affection which were both intense.

Of the second series of *Outspoken Essays* four thousand five hundred copies were sold on the day of publication. Its success was no less and no more than that of the former volume, and this is what was to be expected of works so similar, almost exactly the same in length, and each consisting of eleven essays. But the topics are mostly not of quite the same character; there are no essays on directly religious questions here. On the other hand the first in this book, 'Confessio Fidei,' is indeed the most deeply religious in the whole two volumes. Of the remainder, 'The White Man and His Rivals' was contributed to the *Quarterly* in April 1921, and 'The Dilemma of Civilisation' and 'Eugenics' to the *Edinburgh Review* in June 1921 and July 1922 respectively. The rest of the book had been made public in the form of lectures. The Hibbert Lectures number five, and extend to almost a hundred pages, under the general title 'The State Visible and Invisible'; they were delivered at Oxford in April and May 1920. 'The Idea of Progress' was the Romanes Lecture given at Oxford on 27 May 1920, and 'The Victorian Age' was given as the Rede Lecture at Cambridge on 5 May 1922. The 'Confessio Fidei' and the Hibbert Lectures had not been printed before.

The three review articles scarcely call for much notice. They are similar to the previous ones, but rather less optimistic, positively gloomy in parts, 'Eugenics' most of all, but it has a distinctive feature in that a footnote gives a table of the twelve male descendants of the Dean's great-grandfather Ralph Churton, Archdeacon, Scholar, and Divine, showing that "no male member of the family failed to win a certain degree of success in scholarship or theology or both." He gave it, he said, "not from conceit or egotism, but merely as an instance of the way in which a quite ordinary family record will confirm the views of Eugenists."

With the Hibbert Lectures on 'The State Visible and Invisible,' the Dean was never satisfied. They exhibit a great deal of reading, more perhaps than any of his other works except the *Plotinus*, and it looks as if they emerged out of the project he had formed in 1917 of writing on "the future prospect of religion and social organisation," the project which was not shaping well in April 1918, and proved abortive.

He wrote in his diary after delivering the first to a great crowd: "I do not wish to publish this course, which had to be composed hurriedly, and contains little that is really original or valuable," and after the course was finished he was of the same opinion: "To me they seemed superficial and wanting in originality: I have not had time to work them out properly." The audience kept up, however, not a common thing in Oxford. Whether they were altered or added to before publication cannot be told, probably they were not; the Dean still thought and wrote in the Preface: "the treatment is necessarily cursory and superficial, mainly from lack of space, but also, as regards the medieval period, from insufficient knowledge." This suggests a greater scale for the volume he had previously planned. The publication of what he regarded as unsatisfactory also suggests that he had found out that he had now reached a highly appreciative public much less critical than himself, and this was no doubt true. His readers would mostly be quite content with the new knowledge they acquired and the many ideas put into their heads which had a substantial bearing on their own times.

The Romanes Lecture at Oxford is one of the great public

events of the year, and to be asked to give it is a mark of great
distinction. The Rede Lecture corresponds to it at Cambridge,
but it is perhaps not of the genius of Cambridge to assign it quite
as much prestige. Of his Rede Lecture the Dean said, "it was
not really good, though I did my best with it." As to the subject
of it he had been in some doubt. In December 1921, not much
more than four months before it was delivered, he first thought
it would be about The Flowering Times of Civilisation, then
about the Platonic Tradition in English Literature, the subject
which in fact he took for his four Hulsean Lectures in 1925–26.
'The Victorian Age,' which he subsequently decided on, gave
him great opportunities for airing some of his favourite views.
It is lively stuff, which looks as if it were directed consciously
or unconsciously to the undergraduates. It is not so polished
as usual, in places almost rough and ready. Its laudatory appreciation of Tennyson may have a lasting interest, as having been
said when something needed to be said in praise of Tennyson,
who was going or had gone entirely out of favour. As literary
criticism it is perhaps not very successful.

The Romanes Lecture calls for closer examination, because
the Dean described it as "the best thing I have written, as far
as workmanship goes." What would he say were its particular
merits, and what particular aspect of writing did he call 'workmanship'?

I think he must have had foremost in mind that it is very
orderly. It begins by observing that the belief in progress is not
new, but has always existed side by side with the view that the
golden age lies in the past or that the history of the world moves
in cycles. Evolution does not support a belief in progress : the
scientists at first put this interpretation on Darwinism and then
abandoned it. The historians maintain the doctrine of progress
wrongly : political science has detected it where it does not
exist : philosophers have misused the word : Christianity has
been distorted by it "almost beyond recognition." Optimists can
be answered. Nevertheless Christianity has erected hope into
a virtue. The relation of hope to progress is discussed ; its
validity defined. The Lecture ends with a long peroration on
ideas and values and a modest hope for the future qualified
by a "perhaps" ; "of our more worthy visions for our race we

may perhaps cherish the faith that no pure hope can ever wither, except that a purer may grow out of its roots." These are the concluding words. There are several places where some favourite notion is briefly presented, as for example the relevance of Plato, or the value to mankind of the experience accumulated from the past, or the probability that the world does not tend to one universal end, but to a multiplicity of ends.

Finally there is the 'Confessio Fidei.' It is the first and longest of the *Outspoken Essays*, Second Series. The Dean describes the circumstances under which he wrote it "on the terrace in front of an hotel at Mürren." "A Swiss alp, five thousand feet above the sea, and in full view of a majestic range of snow peaks and glaciers, opens avenues of communication with the *magnalia Dei* which are less easy to maintain amid the dark and grimy surroundings of my London home." This was in August 1921. He was working at it again in the following December, and in the April after that. His object was primarily to benefit himself. "The object of studying philosophy is to know one's own mind, not other people's. Philosophy means thinking things out for oneself." These are the opening words of the essay. And eight lines on. "We cannot make a religion for others, and we ought not to let others make a religion for us. Our own religion is what life has taught us. If we can clarify this body of experience, which comes to us so turbid and impure, we shall have done what is best worth doing for ourselves," but he adds "and we shall have to offer to others the best that was in us to give. . . ." "And so I will employ myself here in trying to formulate my articles of belief, primarily for my own sake, but also in the hope that what I write may fall into the hands of some like-minded or sympathetic reader."

There are three tasks then before him, or perhaps more exactly three stages of one task: to think things out for himself, to clarify his experience of religion, and to formulate his articles of belief. The reader may expect therefore first a certain amount of arguments or dialectic or exercise of the discursive reason, call it what you will; then an evaluating of a number of experiences with the acceptance of some as what really matters, and the setting aside of others as unimportant or misleading;

and finally, based on this evaluation, a statement of personal convictions as to what a Christian man ought to believe. This is in fact what the reader does find. He will learn of some religious difficulties which the Dean encountered, a good deal of the things he values most, incidentally a few of his anti-pathies, and finally the grounds on which he held that Chris-tianity is unassailable, unless betrayed by its apologists.

Here is the Dean's inmost mind. He is expounding the solu-tion he has accepted for the difficulties he has felt. He had been dealing with them for years, and they so intimately concern the growth and shape of his thinking that it would be inexcusable not to attempt some account of them. In such a summary he must seem to be moving rapidly from one problem to another. In fact of course the process occupied many years, and different problems engaged him at different times with long intervals intervening. In setting it down, however, he has ordered it so as usually to let one problem lead on to another.

The first difficulty would concern the existence of God.[3] But this gives way at once to another. "Alike in religion and philo-sophy the important question is not whether God exists, but what we mean when we speak of God." This confronts us with what is called the conflict between religion and science. Clearly religion cannot deny the findings of science in its own sphere. "If for example an outbreak of cholera might be caused either by an infected water supply or by the blasphemies of an infidel mayor, medical research would be in confusion." But mechanical physics cannot account for mind; mind is not a cunningly con-trived clock. Science is concerned with quantity; quality or value is not its concern, and "the main thesis of this essay is that true faith is belief in the reality of absolute values." But to put mind and consciousness into a world of their own will not do; the unity of the cosmos must be maintained. The dis-tinction between natural and supernatural must be rejected, but so also must determinism be rejected. The place of life in what seems otherwise to be an inorganic world is acknowledged to be "extraordinarily difficult."

The next difficulty can be put in the form of a question, "Is the directing mind which orders all the events of the universe merely immanent?" If so, we ought to be pantheists and pessimists. But here "the hypothesis of creation expounded by the guardians of the Catholic tradition must be accepted." In other words a transcendent God outside the creation must be accepted. But this raises a fresh problem. "The question whether and how the transcendent God of Christianity can be known is a very difficult one." Here, by way of a preliminary, God's existence may be questioned, and the answer given that the famous proofs by human reason that God exists have their value if properly stated, but that the line of proof from religious experience is decisive. "The God revealed to us in prayer and meditation is both immanent and transcendent. He is within us, yet far above us." But supposing then that a transcendent God can be known, what can be known about him? The answer is Neoplatonic. The world is a Thing, but it is God's Thought, and with him to think is to create. "The world of time and space touches reality most closely when the eternal thoughts of God can be discerned creating after their own likeness."

Immediately we are up against the world's obvious imperfections, and the problem of evil must be tackled. The partial solution which the 'Confessio' suggests is based on a daring judgement of value, namely that the moral is less ideal than the true and the beautiful.

> We magnify the problem of evil by our narrow and exclusive moralism, which we habitually impose upon the Creator. . . . It would be easier to justify His ways to man if we pictured him more genially. . . . The unsolved mystery of evil is not so much the prevalence of suffering as the apparently reckless waste and destruction of the higher values . . . but there is no reason to doubt that those values which are the objects of the soul's love and aspiration are the atmosphere which the perfected spirit breathes when it awakes after the likeness of its Maker and enjoys His presence for ever. If this is so, the apparent waste of spiritual values in time is analogous to the wastefulness of nature in the creation and destruction of lower values. It is the lavishness of a Creator who draws from inexhaustible stores. I do not suggest that this is an adequate explanation of the problem of evil; I do not think that an adequate explanation has been or can be given. But the problem seems to me to have been made much worse than it really is. It is, on the whole, the least worthy conceptions of God which have most to fear from this difficulty. (pp. 24, 25.)

It is easy to see how much the Dean owed to Platonism in the solution (or partial solution) of his difficulties, and the central part of his 'Confessio' is concerned with a positive exposition of various aspects of the doctrine of values, and he begins it by asserting that "Rightly interpreted, this doctrine of values seems to me identical with the Platonic doctrine of Ideas," and twenty pages on he makes an admission: "So far I have kept almost entirely to that religion of philosophy which is common to Platonism and Christianity. I make no apology for thus emphasising the debt of the Christian Church to 'its old loving nurse, the Platonick philosophy.'" In all this part the Dean is not dealing with difficulties but expounding his convictions. He ends by reiterating his cherished doctrine of the Incarnation as the crown of Platonism, if only it had been revealed to Plato or Plotinus. But here he squarely faces the special difficulties raised by miracles and Modernism, and says quite frankly "To make our belief in Christ as a living and life-giving Spirit depend on any abnormal occurrences in the physical world seems to me an undetected residue of materialism."

His true personal confession of faith occurs almost incidentally a quarter of the way through the essay, and it must find a place in a Life of him, because it was what he lived by:

At the core of our personality is a spark lighted at the altar of God in heaven—a something too holy ever to consent to evil, an inner light which can illuminate our whole being. To purify the eyes of the understanding by constant discipline, to detach ourselves from hampering worldly or fleshly desires, to accustom ourselves to ascend in heart and mind to the kingdom of the eternal values which are the thoughts and purposes of God—this is the quest of the mystic and the scheme of his progress through his earthly life. It carries with it its own proof and justification, in the increasing clearness and certainty with which the truths of the invisible world are revealed to him who diligently seeks for them. The experience is too intimate, and in a sense too formless, to be imparted to others. Language was not made to express it, and the imagination which recalls the hours of vision after they have passed paints the vision in colours not its own. Remembered revelation always tends to clothe itself in mythical or symbolic forms. But the revelation was real; and it is here and here only—in the mystical act *par excellence*, the act of prayer—

that faith passes for a time into sight. Formless and vague and fleeting as it is, the mystical experience is the bedrock of religious faith. In it the soul, acting as a unity with all its faculties, rises above itself and becomes spirit; it asserts its claims to be a citizen of heaven.

I am very far from claiming that I have had these rich experiences myself. It is only occasionally that I can 'pray with the spirit and pray with the understanding also,' a very different thing from 'saying one's prayers.' Nor have I found in the contemplation of nature anything like the inspiration which Wordsworth and others have described. At times 'the moving waters at their priest-like task' seem to have the power which Euripides ascribes to them of 'washing away all human ills'; at times the mountains speak plainly of the Ancient of Days who was before they began to be; but too often nature only echoes back my own moods, and seems dark or light because I am sad or merry. The sweet sanctities of home life, and especially the innocence and affection of young children, more often bring me near to the felt presence of God. But for the great testimony of the great cloud of witnesses, who have mounted higher and seen more, I should not have ventured to build so much on this immediate revelation of God to the human soul. But the evidence of the saints seems to me absolutely trustworthy; and the dimness of my own vision would be disquieting only if I felt I had deserved better (pp. 14, 15).

14

Mysticism

In languages like English, where words have flowed in freely from many sources simply by usage, meanings of words of the same derivation may vary widely. We usually associate ancient Rome with law and order and a certain want of imagination, yet the attributes of romance are almost precisely the reverse of these. We are taught that the Goths and Vandals invaded and overwhelmed the Roman Empire, yet to destroy a Gothic building is, or was till lately, described as an act of vandalism. But with Greek it is otherwise. The ancient Greeks admitted very few foreign words to their language, because they never learnt foreign languages and so they knew the meaning of very few foreign words. But they formed endless derivations and compounds from what they had and came to use a very large vocabulary. In the Greek lexicon the word *myeo*, I initiate into secrets, shows more than twenty other words formed from it, and of these the adjective *mystikos* and the noun *mysterion* have acclimatised themselves in English as mystic and mystery. From them by analogy we have got mysticism, though *mystikismos* is not a Greek word of the classical period.

The word mystery came in Greek to apply to secrets imparted in a religious atmosphere consciously created by rites and ceremonies, but since they were secrets, not much is known of them for certain. The most famous mysteries were at Eleusis, about thirteen miles from Athens. Beginning independently and (for us) obscurely they were taken over by the Athenian State before the sixth century B.C. and survived to the very end of paganism. The initiate, it appears, was told something, saw something, and after a year's probation, had things shown to him or enacted before him. Conjecture as to what these things were varies between obscenities and as innocent a thing as a cornstalk, with some probability in favour of the cornstalk. That a genuine sense of purification or release or new life was to be had at Eleusis, and other places too, is not to be questioned. Eleusis is now only a jumble of ruins where not much can be discerned, but the great hall of Rites and Ceremonies is still identifiable with its banked rows of seats running down each side.

It must be because not much that was definite was associated with it in most minds that Christianity was not afraid to take over the pagan word *mysterion* and give it new associations. It occurs nearly twenty times in the New Testament, but it suffers a distinct change of meaning on the lips of the Christian. It means a piece of news which has hitherto not been known, but which God has now told to some community or individual with the express purpose of its being made known to the Church and through it to the whole world. It might perhaps cover anything that we include under the heading 'revealed religion,' though apocalypse would be a more accurate term if the revelation seemed to be of the nature of a drawing aside of a curtain, which is after all just what *apocalypsis* means. A mystery would tend to be a soberer, more doctrinal thing.

The revelation of the secret counsel or intention of God is commonly made to men and by men who have the sense of a personal contact with God, and so Christian mysticism comes to mean nothing less than that whole field of experience and its accompanying literature which considers and speculates upon God realised in individual lives directly and otherwise than by participation in the Church and its ministry of the Word and Sacraments. This does not entail neglect of the Sacraments or the Bible by the mystic; either may in fact be the occasion of mystical experience, but mysticism is a third way to God which is not the way of an institution or of doctrine.

With a view to his Bampton Lectures on *Christian Mysticism* the Dean had begun to write about mysticism and the mystics in the Long Vacation of 1897. In 1948 he published another work entitled *Mysticism in Religion*. These two books, separated in the writing by more than half a century, both exhibit the mind of an author who had a particular insight into the interpretation of the mystical experience, and the long roll of his intervening works makes it very clear that he never relaxed his study of the subject or his deep feeling about it. Much of the material he accumulated is of great interest and his criticism of it striking, but it is when he reveals his own convictions that he is most impressive. His views on other matters, often matters of serious import, seem even when most concentrated to be those of one who is the spectator of a passing show, but mysticism is for him concerned with eternity and resolves all transitory fears and hopes and illusions. "It is a vision of time-less reality," he wrote towards the end of *Mysticism in Religion* (p. 135), "which is neither born nor dies, being raised above the changes and chances of this mortal life. We pray God that we who are careful and troubled about many things may repose upon His eternal changelessness." This is the old man nearing ninety years, saying in simplified terms what the same man before he was forty had expressed as follows: "Religious Mysticism may be defined as the attempt to realise the presence of the living God in the soul and in nature, or, more generally, as *the attempt to realise, in thought and feeling, the immanence of the temporal in the eternal, and of the eternal in the temporal*." These words are taken from the third page of the Bampton Lectures. No Life of Dean Inge could omit some attempt to sketch what he himself meant by mysticism and thought about it. It is an attempted sketch of the contents of a mind. If the reader reckons this no part of biography he might well pass on to the next chapter.

When the Dean tells us in the Preface to the Bampton Lectures that until he began to write them his study of the mystical writers had been directed solely to his own intellectual and spiritual needs, it is noticeable that he puts intellectual before spiritual. Mystical religion is generally held to begin with disillusionment and to proceed next to detachment, and there is no doubt that the young Inge had found the religion he was so carefully brought up in intellectually untenable, and had detached himself from it gradually, or at least without any violent crisis of disbelief. His intellect was strong enough to cope with the difficulties as they arose, and diffident though he was about his prospects, he fully trusted his powers of mind. He did not have to detach himself from the world; for in spite of his eclectic pleasure in society and his careful management

of money he never really belonged to the world. Nor did he
have to detach himself from an interest in social problems as
the call of Christian duty, for he never had this interest until
late in life and he thought it a worldly interest, which often
distracted the ministers of religion from their proper work.
Private benevolence he took for granted, and what is perhaps
his sharpest criticism of Plotinus is Plotinus's depreciation of
action as a shadow of contemplation, which leads, he says, "to
the heartless doctrine, quite unworthy of the man, that public
calamities are to the wise man only stage tragedies." He did
not detach himself from church-going, of which he always
made an unquestioning but moderate use. But he did detach
himself from a good deal of religion as it was taught up to the
end of last century and beyond. He detached himself from
Anglo-Catholic teaching: he detached himself from Evangelical
teaching; he detached himself from a belief in miracles as a
support to faith; he detached himself from institutional religion
as being in any way an end in itself. It might be thought after
all this that there would scarcely be enough left for an ardent
Christian to live by. But the Dean had his mysticism. He looked
where true joys were to be found.

That union with God is possible in experience, and that it is
an experience which surpasses all others in satisfying man's
spirit, is the basic article of the mystic's creed, and the Dean
found in the course of his studies that the terms in which this
experience was described were similar in ancient and in modern
times, in Europe and in Asia, in wise and simple minds alike.
He believed this guaranteed its reality and its value. He found
that it was always represented as a path of ascent. He professed
to have set himself upon the path, though he never claimed to
have got very far upon it, but it was a path which any man
could traverse, for it was simply the way of prayer. He was
fond of quoting Plotinus's saying that for the apprehension of
divine truth we only need a faculty 'which all possess, but few
use.'

The mechanics of this way of prayer after Detachment has
been won are generally described as a sequence of Meditation,
Contemplation, Rapture, Ecstasy, and Mystical Union with
God, who is named amongst other names as the One, the

Absolute, or the Good. The Dean used all these terms in their accepted meaning, but the milestones in the path were for him Purification or Purgation, Enlightenment or Illumination, and a third and final stage to which he hesitated to give one special name, but it was Union, Vision, Absorption. He expresses his own view no doubt in his report of a passage from St Augustine (*De Quantitate Animae* XXX): "St Augustine arranges the ascent of the soul in seven stages. But the higher steps are, as usual, purgation, illumination, and union. This last which he calls 'the vision and contemplation of truth,' is 'not a step, but the goal of the journey.' "

It is natural to speak of the 'higher' steps in the mystical experience, but in *Studies in English Mystics* it is said that the experience in a sense describes a full circle in accordance with a principle enunciated by Proclus which the Dean quoted in the following passage and often elsewhere:

We may say that the religious consciousness begins as pure feeling. It begins with a lower kind of immediacy, which I should express in religious phraseology by saying that it begins with God's self-revealing presence in our consciousness. God lends us a portion of His eternal life, that we may at length make it our own. But it can only become our own by passing for a while quite out of the sphere of immediate perception. Feeling must pass into will. In so passing it does not cease to be feeling, but becomes conscious of itself as feeling. And Will, when it becomes conscious of itself as will, passes into intelligence without ceasing to be will. The reconciling principle between will and intelligence or knowledge is love, as has been recently well shown by McTaggart (*Studies in Hegelian Dialectic*). This corresponds with the thesis of some mystical theologians, that what they called the "mixed" state is higher than contemplation, being the perfect union of contemplation and action. But this "intellectual love of God," as Spinoza called it, is a reversion, on a much higher plane, to the pure feeling, or immediacy, with which we said religion begins. The religious experience has described a full circle, and has entered into the inheritance which was shown to it, as its own, at the beginning of its course. "The highest and lowest things are simple," says Proclus the Neo-Platonist; "the intermediate are complex" (pp. 29, 30).

This "immediacy" is what gives the mystic his conviction of

the truth and reality of his knowledge of God. But unless he is quite without intellectual interests he will have to fit it in to the rest of his experience, both for his own satisfaction and in order to commend to others what is in essence incommunicable just because it is immediate. Mysticism must be philosophised. The Dean studied earnestly the attempts which had been made to do this. He attempted it himself over and over again, and found it very difficult. In a lecture to the Institute of Philosophy in 1938 he summed up his findings, and he reprinted the lecture in 1948 as the conclusion of *Mysticism in Religion*. Its closing paragraph runs as follows—a kind of last words:

> Mysticism as a philosophy will not satisfy anti-intellectualists or pragmatists, or sceptics or agnostics or materialists or those who take time so seriously as to put God inside it. It is a philosophy of absolutism, which offers an experimental proof of itself. The proof is terribly hard, because it requires the dedication of the whole life to an end which is not visible when we begin to climb. Our world must change again and again, and we with and in it. The pearl of great price is there, and within our reach; but we must give all that we have and are to win it (p. 165).

The proof must show that the individual may reach to a real place and there really be with God. An experimental proof of this is to be found, the Dean said, in the fact that so many people believe they have had this experience and it has been an experience of marvellous happiness. This is an argument of the same kind as to say that many people pray and believe they are really speaking to God, and that at least raises a strong presumption that they can and do speak to God and are not deceiving themselves. It is a strong presumption, but it is open to flat contradiction. This is, of course, equally true of more advanced mysticism, especially as a great deal of self-deception, not to say magic, is apt to pass for mysticism. Some more strictly philosophic proof must be found. It would turn on three questions: first, the mystic is not materially with God: what part of him is with God then? This is a question of psychology: secondly, to speak of a place of meeting between man and God may be biblical, but it is not metaphysical: in what sense is the meeting real? (Here there was a hint of where to look for an answer; the Jews were not metaphysicians but the Greeks were): thirdly, there is the question of what God is: what do you mean by God? The Dean never doubted that the answers to these questions were to be found in Platonism. But Plato dealt with an immense variety of topics, and an author who speaks of Platonism may have many different things in mind, and some things which were never in Plato's mind. It would be impossible by quotation from the Dean's writings to bring together all that it suggested to him, but some sketch of what his Platonism clearly was must here be introduced.

The word Platonism is used in two senses: it means what Plato said: it also means what the students of Plato say he said and say themselves. And this is confusing, all the more because Plato wrote Dialogues and we cannot tell *for certain* whether he was speaking for himself, especially as he was particularly good at discussing and analysing sympathetically views and assertions which he thought false. But whatever he thought himself he has put notions into men's heads so original and important as to have given Europe a particular outlook and a particular way of life. The Christian world owes to him most of what it thinks about education and government, and a good deal of what it thinks about justice and immortality, and about many minor matters as well. All this is Platonism. But the greatest debtor to Plato is mysticism, when he asserted that the real world is not the world about us, but a world of ideas laid up 'in heaven.' He connected these two worlds by saying that the particular things we see here are copies or projections or shadows of corresponding ideas. He took tables and couches as his instances. We are aware of a table from time to time and of many different tables in the course of time, but they pass out of consciousness and in the end they perish. But all these tables are copies of the ideal table, or the idea of table, which is indestructible and eternal, and all the ideas together form an indestructible and eternal world. He would have agreed that all these ideas are related to the master ideas of Beauty, Truth, and Goodness, and these three might comprise The Good. The Good was perhaps the whole mind of God.

But here there is a deep confusion lying in wait for us, because Plato used the word god much less warily than we do. Though he speaks of God as one, he does not think that inconsistent with speaking of 'the gods' and having in mind the gods and heroes of ancient Greece and also the chief luminaries of the sky, to which with his contemporaries he ascribes the government of men's lives. Furthermore, by the Good he does not mean the system of ultimate moral values which we think of. The Good for him includes all that realises itself as what it is meant to be, so that knowledge and art stand on the same footing as morality. We take it for granted that we have improved upon his notion of God by limiting it. We have probably spoilt his notion of the Good by limiting that too.

It is not difficult to see that in Plato the Dean could find a great deal of mysticism: for the world of ideas looks like a place where we could be with God; and since the ideas are apprehended by the mind and not touched or seen with the bodily senses, it must be the mind, and not the body, which is with God; meaning by God that single Mind which creates and thinks and is the all embracing idea of the Good. All this is implicit in Plato. He expounds it with great power and charm, but not systematically. Only readers with a turn for it have seen its power and felt its charm; they seek it out, and can make of it an intelligible and systematic philosophy by which to live.

The Platonic doctrine on these lines could be extracted from Inge's writings in an abundance of passages. It had a double hold upon him, on the one hand because he felt an affinity with it; he had the turn for it, and he could shape the doctrine to his own uses from the Dialogues; on the other hand because he had that intellectual urge which desires to find out what other men have thought, and particularly he looked for the mystical element in their writings. In his own writings you find not a little about mysticism as a rule of life,[1] but you find much more of the history of what he called speculative mysticism. He thought St Paul more of a mystic than St John; he highly valued Origen and Clement of Alexandria, but more than in them he found in the New Platonism a system both philosophical and practical which seemed to solve most problems or else make them quite unimportant. His study of mysticism probably began with the devout, experimental mystics such as the lady Julian of Norwich, or the German Tauler. He calls their mysticism "Introspective Mysticism" or "Practical and Devotional Mysticism." But he gradually filled out the picture, and got a deeper view, and after he had mastered Plotinus he gave his attention mainly to those who aimed at a system; he wrote at some length on Dionysius the Areopagite so called, and Eckhart, and he delighted in the Cambridge Platonists, particularly Whichcote. He also diligently culled the testimonies and the asides of Platonic minds like Wordsworth's wherever he came across them.

But of course it is in Plotinus that the Dean found the most complete, consistent and systematic expositions of mysticism. It is instructive to see how in his earlier lectures on Plotinus he was mainly engaged in showing its superiority to other systems, as for example in his Essex Hall Lecture in 1914. As Plotinus was very little known, he had to bring in other philosophies which were then being canvassed. In 1917–18 in his Gifford Lectures, where he had time and occasion for detailed exposition, after setting the scene with an admirable historical review, he kept quite closely to the text of Plotinus, and what he could make of it. But if he tended a little to find satisfaction in correspondences between Plotinus's Neoplatonism and Christianity, in 1929 in the Annual Lecture on a Master Mind at the British Academy he left Christianity on one side, and accepted the fact of Plotinus ignoring it and refusing to introduce God into his system as being, to say the least of it, a useful simplification. At the same time he opined with Eucken that no thinker has influenced Christian theology more than this pagan, and he agreed with Troeltsch that 'the sharper stress of the scientific and philosophical spirit in modern times has made the blend of Neoplatonism and New Testament Christianity the only solution of the problem at the present day.'[2] He held firmly with Augustine to the belief that this New Testament Christianity could and must supplement the philosophy of Plotinus and to some extent correct its values.

The Dean accepted Plotinus's picture of the interior life of man, and he made it his own. By looking at Plotinus's picture then we look from a point of vantage at the interior life of Ralph Inge, and see much of what he most valued and revolved

most deeply in his mind. But the system of Plotinus is not easy
to explain, and cannot be expounded in very simple language.
Its basic Platonism consists in the conception of the world as
an ascent or descent from one level of reality to another. At
the bottom is matter (*Hylé*), which it is very difficult to understand. In his Essex Lecture the Dean describes it as "that which
hypothetically would be left if we could abstract from objects
all that gives them form and meaning—all, in fact, which makes
them possible objects of thought." This certainly asserts that
matter is not material in any ordinary sense. It is "no thing,
an aspiration to exist," which is needed to make objects of
thought possible. And so we can leave it and go up one floor
to the level of sensation, and here we have an essential
co-existence, of things perceived and persons of some kind
possessed with bodily senses to perceive them. Both the things
and the persons are necessary to one another. But the persons
must be alive, and therefore they must be attached to souls.

But it is obvious that the soul has many more faculties than
mere sensation: it is also connected to the body by pain and
pleasure: it is largely free of the body in Memory and Imagination: it is capable of Opinion and Reasoning in an ascending
scale, and Reason is the characteristic function of the soul. Thus
we ascend "by an inclined plane" to a new floor, and a wider
view spreads out before us, because it is clear that the function
of soul is not only exercised by individual souls; it must be a
World Soul which has created and maintains the world. But
Plotinus is not prepared to have individuals absorbed into the
World Soul. The individual soul is the one imperishable fact,
but each individual is a manifestation and an activity of the
World Soul. The World Soul "is not in the world: rather the
world is in it." It is perpetually active and creative, which is
equally true of individual souls.

But this is not the height of the ascent. The soul, while it
belongs to the world of sense and things sensed, is also lifted
by its faculty of reason into the world of Spirit. And here it is
necessary to emphasise that *Spirit* is according to Inge the right
equivalent of the Greek *Nous* usually translated *Mind*. Mind as
generally understood is certainly not adequate; and by avoiding
the word Mind for *Nous* we avoid conceiving of the world above

reason as the intellectual world, and can conceive of it rightly as the spiritual world, and here we come to the real world. The world of sense is not real, the 'things' are not in themselves what they seem to us. The soul by its faculty of reason gets nearer to things as they really are through knowledge and understanding, but in the spiritual world there is a complete transparency, as it might be called, and "spirit is what it knows." "Reality is neither thought nor thing, but the indissoluble union of thought and thing."

But beyond reality and beyond any relation, as for example, the relation between thought and thing, Plotinus, and most philosophers with him, see the necessity for the Absolute, the One, the First. But the Absolute, the One, the First, comes peculiarly near to being the Nothing. Properly speaking it ought not to be possible to say anything of him. But Inge points out that a good deal has been said about the Unknowable and the Unconscious, and zero at any rate is a most fruitful conception. So likewise the One with Plotinus takes on the attributes, without the name, of God. He thinks the One is certainly active, and perfectly free; he does not think that he comprehends everything. The One does not will, but he *is* necessity—and so forth. But "the real question for the student of Neoplatonism is not whether the dialectic really leads to an Absolute 'beyond existence.' It does. The question is whether this Absolute can be the object of worship or of contemplation, without at once descending into the sphere of Nous." (*Plotinus*, II, p. 115.)

And this is the important question for the life of the Dean himself. And here it must be explained that in the Plotinian system, although there are no barriers or hard and fast lines between the different levels of the world, yet it is a fixed principle that a lower level can contribute nothing to one above it, but each level above the lowest (i.e. matter) is by its nature bound to penetrate the lower level and create the possibility of ascent into itself. Souls might descend, perhaps might be said to fall, and they might refuse to seize the opportunity to rise again, but this was matter of speculation. What was certain was that ultimately contact of an individual soul with the Absolute was possible, and had been experienced. Plotinus had experienced it himself several times; his disciple Porphyry only once. It was reported to be a scene of bliss which could not conceivably be surpassed. Inge perhaps never attained to it: he always spoke of his own experience with caution.

It is obvious that such a conception of life and the universe raises many problems. It seems after all that the Absolute is not absolute, and that matter is more material than Plotinus would allow. Time and immortality have to be put in their proper place. Why the One should shed himself abroad (like sunlight, Plotinus said) is just as unsearchable for the Neoplatonist as for the Christian is the question why God should create the world. Can a disciple of Plotinus avoid pantheism? But theological theory does not need to be either complete or consistent before it can be a source of rapture or commend a rule of life, and so the British Academy Lecture ends by testifying:

> Plotinus is the greatest of all truly religious philosophers. His is a deep spiritual religion resting partly on philosophic thought and partly on intimate personal experience. It stands free of any historical events in past or future. For this reason, he has a message for us today. To speak for myself, I have lived with him for nearly thirty years, and I have not sought him in vain, in prosperity or adversity.

It is natural to ask oneself whether a devoted disciple of Plotinus could be also a devoted Christian. The Dean asked the question himself and had no doubt of the answer. In the 'Confessio Fidei' he wrote (p. 46):

> Can a Platonist be a Christian without renouncing the philosophy which he has found satisfying, both as an interpretation of the universe as it reveals itself to human experience, and as a rule of life, a path of ascent up the hill of the Lord? I believe that not only is it possible, but that the Christian revelation puts that keystone in the arch, and completes what the long travail of the human spirit, during many centuries of free and unfettered thought, had discovered about the nature of the world in which we live, the laws of God and the whole duty of man.

This keystone, as he had already declared in his *Plotinus*, was the doctrine of the Incarnation, and the Dean did not tire of recalling the passage in St Augustine's *Confessions*, where Augustine ascribes his conversion to Christianity in some part to his coming to the same conclusion, and when he recalled it in the 'Confessio Fidei,' he continued:

> As St Augustine rightly discerned, there comes a point where our non-Christian guides can conduct us no further. The great Bishop of Hippo had learned from the Platonists the meaning of 'God is a Spirit,' a doctrine which many Christians of his time did not understand, and which many do not understand today. But that 'the All-Great is the All-Loving too,' he could not learn from the sages of Hellenism. 'The Word made flesh—that I found not among them,' he says. And so, after due deliberation, he threw in his lot with the Christian Church, which had already assimilated the spiritual philosophy of Platonism, as well as the moral discipline which the later Platonists had taken over from the Stoics (p. 45).

Thus Augustine embraced "the Platonism of Plotinus with the Incarnation added to it"; but this addition to Plotinus was enormous, at one end the central doctrine of the person of Christ, at the other end the true and original Plato. The Dean never doubted that the Christian religion was Platonist before Plotinus.

The Dean called his religion "the religion of the Spirit," and he contended for it, not only as embodying the highest wisdom of the past, but as a much needed "third element" in the Church of today:

> My contention is that besides the combative Catholic and Protestant elements in the Churches, there has always been a third element, with very honourable traditions, which came to life again at the Renaissance, but really reaches back to the Greek Fathers, to St Paul and St John, and further back still. The characteristics of this type of Christianity are—a spiritual religion, based on a firm belief in absolute and eternal values as the most real things in the universe—a confidence that these values are knowable by man—a belief that they can nevertheless be known only by whole-hearted consecration of the intellect, will, and affections to the great quest—an entirely open mind towards the discoveries of science—a reverent and receptive attitude to the beauty, sublimity, and wisdom of the creation, as a revelation of

the mind and character of the Creator—a complete indifference to the current valuations of the worldling. (*The Platonic Tradition in English Religious Thought*, p. 33.)

This goes a long way beyond pure mysticism, but it contains the essence of mysticism, for it maintains that there is a spiritual world more real than this world, and that God is in it, and that we can get there while we are in the flesh or out of it.

If it is suggested that all this mysticism is escapism, self-deception, wishful thinking, auto-suggestion and entirely arbitrary, and this is what its critics do say; if 'the world yonder' or 'the negative way' or 'the flight of the Alone to the Alone' or 'mystical union' are from the beguiling phrase-book of Unreality, the Dean had his answer, often repeated in his writings and finding its latest expression in 1948:

In attempting to answer this objection, one is rightly chary of speaking of experiences which we have not had ourselves. I know well that I am very far from having earned the divine knowledge which is only imparted to the chosen few who have offered up all that they have to gain it. I can only speak of rare and fitful flashes of light which have seemed to come from some higher source than my own personality. But those who have mounted higher are sure that they have been in contact with ultimate reality, and heard the voice of God Himself, or of the glorified and indwelling Christ. Ought we not to believe them? It is conceivable, of course, that they may be deceived; but if our highest and deepest experiences cannot be trusted, it is useless to seek for truth anywhere. (*Mysticism in Religion*, p. 149.)

15

Modernism

Novelty is not a word of high standing. It generally brings with it a trace of disapproval or contempt. Novelty soon wears off, they say. If a shopkeeper tickets his wares as Novelties, they are generally not of the best quality. The newspapers which emphasise the newness of their news with the biggest headlines are not the best newspapers. Novels are the lightest kind of literature. Milton makes Adam, regretting the creation of woman, call her a novelty.[1] St Luke's remark about the Athenians that they spend their time in nothing else but either to tell or to hear some new thing is derogatory, though it sounds like the very attitude which St Paul would have wished to find in every city where he preached.

It is not surprising then that novelties which deserve respect often fail to secure it, and a classic instance of this is the new notion propounded by Copernicus that contrary to all appearance the earth is in rapid motion round the sun. It radically altered men's ideas of the world and of God, and in consequence it was on the one hand vehemently maintained and on the other hand passionately rejected. It is now almost universally accepted as a fact, but since it has (so far) made no difference to our way of life, most people have ceased to bother their heads about it: we all know the true explanation of what we still call sunrise and sunset, but only a few of us think deeply about the matter, for thinking is hard work, and most people do not seriously undertake it unless they must.

But for those who do think of it, this new astronomy has led on to speculation about laws of nature and miracles and God's omnipotence and existence which are disquieting for the adherents of a religion which took a fixed shape in the fourth century and has its roots in ancient wisdom and revelation long before that. The wide diffusion of reading and writing has augmented that disquiet. And so at least since the Renaissance there have been Modernists, people who in one way or another think that religion, and Christianity in particular, need to be brought up to date. To them this need is very obvious, and they are apt to be impatient of opposition. They forget perhaps that the things which go most to making man what he is remain unchanged, human nature and its affections, land and sea and air and climate, and most of all men's love of God.

The Dean was associated with Modernism in two quite different ways. He was a very strong opponent of what we may call Continental Modernism, he was a leader of Anglican Modernism. Both these activities played a large part in his life; they occupied a great deal of his thoughts and filled a good many pages of his writing. They demand to be studied a little.

They are quite distinct. Although strongly opposed to the authoritarian character of the Papacy, the Dean was of the opinion that the Pope could not do otherwise than suppress the Modernist movement in the Roman Church, but he did everything he could to help the movement in England. Nevertheless both movements arose out of the same situation, a situation which was troubling the whole of Christendom in the latter part of the nineteenth century and in a less oppressive shape troubles it now. It is the difficulty of determining the authority of the Bible in view of the critical study to which it has been subjected, and the difficulty is all the greater, since the critics are not agreed as to how much historicity can be assigned to the various books, and in particular to the Gospels. The critical process in its modern form, described as scientific and certainly influenced by scientific methods, had been going on for many years before 1902, but it was in that year, according to Dr A. R. Vidler, that the Modernist movement 'may be said to have come to a head, in so far as it ever did this.'[2] In any case it did not come to a head except in the Roman Church. There the situation was particularly difficult, because some of the most assured results of the criticism had been formally declared erroneous, because also the critics themselves had in some quarters published conclusions which were, to say the least, precarious, and because the laity were only interested to a very small degree. In the end the complex unravelled itself.

Alfred Loisy (1857–1940), the leader of the movement in France, left the Church; George Tyrrell (1861–1909), the leader in England, died, perhaps of grief.

In theology neither of them was of very great importance. But they had it in common that both assumed that the historic Jesus was a peasant of exciting but deluded Messianic views, belonging entirely to the place and age in which he lived. Loisy was much more drastic than Tyrrell, and there is a good analysis of his idea of 'the career of Jesus' in *Outspoken Essays*, I, pp. 150–2. The Dean concludes it with the comment: "Readers unfamiliar with Modernist literature will probably have read the foregoing extract with utter amazement." Tyrrell was more moderate, but he would have allowed quite as frankly as Loisy that criticism had made much of the accepted dogma of the Church untenable. At the same time they both wished to maintain their allegiance to the Christian religion in the form in which Roman Catholicism presents it. They were in contact with one another, but they did not work together, and in some ways they were singularly different. Loisy was a *savant* with a logical mind, and it was a very good mind. The Dean calls him "not only a brilliant controversialist, but a very acute critic" ('Confessio Fidei,' p. 51). But as a writer he was a bit sour and a little bit of a bore. Tyrrell, though very hot-tempered and often hopelessly indiscreet, was much more attractive and in a way sympathetic with his opponents. Although dismissed from the Society of Jesus and subsequently excommunicated, he clung to the Church, hoping that his views would one day prevail, until his death in 1909. Baron von Hügel's analysis of his temperament in a letter of 1905 is relevant. It ends with the words: 'A German brain, an Irish heart: can there be a more fruitful combination if the owner is heroically faithful?' (*Selected Letters*, p. 132).

Different as they were, Loisy and Tyrrell both took the same line in defence of their religion. It was the time when pragmatism was fashionable as a philosophy, or at least as a philosophic approach. The value and the validity of Reason were being questioned and the Will was being exalted. So it seemed good to Tyrrell to write: 'Certain concrete historical facts enter into our creed as matters of faith. Precisely as historical facts they concern the historian and must be criticised by his methods. But as matters of faith they must be determined by faith, i.e. by their proved religious values' (*Lex orandi*, p. 169). This position looks easily assailable, but it was expounded by Loisy with great force, and was strengthened by a doctrine of development which asserted that a religion had sprung from the life of Jesus of Nazareth inevitably, though quite unforeseen by himself; and further, that the whole history of this religion was bound to be what it successively was, as it defended itself against its environment century after century. In this sense it might be said to be inherent in the gospel, and at any period to be not only the Christian religion but Christ in the world.

This was the Modernism against which Inge contended so vigorously. He would have nothing to say for it. He often referred to it in his writings and he dealt with it directly in *Faith and Knowledge* (1904, pp. 281–92), *Faith* (1909, pp. 102–5, 161–77), *Outspoken Essays*, I, 'Roman Catholic Modernism,' pp. 137–71, reprinted from the *Quarterly Review* for April 1909, *Outspoken Essays*, II, 1922, 'Confessio Fidei' (pp. 51–3). Its anti-intellectualism he examined more particularly in *Personal Idealism and Mysticism*, Lecture V. The literature and the story of it he dealt with mostly in his article in the *Quarterly Review*, and the philosophical aspect in *Faith*.[3] It is not necessary here to restate Inge's answer to Loisy at length: one or two passages must suffice: their cogency may perhaps be more obvious to an average English Christian than to an average French Christian, whose objection to Modernism might be equally strong, but different.

> St Paul, who is often invoked by this school, made it his hope and aim that the Church might grow up *into* Him in all things, which is the head, even Christ. We are now told that we must be content to grow up *out* of Him. (*Faith and Knowledge*, p. 288.)

> It is plain that the facts of religion are no facts for them [the Modernists]. M. Loisy's Jesus may have been a more respectable Messiah than Theudas, but he belongs to the same category. There has been, after all, a real breach of continuity, and no mere development, in the Church as they conceive it; and it is a breach which divides the Church from the historical Christ. It is as if one were to trace one's descent from some great man, and to

establish every link except the first:—our ancestor was after all wrongly supposed to be the son of the great man; or the great man was only a myth. It is quite impossible to justify this position by disparaging existential truth. If it does not matter whether the Incarnation was a fact or a legend; if Faith can create dogmas with the same freedom which Plato's Socrates claims in inventing his myths: if things exist only as instruments for the will, and all events are plastic under the hand of the religious imagination; we are transported into a world where there is no difference between fact and fiction, and where it is difficult to suppose that human conduct can matter much. Such a contempt for actuality is far removed from the Christian view of the world. (*Faith*, p. 174.)

A more personal reaction is expressed in 'Confessio Fidei' (pp. 52, 53).

I have tried to ask myself what would be the effect upon my personal faith if I were driven to accept the interpretations of Loisy and his followers as true history. The figure of Christ as an object of true worship would be gone. We could take no interest in a deluded Jewish peasant, who, believing that the world was coming to an end, preached only an *Interimsethik* of no value to a world which had thousands of years before it. Cut off from its roots in a historical Incarnation, the Church appears in Loisy's 'L'Evangile et L'Eglise' as a very human political institution, adapting itself adroitly to the task of self-preservation, and perhaps incidentally doing rather more good than harm in the world. Devoted loyalty to such a political organisation is possible, as history shows: but on the whole I think that my country has had a better record, and the name of England moves me more than the Church without Christ.

Here there is certainly something of self-revelation. The Dean in opposing Modernism was partly actuated by his general dislike of Roman Catholicism, and partly by the fact that he did not accept the more speculative and extreme assertions of criticism, both thoroughly English attitudes, which reinforced his objections on philosophic grounds. But it is very interesting to notice how near he was in fact to the Modernists, especially Tyrrell.

He accepted the unfettered criticism of the Bible which was the beginning of their movement, and he felt very much the tension which it created for orthodoxy. He rejected the miracles as props or proofs of the Christian creed. "The famous arguments from miracles and prophecy are in principle condemned by our Lord, whose warnings against seeking after a sign have been preserved by the candour of His biographers, though they themselves attached great value to such evidence. They are no longer arguments for us" (*Faith*, p. 81). He shared with the Modernists what A. L. Lilley called 'their eager and enthusiastic confidence in the achievements of the modern mind,' at least in so far as it concerned natural science, and he frequently urged that the distinction between natural and supernatural must go, because it was not possible to draw the bounding line between them. This was implicit in the Modernist position; there was 'a tendency to close the long period of divorce between the natural and the supernatural,' Lilley says, and he goes on to say that Loisy 'had yielded to its uncompromising logic.' But in fact Loisy had been illogical enough to exclude the supernatural; he was no mystic. Here Inge walked more closely with Tyrrell. Tyrrell's *Much-Abused Letter*, if it had been slightly more astringent in its indignations, might well have been written by Inge. It goes beyond Inge in the Protestant direction in its attitude towards 'the invisible Church':

> I think you agree with me, that though the one thing needful is communion with the invisible Church (i.e. with God as presented to us in Christ and in all Christ-like men past, present, and future; with all those who, whatever their professed creed, in any way or degree suffer and forsake themselves for God's cause and God's will), yet communion with the visible Church, with those, namely, who *profess* to be Christ-like, is a great *desideratum*, is a condition of more fruitful communion with the invisible (p. 62).

This would be regarded as an understatement by orthodox Anglicans, for whom visibility is a necessary mark of the Church, and Inge, I think, accepts that. But he and Tyrrell would be in step again, when Tyrrell two pages later comes to what he calls the main purpose of his letter, and this proves to be to suggest recourse to pure mysticism.

> Faith is a *seeing* of God, not face to face but through a glass darkly: still it is a seeing for oneself; not a believing on hearsay. . . . this vision is not at command but is given us; and that,

most clearly in moments when we seem most filled with God; when we are truest to all that is best in our spiritual nature; when we are lifted up above the plane of ordinary vision, not by some narrowing excitement or intoxicant that excludes the data of sober sense and so produces an illusory transformation of reality; but by an access of inward light which shows us all we knew before, included in a vaster and deeper knowledge, transcended but not contradicted. In such moments we seem to gaze with God's eyes and from the standpoint of the whole. It is as though by certain moral self-adjustments and self-dispositions the soul had first to set its face and strain its eyes in the right direction; and that then God could lift it up to command a wider horizon. To live by the memory of such moments in the teeth of the doubts and negations of our lower and narrower states is to live the life of Faith (pp. 69, 70).

One would hardly have to alter a word of this to make it a convincing piece of Inge. One might add that Tyrrell could have written almost any part of *Speculum Animae*.

So Inge and Tyrrell took the same way out of the modernist situation. They found it in Mysticism. Inge claimed that the religious problems of the day, the world of science, the slender merit of the scriptures, were seen in their right place, when mysticism was allowed to stand on its own feet, but it is just a question whether he was not denying the pragmatist philosophy and yet accepting its inevitable conclusion. In the light of truth, as he saw it, a number of traditional dogmas were given notice to quit, but somehow they stayed on.

In this *Much-Abused Letter* of his Tyrrell was telling an imaginary friend that with this kind of Faith he need not worry about the Church, but he took it for granted that the Church must reform itself and meanwhile men must not break away from it. He pictured the reform as being effected by authority when authority was liberalised. Inge really saw more clearly what would actually happen. "Of the Modernists a few will secede, others will remain in the Church, though in open revolt against the Vatican: but the majority will be silenced, and will make a lip-submission to authority" (*Outspoken Essays*, I, p. 167). This is in fact what happened. The Modernist movement in the Roman Church was successfully suppressed. But with Inge and those of like mind the situation was different. They were not in the least disturbed by the thought of the authorities. Anglicans seldom are. They believed that the Truth would prevail. "We must wait in patience for the coming of the wise master-builders who will construct a more truly Catholic Church out of the fragments of the old, with the help of the material now being collected by philosophers, psychologists, historians, and scientists of all creeds and countries" (p. 170). What subsequently came to be called Modernism in this country was a liberal Protestantism which strove consciously towards this objective.

The word Modernism was rarely used in the controversy over the heresies of Loisy and Tyrrell until it was used by the Pope himself in the encyclical *Pascendi Gregis* which condemned them. In such a Church as that of Rome it is difficult not to suppose that there is always Modernism in some quarters, but its adherents since the encyclical do not care to have this label attached to them. In England, however, the name survived and has had an honourable history, and Dr Inge was no doubt in the English sense one of the leading Modernists of his time.

The Modernism in which he was so prominent was much more of a movement than Continental Modernism ever was; but generally speaking it was less modern. It may be said to have been founded in 1898, when the Churchman's Union was formed; and presently its energies were directed and publicised by the *Modern Churchman*, a periodical of great interest and ability begun in 1911 and edited for many years by the Revd. H. D. A. Major, still happily among us. Dr Inge made his first contribution to it in September 1917. Henceforward he attached himself actively to the cause.

From 1924 to 1934 he was President of the Churchmen's Union, changed to the Modern Churchmen's Union in 1928. He succeeded his old Hertford College colleague, Hastings Rashdall, who died after a very short tenure of the office. It is interesting to recall that Rashdall was a strong opponent of mysticism and Inge its strongest advocate. It is in fact the varieties in Modernism which make it difficult to succeed as a 'movement.' In his presidential address at the Annual Conference in 1925 the Dean glanced at this obliquely, when he spoke of "the tradition which we wish to follow, whether we

THE DEAN & CHAPTER ASK YOU TO JOIN IN THE
THANKSGIVING FOR THE PRESERVATION OF
ST. PAUL'S CATHEDRAL ◇ JUNE 25TH 1930, 12 NOON

The restoration began just as Dr Inge was appointed to the Deanery, was
interrupted by the 1914 War, and only completed in 1930.
The drawing is by Henry Rushbury.

call it Greek, or Platonic, or mystical, or Liberal, or Renaissance." This tradition he described as "what was best in the old [Greek] civilisation, its spirit of unfettered enquiry, its long tradition of deep thought, its reverence for knowledge, its robust faith that divine truth is accessible to man." This was what he at any rate meant by being a Modernist, though he confessed that he disliked the name.

> We are not Modernists, because our Christianity is no new thing, but older, we may venture to say, than Catholicism, and much older than Protestantism.
> We wish to deal with the new knowledge which has come to us, whether scientific or historical, in the same spirit in which the Greek theologians dealt with Greek philosophy, the Schoolmen with the partially rediscovered Aristotle, and the Renaissance scholars with the newly-recovered Greek Testament. We try to be up-to-date with our science and our scholarship; but there is nothing 'modern' in our desire to add to our faith knowledge, or in our hope that the Spirit of Christ is still with us, to guide us into all truth. (*Modern Churchman*. Sept. 1925, pp. 276, 277.)

Every year at the conference he delivered a presidential address, clearly with the intention of keeping the discussions at a high level, and he certainly succeeded. Men of real powers of mind were got together to give papers, and these were collected each autumn into an issue of the *Modern Churchman* three times the size of an ordinary number and of remarkable quality. The contributors' handling of their theme was very able, their knowledge was ample, and they had thought deeply. But for the most part they could only appeal to readers with some academic training, people like Sir Arthur Hort who wrote in a 'Confessio Fidei' of his own in the *Modern Churchman* (Vol. XV, p. 463): 'I do feel it most highly desirable that those whose education enables them to think for themselves should face the "religious question" and make up their minds.' But to help those who can think for themselves to make up their minds is very difficult and just what these writers could not do. They could not offer satisfactory conclusions on such problems as are presented by miracles or the notion of immortality or the relations between science and religion: the best they could do was to dislodge erroneous convictions and urge a suspension of judgement. They appealed therefore in the main to those who found satisfaction in discussion for its own sake. Even the Dean seemed to have resolved to be far less dogmatic and therefore less popular than usual. He realised that it was advisable, if you were objecting to dogma, not to be dogmatic yourself, and he saw on more than one occasion that when his friends were attacked for their Modernism, it was because they had said things which were not easy to defend. In his earlier presidential addresses he showed that he had thrown in his lot with the Modernists only because he thought that to liberate Christianity on their lines was the way to leave it free to be the spiritual religion it should be. This is what he urged for a number of years, whatever the theme of the conference might be. From 1930, however, he turned his attention to problems of conduct. Here he showed his usual wisdom and individuality, but he was not specially Modernist. All he wished was the improvement of society.

Modernism has never looked like becoming a widespread attitude in this country, much less has it created a party. But in the years through which the Dean presided over the Modern Churchmen's Union there began to be in religion more tolerance without indifference, more respect for science without loss of faith, more truth without alarm. This change was to be found largely among people who had never read a word of the *Modern Churchman*, but it was a team of Modernists who brought it about, and the effects are by no means fully worked out yet. It was a work wrought within the confines of the Church of England, but felt far beyond its bounds. The Dean recognised it when he wrote apropos of R. H. Lightfoot's Bampton Lectures of 1935, "The change during the last thirty years in what the clergy are allowed to say without getting into trouble is amazing."

16

Fame and Family

One would suspect Francis Bacon of giving us an Essay of Fame, but there is none, and he scarcely seems to have regarded it. In his Essay of Vain Glory he makes this observation: 'Neither had the fame of Cicero, Seneca, Plinius Secundus, borne her age so well, if it had not been joined with some vanity in themselves, like unto varnish, that makes seelings [i.e. woodwork] not only shine but last'; and in the early and slight Essay of Honour and Reputation he says, 'Discreet followers and servants help much to reputation,' all of which is as much as to say that a man's fame depends most on himself and his household. Of course there is always truth in what Bacon says. To be well-spoken of by one's servants, if one has any, is an impressive testimony. It is also true that some men have a personal trick or flair for publicity which helps them much. But Bacon has mostly politicians in mind, and it is not quite the same with authors, those other great candidates for fame. Some good writers, to be sure, have failed to become famous not from want of merit, but from want of will or want of care. This is not at all the main cause of success or failure, however. Most good writers grow famous because their books are liked. But if they are liked when they are new, most of them will experience vicissitudes of fame, as they and their authors grow old. There are not many Immortals, and all the rest will go out of fashion sooner or later. The question is whether they will be revived, and one would like to think that a secure reputation with posterity was more valued than a large circulation and fame here and now. But the famous author hopes for both.

The *Outspoken Essays* had established the Dean's reputation with the reading public, and in the years that followed his fame became very great. Honours and offices were showered upon him. He was stimulated into a life of great activity which was

good for him. It diminished his diffidence and improved his
health. He still got through a wonderful lot of writing; he did
a great deal of travelling: he went to more meetings than ever,
and he entered more and more fully into the life of London
society as it revived after the war. He admitted that the revival
was much greater and more rapid than he had expected, though
he still persisted in prophesying financial ruin and political
revolution. There is a unity and a progress about the years 1919
to 1927, various aspects of which now fall to be considered.
The period ends with the first thoughts of retirement. His
distinctions were numerous. He was elected a Fellow of the
British Academy on 7 July 1921, an honour he had coveted.
He was made an Honorary Fellow of King's on 30 November
1922. He received an Honorary LL.D. at Edinburgh at the same
time as Mr Winston Churchill on 12 July 1923, a D.Litt. at
Sheffield on 4 July 1924, an Honorary D.D. at Oxford on
1 July 1927. In the year 1922 great efforts were made to lure
him back to the University. Lord Curzon as Chancellor of
Oxford University offered him the Principalship of Hertford
College, which he refused, in April. Two months later he was
approached from Cambridge about the Regius Professorship
of Divinity, vacant by the retirement of Dr V. H. Stanton. In
December of the same year the Prime Minister, through one of
his private secretaries, sounded him about the Regius Professorship of Divinity at Oxford. He answered that he did not wish
to leave London or to be considered for the post, but if they
could not get a good man they might of course ask him to
reconsider it. He thought Vernon Storr would be the best man,
but was afraid of a thoroughly bad appointment. He confided
to his diary three names in this connection. He was always
jealous of the reputation of Theology.

He was invited to give a great many special lectures and
sermons. Some peculiar circumstance attached to them from
time to time. In October 1920 he preached the University
Sermon at Oxford after an interval of sixteen years. He believed
that Canon Scott Holland, the Regius Professor, had kept him
out all that time. He preached in Repton School Chapel in June
1922, when the Headmaster was the Revd. Geoffrey Fisher,
destined to be Archbishop of Canterbury. He was favourably

impressed "by the nice look of the boys. It seems to be a very good school." What he said in his sermon was not immediately known to the public: the would-be reporter of it went to the parish church and took down the curate's sermon. In September of the same year he preached in St Paul's to a very large congregation. "At last the poor little prophet is beginning to have honour in his own country," he observed.

The Dean recorded very little of the Cathedral business in his diary. Many stories were told of his supposed indifference to it, and no doubt he did not think all the business was his business, and he did not think most of it mattered as much as his colleagues were apt to think. The story was told that at Chapter Meetings he used very often to get up and leave them to it after a short time; and further, that on one occasion they were determined that he should stay until a vote had been taken on a certain matter, so, when he got up to go, one of the more active canons rose to bar the way; in vain, for the Dean successfully brushed him on one side and passed by. One of the things he still took much interest in was the patronage of the Dean and Chapter and the livings of which they were patrons, but he was only chairman at the Chapter Meetings and could be and often was out-voted; he could not get liberal churchmen appointed. Attempts to make the services more 'catholic' and more ornamental did not meet with any sympathy from him. He was present in Westminster Abbey at the Installation of Dr Foxley Norris as Dean on 21 December 1925. Of this he had the following impression: "The ceremonial was most elaborate and magnificent, crimson and gold copes, quaintly attired acolytes, a huge procession round the church, etc. I dislike this sort of thing, but if it has to be done it could not be done better. Norris did his part very well, looking very dignified, and his address was in perfect taste." In the published version of the diary he added: "I remember my own quiet entrance upon my duties." To judge by a photograph of that occasion which has survived it certainly was the quietest thing under the sun.

The really grave matter which the Dean and Chapter had to contend with was the state of the Cathedral fabric. When the new Dean arrived in 1911 the alarm had already been raised as

to the probable effect of a proposed subterranean tramway close
to the East end of the Cathedral. This led on to anxiety about
the existing state of the building in general, and when extensive
repairs were deemed necessary the main part of the effort to
raise funds for the purpose fell upon Canon Alexander, a
difficult character, but with a remarkable portion of that special
gift which runs a successful appeal. It is a gift which in some
eyes is apt to appear rather unlovely, and it did appear so to the
Dean, but it was generally allowed that Alexander was the
leader in three successive appeals, in 1914, 1922, and 1925:
they raised altogether £400,000. Alexander was perhaps rather
too well aware of what the Cathedral owed to him; the Dean
perhaps did not appreciate his methods as generously as he
might have done, and he refused to be an alarmist. But alarm
is the spring-board of an appeal, and Alexander knew it. The
Dean was really stirred up, however, when the City Surveyor,
on Christmas Eve, 1924, served a notice on the Dean and
Chapter that St Paul's was 'a dangerous structure.' He was
correspondingly pleased when he found that the Lord Mayor,
who was a Roman Catholic, "played up splendidly" and backed
the new appeal which had to be made. *The Times* took it up,
and that, together with the excellent publicity afforded by the
City Surveyor's action, brought in £200,000 in a short time.
The first series of repairs had gone on steadily all through the
1914 War; the final phase was only completed in 1930. When
Dean Inge began his reign, the fabric was in poor condition:
twenty years later it was sound. The story is told in more detail
in *The History of St Paul's Cathedral* by Matthews and Atkins
(pp. 286–7, 291–4).

Outside St Paul's he was certainly growing famous, and with
an ever extending fame among various types of hearers. His
four Hulsean Lectures at Cambridge were given to a record
crowd. He lectured to an audience of 2,000 at Wigan on 'English
Literature in Education': many were turned away. He gave an
address at the Royal College of Physicians which was printed
in extenso in *The Lancet*. After mysticism the borderland of
medicine and psychology was perhaps his second special subject, but he was versatile. There can scarcely have been anyone
who gave so many lectures which were afterwards printed

separately or in some professional organ at various intervals
from 1913 to 1951. And all the time he was Dean he was a very
frequent preacher. From 1923 it was an ordinary experience
for hundreds to find a church already full when he was to be
in the pulpit. In 1926 he seems to have been particularly active,
and his diary is more detailed than usual. He was away from
St Paul's on seven Sunday mornings in succession in October
and November, once as far afield as Southport. He often enjoyed
a week-end away with a sermon and frequently two sermons
to preach. But it must not be thought that he neglected St
Paul's; at the end of 1924 at any rate he had noted with satisfaction that his attendances at Cathedral for the year were 442,
and even Canon Newbolt's only amounted to 439. He had still
to say, however, that the Cathedral services did not help him
at all.

He was also increasingly in request as a speaker after dinner.
He quite enjoyed it, and was most amusing. Attention was
particularly drawn to this when he became one of 'Mr Punch's
Personalities.' This was a fortnightly feature in *Punch* from the
latter part of 1925. There was a full-page drawing of the
Personality by Bernard Partridge or George Belcher, and some
verses beneath. The Dean was drawn by Partridge in December
1925. He is seen at his desk having just suspended the writing
of his diary; the leather-backed book is unmistakably a volume
of it. Beneath the picture are twelve lines by Owen Seaman,
the editor of *Punch* at the time, beginning

> 'The Gloomy Dean' they call our Inge,
> But he is really no such thing.
> For, though I never heard him preach,
> I've known him make a funny speech:

The lines went on to chaff him about his journalism. Seaman
wrote a note to Mrs Inge after it appeared and said: 'I am so
very glad you and the Dean liked Bernard Partridge's picture
and didn't mind my verses.' The Dean was more than pleased:
he called the picture "an excellent portrait," and so it is. He
added: "The Provost of Eton wants to buy the original to
frame and hang in the gallery in the Cloisters. This is an honour

which gives me peculiar pleasure." The picture is in the gallery.

The funny speech to which *Punch* alluded was presumably made after dinner. At City company dinners and at learned societies he was equally at home. His serious speeches too were not without their pleasantries, and it is noticeable that in this period the diaries frequently record meetings with "very nice people." Mrs Inge had always been a very good mixer and easily made dear friends with many people. This could not always be said of the Dean, but he often melted now. Strangely enough it was so in part, it seemed, because of a great sorrow, the death of his daughter Paula on 29 March 1923, in her twelfth year.

This must be viewed in the setting of the family life. As we have seen, at the close of the war none of the five children had emerged from childhood. In 1920 Craufurd failed to get a scholarship at Eton and went to Shrewsbury, which he did not care for, but it is scarcely possible that he himself or anyone else should know whether he would have cared for any school. Edward followed him from Summerfields in September 1921. Catharine went to St Margaret's School at Bushey where she was very happy. Paula went to school in Oxford at Miss Owen's, where she would have got a good start. But she was only able to be there a very short time. It was in the autumn of 1921 that she developed the symptoms which on 16 November were diagnosed as diabetes, then very dangerous for the young. Nurses were called in, the 'Allen treatment' was tried, but the Dean confessed that he had no real hope that she would be spared. Yet she was spared for sixteen months, and accepted her invalidism with perfect patience. After a whole year of it she told her father that 1922 had been a very happy year for her; he wrote that "it has been a privilege to have the dear little heroine with us." She had "the new insulin treatment," but the disease could not be arrested. She died on Maundy Thursday, 1923. The Dean felt "a terrible loss. Next to Kitty my little daughters have been the joy and pride of my life, and I have often thought what a perfect wife and mother Paula would be for some good man." The funeral service was in the Cathedral, and the interment the same day in Holywell Cemetery, Oxford. As they left the Cathedral "crowds lined the pave-

A copy of the portrait published in *Punch* (December 1925) made specially
for the Dean by the artist.

ments on Ludgate Hill from top to bottom. Paula was buried like a princess."

The Dean was a naturally reserved man. He first expressed his sense of this bereavement in Latin verse, but in January 1924 his *Personal Religion and the Life of Devotion* came out, and he gave in the last pages a very intimate account of Paula's illness and death. It was, one would say, not like him to do it, yet it seemed to break down a barrier and cure an inhibition. Personal sorrow seemed to have two effects: it made him gentler, and it made public anxieties of less concern. He was not in any sense a changed man; he recovered his spirits and retained his energy and his wit, but in the face of so great a loss he appreciated more fully what he still had, and what he had was much. One disappointment perhaps he now felt keenly, and that was that his sons were not particularly clever. He remarked that their four grandparents being who they were, this was surprising. Eugenics had not worked. But he praised their manners and hoped and believed they were good boys. When later on they sometimes failed to keep in touch with home, he did not quite realise that even good boys are sensible enough to break away, and he had done it himself. About his daughters he never seemed to think whether they were clever or not. They charmed him. Summing up 1923 in his diary he wrote: "So ends 1923, a year which has made the first break in our home circle. Our darling Paula will always be with us in memory; it is a purely happy memory of a most beautiful and not incomplete life. . . . Catharine is all that we could wish, a most dear little girl." Three weeks after writing these words he had occasion to send Catharine a letter which has been preserved:

My darling Catharine,

You cannot think how unhappy it makes me to think of you, of all people, being ill. You are a very precious person, at any rate to your poor old father. But I expect Mary Radford and the doctor will be able to put you right soon. There is nothing to tell you about here, as I am all alone, living quietly in my study and thinking about you and mother. Take great care of yourself, my dearest girl.

Your very loving father,
W. R. I.

She was at Oxford with Mrs Inge, and was threatened with appendicitis. She got well again, but had the operation in the following February.

Outside the immediate family circle the Dean maintained the clannish spirit common to the Inges and Spooners. Many of the clan were congregated in Oxford. His sister Sophy had stayed on in Holywell Lodge after his mother's death in 1917. His brother and his family were in St Giles's Vicarage, his Uncle George Inge and Aunt Catty in North Oxford; his cousin Harry Churton was also there for some little time before his death. His cousin Walter How was Fellow and Tutor of Merton. Mrs Inge's Uncle Archie and Aunt Frank and their daughters were at the Warden's Lodgings in New College and subsequently in Canterbury Road; her father and mother left Canterbury for Oxford in 1921. Miss Goodwin, her mother's sister, lived there. The Charles Hows were at Chesterton (Oxon) not far off. Distant cousins were visited too in Staffordshire and Wales: Nearwell at Shrewsbury always made any members of the family welcome. A fortnight's visit there in August 1923 was a pleasure: "The old home is delightfully unchanged, and the manner of life goes on as it has been since I remember. We all played a little tennis, in spite of our grey hairs." They spent very happy holidays at Trengwainton in Cornwall, the home of Robins Bolitho, until 1925 when he died and the house passed to a nephew. The Dean still continued to take a locum tenancy occasionally in the summer: North Cerney in 1926 was a great success: Mrs Inge's parents and her sister Ruth were there and Edward and Catharine, and Richard "scudding about on his bicycle." One time he took a solitary holiday, as he used to do long ago, in the Isle of Wight, and there was the time in Switzerland when he began to write the 'Confessio Fidei.' He went to Sweden for a lecture tour and to be made much of by the Swedish Church. Mrs Inge was with him, and they went on to Norway to stay with our Ambassador and meet the King.

This was in 1922, and only once in these years did he go further afield, on a trip to America from Easter Eve, 11 April, to 18 May 1925. Mrs Inge went too, and this visit was rather different from their former one of 1906. The Dean summed it up as follows: "This has been the most extraordinary experience of our lives. I am being boomed like a first class celebrity. At a railway station I am surrounded by reporters and photographers, and I believe I have been filmed for the 'movies' more than once when I was not aware of it. The Americans say themselves that possibly Bernard Shaw or Kipling would be received in the same way, but nobody else." When the Dean reproduced this passage in *The Diary of a Dean* (pp. 102, 103) he added "Very gratifying, but why don't they buy my books? They don't."

If this was still a just complaint, it is not quite easy to account for the enormous interest the visit aroused. They had started off by being given a cabin *de luxe* on the *Mauretania* when he had only paid second-class fares. He was excused the tedious custom house procedure on arrival at New York, though unfortunately Mrs Inge was not. He was met by twenty reporters. He was driven to a flat in Fifth Avenue. His eight lectures at Yale, the ostensible purpose of his visit, were well attended, and he was most handsomely entertained and met many of the Professors. He gave two lectures at Baltimore on 'The Prospects of Democracy' to a tremendous crowd, 700 people being turned away; he was paid 1,000 dollars for these lectures. He preached in St John's Cathedral, New York, to a congregation estimated at 4,000: he made three extempore speeches which he judged successful: he travelled from Philadelphia to New York in a coach *de luxe* reserved for the President of the Railway Company. They went at eighty miles an hour (beyond the legal speed limit), whether in his honour is not clear, but he was very "sea-sick," he says. Towards the end of their visit they were entertained to a dinner by the Church Club. There were something like 900 diners, and he had to make a longish speech. On their last day he was at a lunch to meet "forty leading editors, etc.," of America.

All this is related in the diary not day by day, but in a continuous narrative with attractive descriptions of the countryside and country houses, and of various things that struck the celebrated visitor. He describes a game of baseball in considerable detail: but what seems to have pleased him most was the American Museum of Natural History. He goes round it in recollection like a schoolboy. They reached home just as the

London season was getting under way, and were drawn into the stream at once.

The Dean's improved financial position did not make much difference to the way of life at the Deanery. First class railway travel was still a luxury worth noting down as much appreciated. The Inges had no car until 1926, and then only because the Dean received a legacy of £2,000 from a cousin, Henry Wagner. "I think I can manage to let Kitty have the motor car after which she hankers, unless we are all ruined in civil war." He was writing this on 30 April, only a week before the General Strike, which he believed to be the work of Communist conspirators. The strike only lasted nine days, but the car was not ordered till 24 November. "Catharine Dodgson came and took Kitty to choose a motor car. I have shelved off this very useless extravagance as long as possible, but the children were so bent on it that I had to give way. They ordered an Austin car, I believe." On 19 March he noted that "the Austin car which my family extracted from me has come, and seems to give general satisfaction."

After the *Outspoken Essays* such time as the Dean found for writing was considerably devoted to journalism, but he did also between 1922 and 1927 produce three short books and a long one. The long one was his book on *England* (1926); the short ones were "Paula's book," published in January 1924, *The Platonic Tradition in English Thought* (Hulsean Lectures) delivered in December and January 1925–26, and *Protestantism* which appeared in October 1927. In the same month what really amounted to a third series of Outspoken Essays came out under the title *The Church in the World*, in which only one item had not been published before. The sale of his writings was now very large indeed, and it is not surprising that in 1927 he calculated that they had brought him £4,000. What is surprising is the immense diligence which produced them amid so many preoccupations.

Paula's book was one of the series of books which the Bishop of London sponsored year by year for Lent, and they always had a large circulation.[1] This one had the added advantage of a famous author and of the widespread sympathy extended to him over Paula's death. Even so the sale of it was extraordinary.

Within four weeks 20,000 copies had been sold, 4,000 of them to America, and 10,000 more, or something like it, in the next ten days. It is not to be wondered at. There is a touch of emotion rather than of passion in the book: it is in places almost lyrical: the chapter on the Soul's Thirst (II) is persuasive and in part intense: the work as a whole exhibits quite simply the characteristic Inge optimism based on pessimism, and the chapter on Joy (V) is very practical, and like one of his best All Saints' Sermons. In all his writings this comes nearest to 'a book of devotion.' It has always been popular.

The Platonic Tradition in English Thought was a promising subject for a short course of lectures, being a detached portion of a large field, and it might be congenial to one who so often quoted and really seemed quite to fondle the Cambridge Platonist's phrase about the Church's "old loving nurse, the Platonick philosophy." But it does not altogether come up to expectation. When the Dean accepted the offer to deliver these lectures, he realised and wrote in his diary, "My acceptance will oblige me to curtail my lucrative writing for the Press." Perhaps he did not curtail sufficiently, for he seems slightly bored with the lectures before they are finished. In places he deserts Platonism for other kinds of mysticism: he finds the material of the lectures in his head (a very full head to be sure) and not in English thinkers. But of course there are many good things: the following paragraph contains several of his favourite notions urged with what is for him a touch of mildness:

I do not wish to be misunderstood as denying the possibility of temporal progress. There will undoubtedly be pleasanter times to live in than the twentieth century. Civilisation is at present in very rough water; after a time it will probably enter a calm channel, when most people will, for a time, be more or less contented. Accumulated experience may enable mankind to avoid some dangers and some mistakes. Science will put into the hands of our grandchildren the means to diminish the amount of irksome toil, though it will also provide the means of mutual extermination on a hitherto unexampled scale. It is just possible that our successors may care enough for posterity to bring about, by selective breeding, a real improvement in the human stock. These reflections give us a ground for reasonable, if chastened, hopefulness. But they have little or nothing to do with the Christian faith, which makes no temporal promises (pp. 109, 110).

Protestantism is a small book on a large subject, and one about which the Dean knew too much. The form is, for him, unusual, twenty-four short chapters of about seven pages each. A good deal of it is history, where the matter has had to be condensed unduly; it is a commendation of the book to say that a longer one on the same subject by the same hand would have been better. The Dean twice called it "my little book," and a little book it is, but a useful little book.

It is perhaps symptomatic of the *savant* growing into the journalist that not one of these three books had a single footnote or an index.

England was a much bigger work, almost three times as long as *Protestantism*, though in the Preface the Dean calls it "this small book." He meant that it was small in relation to the matter he had to deal with, which was no less than the condition of England when he wrote and its prospects in the near future.

It contains [he said in the Preface] the only thing which I could contribute to it as my own—the expression of my personal point of view, with my reasons for holding it. I have tried to be candid; I have made no attempt whatever to be impartial. I love my own country dearly, and I think it is in great danger, not so much from the aggressions of foreign nations, though our international position is far from secure, as from the anti-social and unpatriotic sectionalism which is the curse of industrial civilisation, and which is specially dangerous in a country situated as we are.

The very first words of the book run as follows: "I have found the preparation of this book the most difficult literary task that I have ever undertaken," and at the end of 1925 he had written in his diary: "I am working hard at my troublesome book on England which I heartily wish I had never undertaken."

England sold 9,000 copies in ten days in the middle of September 1926, but under 6–8 October the diary records that it had had "a check." "The reviews have been civil rather than laudatory: as I expected, it was rather a rash undertaking. The only exception to the general courtesy was an impudently insulting attack in the *Guardian.*" What was the matter with it, then? Undoubtedly an apparent want of sympathy with 'the people' and their democratic aspirations. An author who is conscious of class and thoroughly believes in the class he himself belongs to asks for trouble, when he expounds his views. A close perusal of the book would reveal many testimonies to the worth of the whole nation, but the criticism of some sections of it was too pointed, and a few of the observations really inadmissible. In the Preface to the cheaper edition of 1927 he deprecated one of these, but the text remained unaltered. In the fifth edition in 1933 he revised considerably, and the offending sentence was removed. A close collation would reveal numerous changes. The three concluding pages of the chapter on Industrialism, for instance, were entirely rewritten and some economic speculations substituted for reflections on Christianity. But most of the changes were very small, and the book remains substantially the same, and almost exactly the same in bulk.

England was a great achievement in its display of knowledge and its incisive judgements and its love of country. The first chapter, for example, got up from books for the occasion as it must have been, gives an excellent and exciting sketch of the effect upon Britain of its geographical position. As a specimen of forceful writing the account of the events which led up to the war of 1914 may be cited (pp. 117–23),[2] with its characteristic asperity and concluding exaggeration:

> We were, therefore, bound, by considerations of safety, to enter into a struggle which did not immediately concern us; to give help, to the utmost of our power, to Allies who might be expected to show no gratitude; and to mortgage our whole future in an internecine conflict from which we had nothing to gain and everything to lose. No greater misfortune has ever befallen Britain and the British Empire.

The comparatively brief Epilogue is the most generous part of the book. The whole gives the impression of having been written with great ease, which we know it was not.

England was not a complete success, and the Dean perhaps never quite matched his highest successes again. He was in the years immediately ahead no less famous, but there was, it might be thought, a slight falling off in the quality with no falling off in the quantity of his literary output.

The book seems to have increased his reputation in America. Early in 1927 he was offered £2,500 for a book of reminiscences. He tells how, when he refused this offer to write his own life, he was asked to write the life of Christ for a rather smaller sum.

17
Journalism

Dr Johnson took four years to write his *Lives of the Poets*, which is not so very long for something so good as they are, and he says he wrote them in his usual way, 'dilatorily and hastily, unwilling to work, and working with vigour and haste.' This may have been his usual way—must have been if he says so—yet it is hard to think that he would have got his Dictionary done that way, for a lexicographer undertakes a plodding task if ever there was one. But perhaps it is possible to be a plodder, and yet to work by fits and starts. From 20 March 1750 to 14 March 1752 Johnson produced *The Rambler* twice weekly, each time giving his readers a paper of about 1,500 words, some of them notoriously rather long words. All one can say is that if he wrote these papers by fits and starts, the fits and starts must have been fairly reliable. Only four of the papers in their entirety and three in part were contributed by others. In the concluding number (No. 208) he makes some comments on what he calls 'the anxious employment of a periodical writer,' and what he says must be the common experience of all who engage upon this employment: 'I am willing to flatter myself with hopes, that, by collecting these papers, I am not preparing for my future life, either shame or repentance. That all are happily imagined, or accurately polished, that the same sentiments have not sometimes recurred, or the same expressions been too frequently repeated, I have not confidence in my abilities sufficient to warrant. He that condemns himself to compose on a stated day, will often bring to his task an attention dissipated, a memory embarrassed, an imagination overwhelmed, a mind distracted with anxieties, a body languishing with disease: He will labour on a barren topick, till it is too late to change it; or, in the ardour of invention, diffuse his thoughts into wild exuberance, which the pressing hour of publication cannot suffer judgment to examine or reduce.' This is certainly written from experience, but Boswell has fortunately preserved a happier picture of such authorship. Six years after *The Rambler* ceased publication, Johnson began to contribute what he called an 'Idler' once a week to a new periodical, the *Universal Chronicle or Weekly Gazette*. 'Many of these excellent essays,' says Boswell, 'were written as hastily as an ordinary letter. Mr Langton remembers Johnson, when on a visit to Oxford, asking him one evening how long it was till the post went out; and on being told about half an hour, he exclaimed, "then we shall do very well." He upon this instantly sat down and finished an *Idler*, which it was necessary should be in London the next day. Mr Langton, having signified a wish to read it, "Sir, (said he) you shall not do more than I have done myself." He then folded it up and sent it off.'

Similar feats of journalism are no doubt performed very frequently today, and the writing often owes its excellence to the very fact of its having been done under pressure.

The Dean was a very successful journalist. He might quite justifiably have excited the envy of the professionals: indeed it may be questioned whether he did not sacrifice his amateur status, for, although being paid for writing does not in itself constitute a writer by profession, it is difficult to think of one who rises to the very top as a mere amateur. But he was in several important ways genuinely amateur. He did not need to write for his living, although for many years he made enough by writing to live on very well: it was his nature to be diligent, for, although both fame and pay were incentives, he would not have written much less without them: while he wrote what people would gladly read, what he really had in mind was to disseminate the truth as he saw it: in knowledge and in style he was a scholar. But he added to these amateur virtues the talents of a professional. He was a practised writer: he was not a fastidious writer; he enjoyed the money and the success: he saw most things either black or white.

The steps by which he penetrated the jungle of journalism can best be traced in what he himself noted in his diary. The entries are not a complete record, but they are numerous. They do not give a picture of the vicissitudes of the calling, for they are essentially a success story, but, if they have not very markedly their ups and downs, they have their undulations and their interest. The story begins after the publication of *Outspoken Essays* in October 1919. One of the reviews is described by the Dean as "four columns of unmeasured laudation from Bernard Shaw in 'Everyman'! . . . A few days after I received, among several other journalistic offers, a request from the *Sunday Express* to write three short articles for 100 guineas!" Then:[1]

1919. *December 16.* The *Sunday Express* has employed me to write a series of short articles, offering me a magnificent remuneration.

1920. *January.* The *Sunday Express* has paid me £230 for eight short causeries on things in general, and pressed me hard to continue writing for them every week indefinitely. The *Morning Post* made a similar offer, without mentioning terms, and the *Manchester Guardian* wants me to write occasionally for them. It looks as if I might make several hundreds a year in this way, if things get worse, and they are very bad now.

August 14 etc. I have been writing for the London papers—the *Daily Telegraph*, the *Evening Standard*, and *The Times*.

1921. *March 11.* I have been writing a series of articles for the *Evening Standard*, eight in all, at the request of the Editor and my former pupil Macassey, who is on the staff. I can see that my friends think that it is rather infra dig., but I reach a very large public in this way, and the pay is uncommonly good, £20 an article.

June 20, 21. Two quiet days . . . I have lately been busy with my weekly articles for the *Evening Standard*, which are much appreciated both by the proprietor and editor and by the public . . . ; with an article for the *Edinburgh Review* . . . ; with an article for the *Royal Review* on 'Where are we going,' for which I am to get 20 guineas.

August 27–September 4. Cloan. I am contributing to the *Evening Standard* a series of articles on Liberal Theology. I wrote two of them at Cloan.

1921. *November 10.* Lord Dawson, the King's physician, made a speech at the Church Congress on Birth Control, for which he was hotly attacked. I defended him in two articles in the *Evening Standard*.

1922. *January 26.* I had to write in a great hurry for the *Evening Standard* an article on Harold Begbie's *Painted Windows*; sketches of ecclesiastics. An objectionable type of book, but he has made me the hero of it, lauding me to the skies.

February 3. Mr Upward of the *Ch[urch] Fam[ily] N[ewspaper]* came to see me. He wants to make his paper of a higher class, and asks me to contribute one article a month. I think I shall try to help him, as there is more chance of improving an already established paper than of starting a new one, and the *Challenge*[2] is too far committed to Labour politics. But I find that journalism, though profitable, takes up time that might be better spent.

May 29. I have been writing in the *Evening Standard* an earnest remonstrance against the immorality of many modern novels, with special reference to H. G. Wells. Wells, as might have been expected, answered insolently and spitefully. Bernard Shaw also wrote against me, but more civilly. Of the Church papers, only the *Church Family* backed me up, the rest ignored my article.

June 1. I lunched with a young American, Anthony, at Simpson's in the Strand. He is on the staff of the *Century* Magazine and wants me to write for it.

August 4. I wrote, by request, an article on Christmas for the *Royal Magazine* for which I am to receive £21.

1923. *October.* The *Evening Standard* has been sold by Sir Edward Hulton to Rothermere and Beaverbrook, and I don't like writing for them. On the other hand it is a great opportunity for disseminating my views, and is the best paid work I have ever done. I decided at first to give up writing for them, but probably I shall go on a little longer, unless the paper becomes morally or politically impossible.

Summary for 1923. I have not done much solid work and sometimes fear that I shall not do any more. I have continued my weekly articles for the *Evening Standard*, which are not only very lucrative, but give me a very wide pulpit for the advocacy of various things that I care about, the Editor giving me a perfectly free hand. I have abundant evidence that I am exercising more influence in this way than ever before.

1924. *January 19.* Brailsford, the editor of the *New Leader*, a weekly Labour organ, is about to publish a symposium on the advent of Labour to power, and has asked me to contribute an article. I spent yesterday in writing it, and gave it them strong!

March 21. Strachey was very much pleased with the article which I contributed to the *Spectator*, and is going to write to me to invite me to write six more.

May 28. I have decided to give up writing for the *Evening Standard*, which is rather a low paper, and accept an offer from R. A. Gwynne, editor of the *Morning Post*. I went to see him and completed the agreement. I am afraid Thompson (Raymond) of the *Evening Standard* will be very much hurt, but I think I am right. I shall not have quite such a free hand under Gwynne, but it is a better class of paper, and I shall be able to write more seriously, as for educated readers.

May 31. A quiet day. I wrote my first article for the *Morning Post*.

1925. *February 27.* McKenna thought I was unwise to leave the *Evening Standard* for the *Morning Post*, because the circulations are 400,000 and 60,000; but he could not deny that the E.S. is a vulgar little paper.

May 8. On our last day [of a tour in America] I lunched at the Constitutional(?) Club with Mr Leach, to meet the leading editors of America. . . . He is very anxious that I should write for the *Forum*.

May 9. [On the way home] I wrote four articles, three on my visit to America for the *Morning Post*, and one on 'Is our Nobility Decaying?'(!) for the New York *Liberty*.

1925. *July 31*. Putnam, the New York publisher, with his London partner, C. Huntington, want to publish a selection of my newspaper articles in America and I have consented with some misgivings.

October 15. A very pleasant lunch party at home. Mr and Mrs Leach from America (he is editor of the *Forum*, and has just given me 200 guineas for a potty little article), Mrs Clifford the novelist, Geoffrey Dawson, the editor of *The Times*, Sir Edmund and Lady Gosse.

1926. *March 3*. Mr Gwynne tells me he is making certain changes in the *Morning Post*, and that he wants me to write once a month instead of once a week. I am really glad, for I have been making bricks without straw for some time, and I do not want the money. I ought really to have made the suggestion myself.

July 30. I have undertaken to write four articles (and as many more as I like) for the *Sunday Express*, at 30 guineas each.

Summary. I have dropped all connexion with the *Morning Post*, which is doing St. Paul's all the harm it can by scaremongering about the fabric: I now write occasionally for the Beaverbrook group, which is very complimentary about my articles and pays me well; also once a month for the *Church of England Newspaper*.

1927. *May 29*. I finished an article for H. G. Leach of the *Forum* on the Future of Christian Missions in Asia, for which I am to receive 500 dollars—very easily earned money!

November 23. A journalist, Mr Nicholson, came to see me on business. He wants me to write an article in the *Pall Mall Magazine* on 'What is a Successful Man?' for £50.

December 17. I have written on the subject [of the rejection of the proposed Book of Common Prayer] in the *C. of E. Newspaper*, the *Evening Standard*, and the *Empire Review*.

And so on to the same effect.

Although he contributed to a variety of periodicals, it is easy to see from these extracts why the Dean's name became so closely associated with the *Evening Standard*. But his first genuine efforts in popular journalism were in the *Sunday Express*. He occasionally sent up an article to a weekly or daily paper before that: he had one in the *Daily News* on Christmas Eve, 1913. But the article in the *Sunday Express* on 7 December 1919 and the seven following Sundays were his first substantial contribution. They are very good, and perhaps an example of beginner's luck, for the first attempts in the *Evening Standard* seem not quite to come up to them. The Dean at once struck the authentic note of journalism as if by instinct. To instinct he added art; there was something rare about the way he expressed himself. He had also a great stock of facts to communicate and lively opinions to air. He used now one gift and now another. In the fourth article he simply collected together what the sub-heading called 'Utopian Dreams from many Countries and Climes': he remarked that the only one that had come near realisation was Christian Monasticism. He found greater opportunities for giving his own views, as may be guessed, in 'Democracy in Danger,' and its opening paragraph is worth reprinting as being the first words of his first commissioned article as well as a successful effort in superior journalism:

In the articles which the editor of the *Sunday Express* has allowed me to write on the conditions and prospects of the country I have no wish to pose either as a pessimist or as a political partisan. Pessimism, like optimism, is a mood which reveals nothing except the temperament of the writer. If a man is to contribute anything of value to the discussion of public affairs, he needs, above all, the historical sense, a power of seeing through labels and catchwords to the realities which they conceal and distort, and a scientific temper which can diagnose a disease without blaming the patient. It is useless to find fault with politicians, who have to play the cards that are dealt to them—generally a 'spade hand'—and to abuse whole classes of the population is as childish as to complain of human nature for being what it is. There is a marked difference between one class and another; but the class which is in power usually behaves worst, being free from restraint and misled by sycophants. At present it is clear that the chief national danger comes from organised Labour, though the average workman is no worse and no better than the average squire, banker, or tradesman.

A good start, for the reader will now be asking himself, Where do we go from here?

This was rather a provocative article: the second on the 'Labour Revolt against Modern Civilisation' was much less so. Possibly the editor had asked for something slightly milder, and he got it—more or less. There is only one contribution which is directly about religion, that for 21 December. It is a particularly good article, and shows under fresh circumstances that it was on religion that the Dean was most sure to be found at his best. A brief confession of faith sums up one of his deepest convictions. It was printed in heavy type:

> True happiness depends on the possession of those mental and moral and spiritual goods in which one man's gain is not another man's loss, those goods which are increased, not diminished by sharing them, and which no accidents of fortune or injustices of man can take away from us.

He had said this before, but not in the popular Press. The last article was on 'Eugenics,' the Dean's old favourite: it ends with a really eloquent peroration on our precious gains from the past.

The Dean's first contributions to the *Evening Standard* were simply occasional. He was asked to contribute two articles on the Lambeth Conference which had just broken up, and they appeared on 24 and 25 August 1920. They were the ones of which he had written that "they won't please the Bishops." The first was on 'Church Reunion': the second was on 'Social and Industrial Questions.' The criticisms are reasonable and in places constructive. The Bishops probably thought they had been let off lightly, though they did not go scot free, nor did industry of course. The Dean opened his *critique* of the Bishops' findings on social questions with the following modified approval:

> I approached the perusal of this section with alarm, and finished it with relief. After my experience of many recent ecclesiastical utterances, I expected a profession of a vague and sentimental socialism, intended to impress the class who call themselves the workers with the assurance that the Church is their ally. The present excesses of the trade unions have no doubt opened the

eyes of the public to their real aims, and have imposed moderations upon the Bishops in Council.

The Dean took the Modernist view of Church reunion and its possibilities, thinking that the Bishops had laid down conditions which made it waste of time to discuss it. He was for some relaxation in the remarriage of divorced persons. But he did not let himself go.

The regular articles in the *Evening Standard* began on 27 January 1921; eight were commissioned, but they continued long after these had appeared. At first they were not published on any particular day of the week, later on Wednesdays. At the start every other one, roughly speaking, was on a specifically religious topic, and these seem to have created a taste for such topics, for on 23, 25 and 26 March articles of religious interest by other writers appeared. The first of these is noteworthy, because it is entitled 'The Archbishop of Canterbury and Dr Inge.'

This article, which was not signed, arose out of circumstances which the Dean thus records in his diary: "The *Evening Standard* presses for a continuation of my weekly articles, for which they pay me very well—£20 each. An unpleasant incident was caused by the Bp of Woolwich, who wrote to the Archbp asking him to say that I do not 'represent the mind of the Church of England' about popular education. The Abp, who had not read the articles, answered as desired, and the Bp of Woolwich sent the letters to the *Evening Standard*. It was most unfair and improper; I can only suppose that the Abp wished to punish me for criticising the Lambeth Conference. But I thought it better not to answer him." As it is an interesting example of the Dean getting into trouble, and one such example ought to be recorded, this entry in the diary is worth amplifying. What the Bishop of Woolwich wrote to the *Evening Standard* was as follows: it appeared on 22 March 1921:

To the Editor of the *Evening Standard*

Dear Sir,—At a meeting of Arsenal workers in Beresford Square, Woolwich, the men took strong exception to a sentence in an article written for the *Evening Standard* by the Dean of St Paul's early last February.

In it the Dean deprecated the action of the Government in

enabling the children of the working class, who received free
education, to compete with the children of the professional class
for scholarships at the universities.

The Woolwich men asked whether the Dean in this expressed
the mind of the Church of England, and requested me to bring
the matter before the Archbishop of Canterbury. I did so and the
Archbishop sent me a reply, a copy of which I enclose.

I should be grateful if you would publish this explanatory letter,
together with the letter of the Archbishop.

Yours faithfully,
W. Woolwich.

My dear Bishop of Woolwich,—

I am not surprised that some of our friends have been a little
disquieted by a sentence in a recent article by the Dean of St.
Paul's upon our public schools. Like many other trenchant and
witty writers, the Dean of St Paul's uses sentences which ought
not, I think, to be taken too seriously.

I am certain he would at heart be the last to discourage the
giving of every possible opportunity to the clever son or daughter
of parents whose own opportunities had in early life been less.
Anyhow, there can be no doubt at all that the opinion, speaking
generally, of the clergy of the Church of England is whole-
heartedly in favour of all such facilities being placed within the
reach of those who can use them.

I have myself during a long life done everything in my power
to further such opening of doors, or rather of avenues, to all who
can rightly use them; and if it be the case that the Dean of St
Paul's, in his own caustic way, expresses what seems like a different
view, he is undoubtedly not representative of what could be
called the opinion of the Church of England; indeed he would
be the first himself to disclaim the desire to be thus regarded.
Originality and sometimes eccentricity of thought are among his
most prominent characteristics.

Let no one doubt that the Church of England will continue to
do its best to throw open as widely as possible our country's
educational doors.

I am, yours very truly,
Randall Cantuar

The reference was to the Dean's article of 9 February called
'Gentlemen's Schools.' The offending sentence, and it was offen-
sive, in it occurs at the end of the following passage:

The percentage of successes in after life among public school men has been rather high, and the percentage of total failures very low. But we cannot expect that in the future the results will be so favourable, even if educational methods are greatly improved. In the past the public school man has been exposed only to the natural competition of his own class, recruited very sparingly from below. But now our sons have to meet the artificial competition deliberately created by the Government, who are educating the children of the working man, *at our expense*, in order that they may take the bread out of our children's mouths.

This was what roused the Bishop of Woolwich and produced the Archbishop's characteristic tranquilliser, to which Inge wisely decided not to reply. But a reply was forthcoming in the article entitled 'The Archbishop and Dr Inge' which appeared the next day; it was on the whole not disrespectful to the Archbishop, but it was all for Dr Inge. Very near the beginning the anonymous author committed himself to a comparison:

> Dean Inge possesses one of the most daring and original minds of the day, and expresses himself in language of great force and unmistakable clearness. There could hardly be a greater contrast than between the suave and courtly Primate not so much "all things to all men" as nothing in particular to any man, and the grimly decisive Dean, who treads impartially on all sorts of corns and is guilty of everything but platitude.

Later on in summing up the situation he wrote:

> The Church cannot afford to ignore the fact that, while no newspaper editor invites expression of "what would be called the opinion of the Church of England," the "originality and sometimes the eccentricity" of Dean Inge reaches hundreds of thousands of eager readers who are seldom seen in a church. . . . We do not want a regiment of Dean Inges, any more than we want to live on tonics. But it is a great asset to any generation to possess at least one man who says exactly what he believes concerning things in general, and for the moment we can only look for such a man in the Deanery of St Paul's.

Well done, the *Evening Standard*!

When Archbishop Davidson died in May 1930, the Dean wrote in his diary: "He married us 25 years ago, and has always been a kind friend, though I am afraid my goings on worried him sometimes."

Dean Inge's articles were evidently making some impression already, and the impression of several hundreds was cumulative. It would be impossible to discuss them in detail, unless in a book solely written for that purpose, and in any case an author is entitled to be judged by his best work, or at least by the work he thinks worth preserving. In *Lay Thoughts of a Dean*, July 1926, *Assessments and Anticipations*, 1929, and *More Lay Thoughts of a Dean*, 1931, he republished one hundred and ten articles, mostly from the *Evening Standard*. He omitted those which could only have an interest at the moment of publication, some of those that had given most offence, and probably those which would have required any considerable alteration. He added or altered a word here and there; the editing does not seem to have been laborious, and it would be contrary to the Dean's usual practice if it were. But there is, of course, a big psychological difference between a newspaper and a book. Articles anticipated and enjoyed at seven-day intervals do not make the same impression when read page after page. What was so readable in the *Evening Standard* was not designed to be read continuously through a matter of three hundred pages or so, all the more when articles on the same topic are collected together.

But almost every reader, beginning to read one of these volumes here and there, will end by finding he has had to read the whole. They ripple on. Anyone with someone else in the room would soon be reading out aloud one piece after another, many of them pieces which draw attention to what one might have thought of for oneself and didn't, such as "The command 'Be fruitful and multiply' [was] promulgated according to our authorities, when the population of the world consisted of two persons" or " 'Tyger, tyger, burning bright in the forests of the night' (Blake). A naturalist would share his surprise at an arrangement so obviously in the interest of the tiger's victim's, and so little in his own." Or a passage introduces an odd speculation quite casually: "If George III had had the political sagacity of Queen Victoria, should we have lost America? And, if not, would the political connection between the two countries have been terminated in the twentieth century by a glorious war of independence waged by Great Britain?" It was by such wit and wisdom that the author made his reputation for writing short articles. They carried with them his protests and alarms, his statistics, his prejudices, but they also conveyed a great deal of the truth he had to teach. An observation made in *England* is worth recalling: "The distinction between literature and journalism is becoming blurred; but journalism gains as much as literature loses" (p. 37 or 49).

One of these volumes is called *Assessments and Anticipations*, and by that title exposes itself to the test of time. Were the assessments correct and the anticipations justified? Nearly ninety pages of the book are devoted to a section called Prognostications, and in introducing it the Dean considers "whether a minor prophet can justify his existence." He thinks anticipation both easier and more useful than assessment:

> What we know of the past is mostly not worth knowing. What is worth knowing is mostly uncertain. Events in the past may be roughly divided into those which probably never happened and those which do not matter. . . . To predict the future, then, is not only the most important part of the work of an historian; it is the most scientific and least imaginative part of his duties. Our chief interest in the past is as a guide to the future.

A cursory glance at the papers that follow suggests that Roman Catholicism will not advance much further, though it is not likely to decay, that Protestantism will change, but its mysticism will save it; that the very small area of Great Britain makes it inevitable that we shall cease to be one of the Great Powers; that our population will begin to decrease before 1950; that our public schools will be shut up; that with us the institution of marriage will not be seriously threatened; that Democracy will ruin us in the end; that 'scientific morality' will bring blessings; that unemployment is inevitable; that air travel will extend the range of holiday travel almost incredibly; that Russia would not shrink from massacring three-quarters of the population of Europe; that Italy will not go to war. A fine miscellany! Some of these prophecies have been fulfilled, some falsified, some are still subject for conjecture. But it makes no

difference; they are all accompanied by such ingenious observations and arguments that this minor prophet justifies himself
to the full.

The place the author of these articles had won for himself
in the public mind was rather nicely indicated by T. C. List,
a New Zealand journalist who came to London for the Imperial
Press Conference in 1930 and wrote his impressions for a number of Dominion newspapers. He devoted an article to Dean
Inge of St Paul's in which he said:

> Mundane things seem apart from him, yet he regularly dis-
> courses on them from the pulpit and the forum of the Press with
> a freedom and a seeming recklessness that would not be tolerated
> from any other cleric, however high-placed he be, by a people
> even so complacent and indulgent as the English people. The
> fact is that Dean Inge has been given a special dispensation, and
> occupies a singular place in the life of the nation. He says things
> that no other public man would dare say, at times provoking his
> fellow countrymen almost to fury. He exposes their foibles, and
> flagellates them at every opportunity.

At the Press Conference Mr List would no doubt have heard
the Dean both greatly admired and severely criticised, and he
got hold of two important points. The Dean certainly was
reckless, and he had been given a special dispensation. In the
Lay Thoughts and the *Assessments* he would not be likely to
reprint his more reckless articles: we must be content there
with a sprinkling of reckless opinions. He certainly made some
unwise, exaggerated, or inaccurate statements and expressed
dislike or contempt or apprehension (not fear) in language
which might have been and occasionally ought to have been
more reserved. But this was in the first place journalism and
in the second place the utterance of a man who had a special
dispensation. He outraged the public and they loved it. They
felt an affectionate regard for one who viewed them with a
kind of off-hand contempt and was so much cleverer than they,
and yet obviously a man of like passions with themselves. Some
politicians and some ecclesiastics did not care for being flagel-
lated, of course, or for their strongly held convictions being
represented as quite untenable. The Dean sometimes felt him-

self that he had made a mistake, as in October 1928, when the *Church of England Newspaper* asked for an article. He wrote one and soon repented: "I have done an unwise thing. . . . The Editor of the *Church of England Newspaper* asked me to write an article on the Crisis in the Church; and I said that the crux is the question of discipline: the test case must most unfortunately be the London diocese. I ended by suggesting as courteously as I could an exchange between Ingram and Headlam of Gloucester. I now hear that the Archbishop and Bishop have been working for this very thing since July. They have quite failed to move Ingram. My article, if it has any effect at all, can only be to harden Pharaoh's heart. It was a mistake."

Another journalist (A. G. G.) reinforced Mr List's impression with a similar description, to which he added a vivid image: 'He enters the pulpit and reads his sermons as if he were unaware of his surroundings and of the rattle of his own shrapnel.' But the same writer remarked that 'there is a flame in him, and he does not measure life by the things that perish.'

The Dean's contributions to the *Church of England Newspaper* were usually a little more thoughtful and perhaps a little more elegant than to the two other newspapers, but it would be useless to attempt to illustrate this. It is worthy of note that in this newspaper he wrote an admirable appreciation of his old friend Hastings Rashdall, when he died, and a rather relentless article to exhibit his old friend Bishop Hensley Henson changing his mind about the affairs of the Church, to which Hensley Henson replied the next week (9 March 1928) with a moderation which looked not quite effortless.

By way of concluding the present chapter it will be convenient to review the Dean's journalistic work down to the end of 1931 when his activities of this kind were suspended for a time. In 1928 he began to feel that he ought to be writing another book. *England* had been the last major work, and it had come out in 1926 and had not been quite a success. He began to think of giving up the *Evening Standard*, but it seemed as if Lord Beaverbrook with his unerring flair for newspaper work had sensed this. On 11 November 1928, the Inges dined with him for the first time and went on to the Armistice Day celebration at the Albert Hall: "a queer Sunday evening," the Dean called it. Four days later Beaverbrook raised the fee for the Dean's articles to £40 in a very succinct communication: 'Dear Dean, I have arranged with the *Evening Standard* to pay £40 for the weekly articles you so kindly contribute. I hope you approve this charge. Please do not bother to answer this letter. Yours sincerely, Beaverbrook.' The Dean wrote in his diary: "Lord Beaverbrook has raised me to £40 a week, just when I was thinking of giving up writing for the *Evening Standard*. I am having so many requests from publishers to write books that I must consider seriously whether I ought not to give up this very lucrative journalism and try to produce one more serious book before I die or retire." On 22 November he was discussing a new book with Arthur Hind, a partner in Hodder and Stoughton, and in his summary of 1928 he was able to write: "I am glad that I have resolved to write a new book—it will stop the mouths of those who say that I have given up literature for journalism."

But he continued his journalism, and this went on until the end of 1930. The main cause of its coming to an end seems to have been the offer made by Lincoln's Inn in April 1930 to nominate the Dean to preach the Warburton Lectures. It spurred him on to attempt a new philosophical work with which weekly journalism would scarcely agree. And so at the end of 1930 he wrote (19 December):

> I have definitely given notice to the *Evening Standard* that I mean to stop my articles at the end of this year. I have several reasons, all good ones. The paper is going down hill in every way: I am not proud of being connected with it. I have been expecting every week to hear that they can no longer afford to pay me at the present very high rate, and it is more dignified to take the initiative myself. I have really about written myself out; some of my recent articles have not been worth anything like what I have received for them. Kitty has come into her patrimony, and three of my four children have finished their education. I don't want people to say that I am too fond of money, and I think there is some loss of dignity in my acting as a journalist for a not very high class paper if I can do without it. On the other hand, to give up £2,000 a year for half a day's work a week is to surrender a good deal. Still, I am sure I am right, and I could not have gone on much longer anyhow.

To this he added at the end of the year:

I have no doubt that I was wise to give up my weekly articles for the *Evening Standard*. In addition to the reasons given on December 19, the Editor has not even written to me, much less begged me to reconsider my decision. So I probably resigned just at the right time. . . . My ten years (about) association with journalism has made me one of the best known men in England, and has probably somewhat helped the sale of my books. On the other hand it has not increased my repute among scholars, and has exposed me to a fire of insults, anonymous and otherwise, from ill-conditioned nonentities. I shall be able to make good use of the few hours a week which will no longer be taken up with thinking about and writing these articles. For instance I have two lectures, one at the Royal Institution, the other at Aberystwyth, into which I ought to put my best work.

There was a postscript: "The Editor of the E.S. has since written very civilly to say that the discontinuance of my articles is 'a shock,' and that the Wednesday issue will lose 'its most attractive feature'; but I don't think he is really very keen for me to go on."

When he summed up at the end of the following year (1931) he felt he had given up his journalistic work just at the right time, though it was very lucrative: he had saved £20,000 in four years, he said. He was at journalism again before many years had gone by.

18

Towards Retirement

Where men are employed under a Service Agreement, the terms of the Agreement almost always include retirement on reaching a certain age, but the practice is comparatively new, and has not yet affected the clergy of the Church of England to any great extent, except in so far as they can claim a modest pension at the age of seventy if they have been forty years in Holy Orders; and towards this pension they have not had to make any contributions.

This is all to the good, but it still leaves to the individual to decide when to send in his resignation, and the decision will not often be easy. The circumstances on which it depends are so various. Old age comes noticeably on some at sixty, some at seventy and even later, and it not infrequently happens that it is noticed by others long before a man notices it, or at any rate admits it, himself. And further, retirement is not likely to be contemplated until there is some loss of energy; there is no reason why it should be. But retirement itself needs a great deal of energy; there are so many things to settle—where to live, what sort of an establishment one can afford, what to take with one and what to sell, or shall one give this or that away? What of the accumulations of books, letters, junk? And when precisely would it be best to go? Most perplexing of all, it is impossible to know, before one tries it, whether one will enjoy being retired or not. The *New English Dictionary* gives as one definition of the word Retire: 'To withdraw from office or an official position: to give up one's business or occupation in order to enjoy more leisure or freedom (esp. after having made a competence or earned a pension).' It sounds rather delightful, but how will it turn out? Some, and perhaps the most fortunate, will find themselves 'busier than they have ever been before.' Some will find all the occupation they want in looking round the garden in the morning and taking the dog for a walk in the afternoon, or in anything or anybody else that turns up, if anything or anybody does turn up. Some will find the hours drag slow, how slowly, thinking of the days that are gone. Happy is the man who decides on retirement and never regrets it.

In Inge's tenure of the Deanery only the 1914–18 War makes an obvious break. But the year 1927 affords a dividing line, since *England* suggested, if it did not show, a certain falling off in his powers, and so it may be useful to consider the years 1928 to 1934, when he resigned, as a single separate period. Two large books adorned it and two small ones, as well as many contributions to volumes of essays 'by divers hands,' and for several years the weekly article. Undiminished output, undiminished reputation, but in the diary regular references to old age, and in his writings some repetition, some make-do; with the public a still widening influence: in religion a deeper influence, but not upon the Church at large.

The period begins with thoughts of retirement and ends with resignation offered and accepted. Long ago, when they were still at Cambridge, Mrs Inge had an idea that it would be pleasing to her husband to retire to some quiet country place and be nothing but a scholar, and she thought it would be good for him; but things had turned out far otherwise. Now in his late sixties the Dean sometimes felt the strain of his very busy life and its publicity. The symptoms of old age which he thought he detected in himself and Mrs Inge's poor health led gradually but inevitably to his resignation.

He was in fact unusually young for his years. In September 1926 he wrote of himself as having reached (he hoped) the last stage of his earthly probation, but nine months later, on his sixty-seventh birthday, he noted that he had "never been in such good health as during the last fifteen months—not a day's indisposition. But I am getting fat, and somnolent at my work, which is not a good sign." On his next birthday he had an article in the *Evening Standard* on Old Age in which he remarked, "On the whole I hope I may have a few years of complete retirement in my old age." In November of the same year he used in his diary the expression "before I die or retire." Looking back on the next year (1929), "Probably I am really getting old: I do not expect I could write anything as good as the best part of my earlier work"; and in 1931 he was less hopeful still: "I am feeling terribly depressed about public affairs. There is nothing left but religion, philosophy, literature, and science. But that ought to be enough for an old man whose work in the world is done." About this time he had to record the loss of many friends, and early in 1932 death evidently seemed yet nearer. "We decided to put down Richard for Magdalene, Cambridge . . . I have also booked berths for our last journey in the churchyard of St Clements, Oxford." In August 1933 he said he was being very lazy, and again in November, but he was afraid he enjoyed being lazy. This was quite a new feeling for him, which he described as "the feeling that I am already putting off my armour." In the summary for the year he wrote: "I have become rather indolent, going to bed early and reading mainly for pleasure. Perhaps I have earned a rest: anyhow I do not think I have it in me to write another large book." He was, however, writing a small one, *Vale*, his farewell to St Paul's. In spite of his forebodings there were many years in store for him yet, and much work, but it is true that he never wrote any more really great works, though he published a large one, which was also a good one, as late as 1948.

He was wise to leave St Paul's, but he need not have done so, if it had not been for Mrs Inge's failing health. She had always been apt to overdo things, and even at Brook House had often had to spend days and half-days in bed. This continued in London, but it was not till October 1927 that she was ordered away for several weeks. From this time on until they left the Deanery her life was an extraordinary mixture of great energy and considerable prostration. She was ordered complete rest a number of times, but she generally shortened the period which the doctor prescribed and plunged once more into her round of social engagements and immense correspondence. On and off in 1928 and 1929 she suffered from constant fatigue and a loss of memory which the Dean described as "distressing." She was better in 1930, and not taking much care of herself. On the day of a great function at the Cathedral, for example, forty-seven sat down to lunch in the Deanery, and there were

twenty-five at dinner the next day. In August, according to the
Dean, "she showed herself able to do seven or eight miles."
In November, however, she was away for a month "quite ill,"
and came back "looking very weak and unwell." The next year
was a good year. The August holiday was at Harrogate, and
she had some treatment, and seems to have been mostly well
till 14 March 1933, when she fainted at prayers and had to
abandon an Hellenic tour on which the Dean started with
Catharine two days later. Mrs Inge went to their great friend
Mrs Carruthers (Violet Markham) in Kent. "Violet," she wrote,
"has had a long and earnest talk with me about my health and
says I *must* find out what is really wrong, either heart or nerves."
She came home for the return of the Hellenic travellers on
8 April. On the 11th six guests were staying in the Deanery.
"When they left, Kitty wisely went to bed." She would have
been wise to stay there, for by the end of the month the doctor
came and ordered six weeks' rest and a strict vegetarian diet.
It was serious. They began to look at some country houses with
a view to purchase. In May the Dean felt obliged to write:
"Kitty has seen [Doctor] Stannus again. She is better, but she
is to go away for at least three weeks to a convalescent home
near Brighton, and when she returns she is warned that she
must do no work that can be avoided. This means of course
that we must leave London anyhow, and settle down to a very
quiet life in the country, not in a small country house like
Appleton, but on a much smaller scale. I do not think I mind
much for myself, but it is sad to think that she will be a semi-
invalid for the rest of her life. God grant that I may not survive
her." By the end of 1933, however, she seemed to be really
better, perhaps because it had been settled where their new
home was to be. It had not been easy to settle; the house-
hunting was rather prolonged.

But we must return now to other events in the period under
review. In 1927 the interest of Churchmen was largely focused
on 'the new Prayer Book.' After some years of effort a revision
of the *Book of Common Prayer* of 1662 was produced which it
was hoped would be acceptable to all the various parties in the
Church of England. It created a great deal of controversy, but
was accepted with inconsiderable amendments in the Con-

vocations of Canterbury and York, and in the Church Assembly after long debate. It was then rejected by the House of Commons in December 1927, reappeared with slight alteration and was rejected again in June 1928, and a year later printed and published by the authority of the Bishops under the title *The Book of Common Prayer with the Additions and Deviations proposed in 1928*. The '1928,' as it is often called, has no legal authority, but the Bishops have permitted the use of almost every part of it, and some parts, as for example the Baptismal Rite, are in very general use.

The Dean was in the same position as many others. He supported the Book, but without much enthusiasm. He attended the meetings of Convocation, but could not bring himself to sit through the whole of the long discussions in the Assembly. He made no speech at any of the meetings but wrote a number of articles on the subject, and so did a great many other people. The private opinions which he confided to his diary are of more interest and contribute something to a controversy which is by no means dead. It is striking to see how they confirm the comments he had made in July 1911 on a meeting of Convocation when Prayer Book revision was discussed (see back, page 127).

> 1927. *February 7.* In Convocation the Archbishops presented the new Prayer Bk, and made very able speeches. Cantuar was very touching in his final appeal, when he mentioned that to-day he enters on the 25th year of his Archiepiscopate.
>
> [Dr Randall Davidson was Archbishop of Canterbury, Dr Lang of York.]
>
> *February 22* and following days. I attended Convocation every day, since important debates were in progress about the Revised Prayer Book. There were numerous close divisions, but whereas the Anglo-Cats were thoroughly organised and determined to surrender nothing, but to use every means to alter the doctrinal balance in their own favour, there was no organisation on the other side, and crafty motions were now and then allowed to pass, which were contrary to the real opinion of the majority. Darwell Stone and Kidd were the chief speakers for the Anglo-Cats, Guy Rogers for the other side. When the House

broke up after four days, some real mischief had been done. The Bishops however are not likely to accept the new amendments, which would probably wreck the whole scheme in Parliament.

March 29. Important meeting of Convocation to decide upon the new Prayer Book. Speeches, good on the whole, by the Abp of Canterbury, the Bp of Durham [Dr Hensley Henson], (who, as I have long suspected, is preparing to turn his coat again) the Bp of Norwich [Dr Pollock] who opposed the new book, Darwell Stone, and others.

[The next day the proposal that the Prayer Book Measure should be laid before the Assembly of the Church of England was carried by a large majority.]

July 5. I spent the greater part of the day at the Church House, at the great debate of the National Assembly about the Prayerbook. The Archbishop opened the debate very well, after which Sir W. Joynson Hicks and Darwell Stone attacked the measure, ineffectively, from different sides.

[The Church Assembly was then called the National Church Assembly.]

July 6. The voting day at the National Assembly. The whole afternoon was taken up by unnecessary speeches, restricted to five minutes. Nearly twenty others were induced to refrain from speaking under strong pressure from the Archbishop, supported by cheers from the House as each member said, 'I withdraw.' At last, about six, after a rambling and ineffective speech against the measure by Sir Thomas Inskip, Solicitor General, and a fairly good reply from the Archbishop of York, the vote was taken and showed a large majority for the new Prayerbook in all three Houses. . . . The minority were partly extreme Anglo-Catholics, partly die-hard Evangelicals. So the Archbishop has once more scored a signal triumph.

October 10. I attended a meeting at the Church House of members of the Churchmen's Union to confer with the Liberal Evangelical Group Movement, to draw up a letter to the Archbishops about the new Prayer Book. The main point is—will the Bishops assure us that the Jus Liturgicum will not be held to cover the action of any individual Bishop in conniving at a breach of the new rules—e.g. in the matter of Reservation? Storr and I were deputed to draft the letter, to be signed by our two selves, White, Major, Dale, and Hunkin. I don't think it will do much good.

December 17. There has been great excitement over the new Prayer Book. Kitty was able to get a seat for two days in the Lords. The debates in both houses were by common consent the best that have been heard for many years, and in both Houses the weight of oratory decided the result. In the Lords the two Archbishops spoke very finely, Henson cleverly but in bad taste; Norwich and Worcester [Dr E. H. Pearce] on the other side—Worcester better than I thought he could do. The result was a great victory for the Archbishop—241 to 88. In the Commons the Church had no special spokesman, and things went very differently. Bridgeman and Hugh Cecil, for the Book, were ineffective, and Baldwin could only do his best without enthusiasm. On the other side, Joynson Hicks, the Home Secretary, spoke with great earnestness and better than he had ever spoken before; Mitchell, Labour member for Paisley, fulminated like an old Covenanter; these two speeches did most to determine the result, which was the rejection of the Deposited Book by a majority of about 25 in a House of 450. I supported the Book in the Ch. of E. Newspaper out of loyalty, but I am not very sorry to see it killed. There has been an atmosphere of unreality and insincerity about the whole business. The majority of Church goers did not want a new Prayer Bk, and will shed no tears. Most of the clergy were lukewarm, and supported the Book either out of loyalty to the Bishops or under pressure from their superiors. When the Bishops said that the doctrinal balance of the Church is undisturbed, they were not speaking the truth. And when they promised to enforce the new regulations, they had already made up their minds not to prosecute offenders. The rejection of the Book really saves them from a humiliating position; for they would not have been obeyed.

On 23 December the Bishops met and resolved to introduce the Measure again 'with such changes only, as may remove misapprehensions, and to make clearer and more explicit its intentions and limitations.' They believed that the adverse vote was due in part to avoidable misunderstanding. Once more the Measure pounded its way for acceptance through the Convocations and the Church Assembly, and then again for submission to Parliament, where it was again rejected in June 1928.

1928. *January 20.* I find that the universal opinion about the new Prayer Book is that the Bishops are riding for a heavier fall than they got last month. They are making every mistake. Lord Haldane's advice to do nothing for six months was wise. Their fatal mistake was to accept Reservation, when they have no means of preventing its abuse. The public sees that they are not running straight, and will turn them down without scruple. Nor do I see that they deserve much pity.

February 6. Church National Assembly opened.

February 7. At the National Assembly all day—very dreary work, and the Bishops are having it all their own way. I was persuaded by the Dean of Worcester to give an unwise vote—against 'General Acceptance.' Acceptance was voted by a very large majority.

February 8. Church Assembly again. I took a book to read, but was terribly bored.

February 9. I was at the Church Assembly all the morning, but my patience utterly gave out and I stayed away in the afternoon.

February 10. I again absented myself from the Assembly.

March 28 and 29. Convocation on the Prayer Book. It was rather a pitiful debate.

June 14. The Commons again rejected the new Prayer Book by an increased majority—46. The increase was due to a large accession of the hostile Labour vote; the Liberals also nearly all voted against it. I am sorry for the Archbishop, who has now definitely announced that he will retire before the next Lambeth Conference in 1930.

It was the opinion of Bishop George Bell, who ought to have known, that the Archbishop was not really much disappointed, he did not really want the Prayer Book changed, but he did not regard his twenty years' work as wasted. Dean Inge was relieved too, and he felt he had been right in thinking that the Bishops would not be obeyed. At dinner at Lambeth Palace a few days later the Bishop of Worcester was next to him:

> Pearce told me that the Abp of York has taken the lead very markedly in the Prayer Book debates. It was he who put in the clause which makes the administration of the rule about Reservation almost impossible to carry out. As an illustration of the temper of the Bps, when Exeter [Lord William Cecil] proposed that all grants should be withheld from incumbents who contumaciously disobey the law, Manchester [Dr William Temple] asked indignantly, 'Do you wish that those clergy who will not obey shall starve?' Exeter very properly answered 'Yes': but the majority would not look at the proposal. I have been right all through in my diagnosis of the situation.

In his last six years at St Paul's the discomfort of the Dean's situation as Dean was mitigated. The Canons had not changed since he had come to the Deanery, but changes now came quickly. In October 1928, W. H. Elliott came from Folkestone, where he had won a great reputation as a preacher; he took the place of Canon Simpson, who was made Dean of Peterborough. In January 1930 Prebendary E. N. Sharpe, the Vicar of Paddington, was appointed Archdeacon instead of E. E. Holmes who had come to St Paul's just when the Dean came and was now seventy-five years old. In September 1920 old Canon Newbolt died at the age of eighty-six after forty years at the Cathedral, and was succeeded by J. K. Mozley, but already Canon Elliott had left for St Michael's, Chester Square, and Oliver Quick from Carlisle had taken his place. The Dean welcomed these appointments, though he had not been consulted about them. The Inges and the Sharpes soon became fast friends, and the Archdeacon a helpful colleague—not that Holmes had been unhelpful, the Dean had called him "my one friend in the Chapter." Quick and Mozley were both theologians whose minds the Dean respected, though he described Mozley as "a renegade Evangelical, one of Gore's captives." Quick also, who left before long to be Regius Professor of Divinity at Durham, he suspected of being "very Gorian in sympathies." But on Christmas Day, 1932, he recorded "a huge Amen Court tea-party—Christmas tree, etc. I really think the Court is more of a happy family than it used to be." There were no more changes, though Mrs Sharpe's death in July 1931 was a great loss.

One event of this period was the re-opening of the Cathedral after all but the nave had been closed for more than five years, while the restoration of the dome had been carried out. On 7 October 1929 there was a first meeting of the 'St Paul's Re-opening Committee.' Three more meetings were held before the end of the year, and 25 June 1930 was fixed for the great service. The King and Queen, the Prince of Wales, the Duke of York, and the Duke of Connaught were present. "It was a grand affair; we wore new crimson copes for the occasion." The Dean does not say he disliked them, though he had disliked the idea of them.

Two days later he learnt without any warning that the King had conferred upon him a K.C.V.O. He was now staying with Lord Cochrane of Cults not far from St Andrews and had just had an honorary LL.D. conferred on him. After dinner one of the ladies rushed back to say 'the King has conferred the G.C.V.O. upon you.' The next morning this reduced itself to K.C.V.O., "a more reasonable honour." When he got home he found the household "all eager to call Kitty 'My Lady,' a pleasure which they will not have." The K.C.V.O. is now not an unusual honour for a cleric of the standing of the Dean of St Paul's. It was very well deserved in this case; a layman of equal distinction in literature would certainly have been knighted. Whether the clergy should ever be made members of the orders of chivalry might be questioned. On 5 July he attended an Investiture at Buckingham Palace, when he forgot to take his white gloves and had to procure some from the Court tailor. On 9 July at Mercers' Hall he wore his new star for the first time.

In the day to day routine of his life the Dean did not vary much all the time he was at St Paul's. When he was in London, writing all the morning, a meeting in the afternoon, Evensong, and dining out filled up the normal day, and in the last years at the Deanery this programme was carried out more rather than less strenuously than before. He and Mrs Inge were more and more sought after as sure to make a party interesting, his after-dinner speeches were confidently expected to be entertaining, and he himself was more and more eager to discuss public affairs with men in public life. His writing was conspicuous for bulk and variety.

His attendance at meetings was regular, though at many of them he did not say much. He was a Governor of Malvern College from 1912 to 1933. He owed his place on it to Sydney James, the Headmaster: they had been on the staff at Eton together. He continued to be a steady advocate of eugenics and to serve on the Council of the Eugenics Society: occasionally he introduced the topic in a circle not willing to be interested in it: of persons he had known he reverenced none more than "that grand old man Sir Francis Galton." He was on the Council of the London Library; in the early days of his retirement he assisted the Librarian in weeding out the theological section of the Library: he was a Vice-President of the Royal Society of Literature and sometimes took the chair at a meeting or read a paper himself. He was a member of the Classical Association and as President in 1934 read his striking address entitled 'Greeks and Barbarians': he reprinted it in *A Rustic Moralist*. He was nominated by the Prime Minister to be a Trustee of the National Portrait Gallery, and particularly enjoyed the meetings, though he felt at first that the council was not sufficiently active. They waited for pictures to be given to the Gallery, and what they got were mostly bad. He urged the making of a list of desideranda and desiderati, and presently this was done. The Trustees became very enterprising: in April 1929 they thought of trying to raise £5,000 to buy a portrait of Gibbon by Romney. He was on the Philosophy Committee of the British Academy, and later on the Theological Committee as well. Their duty was to recommend candidates for election to the Academy: the Dean always had names to suggest. His prominent place in the Modern Churchman's Union has been described above (see pp. 176–8). He was accused as President of taking a line which would limit the membership of the Union to Evangelicals, and he fully agreed that it would be unfortunate to exclude the Liberal Catholics, though his

sympathies were largely with the Liberal Evangelical movement. Latterly he thought Modernism, as represented by the
Union, was on the decline; but if so, it was simply that it had
done its work for the time being. The Religious Thought
Society was really dearer to him: he had helped to found it in
1912, and the papers and discussions were at times superior to
any in similar societies, but at the end of 1929 the society was
dissolved. The Dean's comment on this runs as follows: "The
Society, which I helped to found seventeen years ago, and have
helped to keep going, has done very useful work, but I quite
concur with the opinion of the Council that it is time to close
down. A society which is neither pro- or anti- anything is
always difficult to run, and perhaps especially in London, where
there are so many other societies and meetings. We have had
a number of excellent papers, some of which, like those of
Baron von Hügel, have been published."

It was these too numerous meetings which account for a
considerable number of flagging and unsuccessful societies
which the Dean addressed or tried to rally. To gatherings which
were mainly social in their purpose he was very faithful right
up to the time he left London; to Nobody's Friends where he
often sat next to Dr Alington, the Headmaster of Eton, and
to the Brotherhood.

With all his other interests and engagements it is astonishing
to find how much serious work the Dean was able to get
through. It was at the height of his first spell of journalism that
he felt the need to attempt a full-size volume. *Christian Ethics
and Modern Problems* had been decided upon before the end of
1928; the writing of it began in May 1929. But less than a
month later the Dean foresaw the danger that it would "fall
into two parts, (i) Christian Ethics, (ii) Modern Problems, with
a hiatus!" This did in fact happen, and the two halves were
almost exactly equal. Having expounded the moral teaching
of the New Testament the Dean proceeded to treat of two
historic interpretations of that teaching, first Asceticism, then
in a chapter which he entitled Theocratic Imperialism the
authority of the Church to give direction in morals no less
than in faith. Then he came on to the second half of his task,
and discussed the moral problems of today. He felt the import-

ance of this task. "The storm-centre of religious controversy
in post-war Europe and America," he wrote in the Preface,
"is, it seems to me, the relation of the Gospel of Christ to
problems of conduct. If the authority of Christ were rejected
in this field, what would be left of Christianity would not be
worth quarrelling over." But in the urgent need for practical
solutions he rather overlooked the doctrine of grace and the
guidance of the Holy Spirit. The result was not altogether satisfactory, and the Dean did not think it was. He recorded in
April 1930 that the publisher was enthusiastic about his book.
"I wish I was," he added. At the end of the year he could only
say that the book was a qualified success.

And it must be allowed that it lacked something in proportion and in unity. The *Irish Times* (26 September 1930) described
it as 'this considerable, but overladen book,' which was perhaps
a fair criticism. There was too much in it, and it tended to
consist of many parts instead of a whole. The chapter on
Asceticism would generally be thought the best, because it
was a well-defined and largely historical subject and almost
inseparably connected with religion; this suited the Dean. Of
course the book is a treasury of information and stimulating
comment.

The following is a characteristic piece of historical criticism,
noticeable for its just estimate of the Papacy:

Let us pause for a few moments in this summary of the strange
and perhaps inevitable transformation of the "little flock" who
gathered round Christ in Galilee into the world-wide domain of
a priestly autocrat. The idea of history as the tale of Two Cities—
the City of God and the City of Antichrist—was drawn out by
Augustine in his most ambitious but not his greatest work ["De
Civitate Dei"]. In the East, after the state ceased its hostility, the
Church became on the one hand the right arm of the monarchy,
on the other hand an organ of spiritual teaching through a
system of ritual. In the West, where the Church was the one
strong society in the midst of a civilisation dying in chaos and
disorder, it was called upon to save what could be saved out of
the wreck. Nor was the Church deaf to this summons. The
monasteries, from being merely schools of asceticism, became
disciplined organisations in the service of the Church. The Saxon

monks, for example, converted Germany from heathenism. It has been said truly that in the dark ages the only citizenship that remained to a man was his membership of the Church. The Church was a world in itself, with its own traditions and its own laws. While secular society was falling back into a barbarous feudal aristocracy of freebooters, the Church was conscious of being the heir of a higher culture. The success of the Papacy was after all the victory of an idea over brute force—the idea of a single religious commonwealth (pp. 161, 162).

The book came out early in September 1930. In about a week three thousand copies were sold, and many reviews had appeared. Although they mostly praised it highly, they did not make him altogether happy. One by "that impudent hussy, Rebecca West" annoyed him. But the royalties were satisfactory: a second instalment in 1931 amounted to £700.

The publication of *Christian Ethics and Modern Problems* left the Dean free to finish off a minor undertaking. In October 1929 he had agreed for £500 to make an anthology from the Bible with an introduction: Longmans gave him two years to do it in. At the end of September 1930 he was getting on with it, but compilation is not the same as composition, and at the end of January 1931 he remarked on something unusual: "I am in the rather curious position of having nothing to do, since I am not writing anything." It was certainly something he had not known for many years, but the situation changed three months later by the appointment to give the Warburton Lectures. "This means six lecture sermons, one each term, beginning in the autumn [of 1931]. I have accepted, and have chosen as my subject 'The philosophical and religious implications of the new astronomy and physics.' This suggestion was accepted with enthusiasm. As far as I can see, it will mean a regular book, much too long for six lectures, and it will involve very stiff work. But I know the British Academy is not quite satisfied with me for doing no serious work in philosophy since my election as an F.B.A.; and this will be a good answer. The subject is very interesting, and is engaging the attention of all thoughtful people. Whether I shall live, and remain *compos mentis*, long enough to finish it, is another matter."

He began work on it, and by the beginning of August was

able to say he had made some progress, "but it is a very difficult task, I think it will resolve itself into a defence of the *philosophia perennis*, based on the Greeks, against the new Time-philosophy of James, Bergson, Croce, Alexander, and Whitehead. I shall find much help, oddly enough, from the Neo-Thomist Jesuit School; also from Urban and Wyndham Lewis. But I have to read the scientific books too." He got quit of his anthology: it appeared under the title *Everyman's Bible* in September 1931. He gave the first lecture on 22 November following, and jotted down some "hints" for next time amongst which were "My 42 minutes was a little short: they were prepared for fifty," and "They do not mind strong meat—the congregation is very intellectual." At the end of the year he wrote in the same strain as before: "I am enjoying my philosophical work, but my task is a very difficult one. I have good hopes of being able to finish my book before the end of next year. I am convinced that there is going to be a great reaction towards the great Tradition in philosophy—the philosophia perennis—and I want to 'get in on the ground-floor,' as I was lucky enough to do with Christian Mysticism and Plotinus. My new work is really a kind of continuation of these, and oddly enough it will please the Catholics."

The second and third lectures were delivered on 17 January and 1 May 1932. The hints he had put down did not prove very helpful, for he was afraid that the second was difficult and unintelligible, and the third too long. The last was delivered on 7 May 1933, but the book was finished by the middle of the previous October. "It has cost me a terrible amount of hard work, and I am not at all sure whether it will be any good. At my age one must expect disappointments, and only be thankful that one's mental powers are not more obviously decaying." *God and the Astronomers*, as it was called, was published at the beginning of September. The lectures as delivered can only have been a selection from it. The first edition sold out in a few days, and its very favourable reception rather surprised the Dean. "There have been a great many reviews, all very kind and appreciative. I have never had such a good press, though the book, I know well, is not first-rate. Samuel Alexander, though of course he thinks me wrong from beginning to end, has written very generously in the *Manchester Guardian*. I think that now my approaching retirement is announced, people are rather disposed to be kind and friendly."

The last sentence but one of this extract is reproduced in the *Diary of a Dean*, and after it there are about nine hundred words not in the diary on what the book was aiming at. He had also covered the same ground, soon after the book appeared, in *Vale*, pp. 105–9. It would be impertinence to attempt to cover it again, and quite unnecessary. Dr Inge did not really like the title *God and the Astronomers* which was adopted at the publisher's request. While he was writing it he called it "my book on Theism and Cosmology," a better description of it; for it was in fact an investigation of the place that might and in his view must be found for God in the world which science offers us, the question, as he says, between theism and pantheism; it was an attempt to put the conclusions of this investigation into language which could be understood by a reader educated, but not in any sense a theologian or a scientist. Perhaps it was rather too long for the purpose: and a sympathetic reader might complain that the authentic Inge was diluted with too much quotation from other writers. In places it was rather stiff reading; it could hardly be otherwise in view of the problem it was tackling. Several of the critics thought the chapter on 'Time' (III) was the best; it well might be, for it was essential Inge, as containing much of Plotinus and much of Thomas Aquinas. It would be worth while to compare it with the treatment of the same subject in *Plotinus*, Lectures VIII and XVI. Time was a problem which always fascinated Inge, because he could not make up his mind about it. In 1936, while re-reading Gunn, *The Problem of Time*, he called it "a subject on which I want to clear up my ideas." Through the whole work the notion of entropy, which compels us to conclude that the world is running down and must have an end, keeps bobbing up like a spectre. It may be the book did not really achieve its purpose—was, as the author thought himself, "not quite first-rate." If so, it was because he was trying to do something too difficult. But who else could have succeeded better, or as well?

As soon as he had finished writing the Warburtons, another task demanded his urgent attention. In February 1932, a meeting had been held in Mr Winn's rooms in Pembroke College, Cambridge, to discuss the 'Mission' which was to be held at Cambridge early in the next year. Dean Inge was to lead it, and he agreed to preach on Sunday, 29 January and the following Sunday and to give an address of about half an hour or more on each of the intervening days in Great St Mary's. The young men were to be encouraged to come to see him, and it was suggested that he might have one or more missioners to help him in his work. The mission was duly held as arranged; Dom Bernard Clements, afterwards Vicar of All Saints, Margaret Street, and R. T. Howard, Vicar of Luton, assisted. The Dean's two sermons and six addresses were published under the title *Things New and Old*. They were already in print before they were delivered, which was fortunate, for on the Thursday he fell ill, and the remaining addresses and the second sermon had to be read for him by Clements and Howard. The book naturally invites comparison with *Truth and Falsehood in Religion*, the six addresses which he had given to undergraduates in the Victoria Assembly Rooms at Cambridge in 1906. The comparison is on the whole favourable to *Things New and Old*. Of course the circumstances were different. This later course was delivered in church, the former in a public assembly room. The later course was delivered on eight successive days, the former at weekly intervals. The later course was delivered in the evening, the former in the afternoon. The speaker was offering *Things New and Old* to men (and some women) more than fifty years younger than himself, and young people will generally listen to an old man more readily than to a man their father's age.[1] The war had altered the social outlook. The religious problems that were most discussed were now more concerned with personal religion than with orthodoxy. All this told in favour of *Things New and Old*, and it is more attractive and more vital than *Truth and Falsehood*, though it is not really so well written or so striking. But in it the Dean speaks more out of his own experience. His wish is more to help than to instruct. He is very serious, so much so that a quip in the old style (bottom of page 63) seems rather out of keeping. In places the book is rather difficult, but on morals it is plain. As with *Truth and Falsehood* and *Christian Mysticism* its best part is in the second

half. The purpose of the addresses is suggested by the title;
and the Dean stated it in *Vale*:

> The addresses contain, I think, most of what I wished to say
> to the rising generation, who are facing fairly cheerfully what to
> their elders seems a not very cheerful prospect. My main thesis is
> that we must build on the old foundation, but fully recognising
> that there are new problems, which cannot be solved by relying
> on tradition. A general overturn is not what is wanted; but there
> must be a courageous adaptation of fundamental Christian
> principles to new conditions, and a readiness to accept new
> discoveries as a divine revelation, the message of the Spirit to
> our time (p. 110).

The following is a comment on a very old text which is con-
trasted with "the secular creed which eliminates God and leaves
only love to men as the foundation of ethics":

> Thou shalt love the Lord thy God with all thy heart and mind
> and soul and strength, and thy neighbour as thyself. Love to
> God is, I know, a very difficult idea: it is hard to speak of with-
> out unreality. It means partly homage to those eternal attributes
> of God of which I have spoken—Goodness, Truth and Beauty,
> the setting of our affections on things above; but partly also a
> much more personal emotion of loyalty and gratitude to our
> heavenly Father. Indeed, the love of God is something more
> intimate than loyalty and gratitude. The spiritual life, as Clement
> of Alexandria says, begins with faith, which is "a voluntary
> assent," or, as a modern writer has put it, it is the resolution to
> stand or fall by the noblest hypothesis. Then faith passes, Clement
> says, into knowledge, or what we call experience; and knowledge,
> as it passes into love, unites the knower and the known. Our
> love of God proceeds from God, who brings His very life into
> the soul of man and receives it back as His own. Our love of the
> good, the true, and the beautiful is united and harmonised in the
> love of Him Who is the source and the end of them all. And this
> love is essentially reciprocal. (*Things New and Old*, p. 77.)

This sums up what the Dean mainly wanted to teach; though
incidentally he taught a great deal else, sometimes pithily as
for example:

> Whitehead says there are no substances and no matter, but only
> "events." Descartes worked with three substances: matter, mind,

and God. Hobbes dropped mind and God, and retained matter. Berkeley dropped matter, and retained mind and God. Some of the absolutists dropped mind and matter, but retained God. Whitehead seems to drop all three, but I am not sure that I understand him (p. 81).

Things New and Old is a small book, but it contains much of wisdom and much Christianity.

In view of his retirement the Dean had undertaken to write for Longmans a Farewell to London, a *Vale*, so called because (in the opening words of the book), "It is, or used to be in my time, the custom for boys who were leaving Eton to write a 'Vale' in Latin elegiacs instead of the regular verse composition which we did every week." *Vale* is a short book without introduction and not broken up into chapters. It will always be the joy and the despair of Dr Inge's biographers; they will never do the job so well. But it does not give more than a one-sided picture of the author, and is a record of opinions rather than of character or actions or affections. It is a most charming book, and in a style which was the great adornment of Dr Inge's writings all through the last thirty years of his life. A page of it on the very matter of his own style will illustrate this well:

The Warburton Lectures were only the nucleus of a large book, and, alas, I found while writing it that my hand had really lost its cunning. I used to be complimented on the "frosty brilliance" of my style. The style of my last effort is neither frosty nor brilliant; and I spent two most exasperating days in cutting out sentences and paragraphs in which I had repeated myself. My kind French critic, the Abbé Nédoncelle, who in his *La Philosophie Religieuse en Grande Bretagne*, gives a whole chapter to "*Le Platonisme Chrétien du Doyen Inge*"—a most careful, appreciative, and just résumé of my life's work—says of my last book, *rien de bien nouveau dans ces pages, pour qui a lu ses ouvrages antérieurs*; *mais un plaidoyer attachant pour la transcendance de Dieu, et un bel effort de synthèse. Rien de nouveau?* It is what I knew myself; my literary work is done. After all, I had nothing else to expect. It is quite exceptional for a man of letters to remain at his best after seventy. To mention two only of the greatest names: Plato, when he wrote the *Laws*, was still a wise teacher, but he was a great writer no longer. The charm of his earlier dialogues has vanished. And

Wordsworth had given his message to the world before 1820, when he had still thirty years to live. The mass of poetry after that date would never have gained him immortality (pp. 104–5).

It may be that Dean Inge had given his message to the world, when he had still thirty years to live. His writings after that would not by themselves account for his fame. But it is not true that his hand had lost its cunning. It had only found a new method. For all his works we know rather precisely the date of composition, but if we did not, we might from internal evidence perhaps put them in chronological order, as Greek scholars have done with Plato's dialogues and English scholars profess to have done with Shakespeare.

PART THREE

Brightwell

1934–1954

19

Peace and War Again 1934-1945

There is a highly reputable weekly journal called *Country Life*, and from its contents we ought to be able to gather what are the pursuits and pleasures of those who live in the country. They seem to fall into two series; (A) gardening, birds, fishing, farming, horses, shooting: (B) female beauty, great houses, furniture, miscellaneous works of art and curiosities, antique buildings whether in town or country. There are other interests, too, but these are recurrent in one number after another. The selection is to some extent influenced by what lends itself to illustration, for the pictures in *Country Life* are always so good, but it is a fairly representative list.

The two series are distinguished by the different relation which the town dweller bears to them. The countryman has the advantage in (A); he generally gets a high pleasure out of these pursuits: the town dweller has often not learned how to get the same pleasure from want of opportunity, but he thinks he would welcome the opportunity, especially if he could have a garden; for almost all the English are devoted to gardening, as many a suburban street otherwise quite undistinguished shows. The pleasures of series (B) are shared alike by the townsman and the countryman; the townsman, it may be, tends to care less for curiosities, and may have rather better taste, because he has seen more good works of art, but taste emigrates easily from town to country. In the country series (B) may be called the Pleasures of the Car, in the metropolis there are more ways than one of getting about.

Your true townsman may hanker after country joys, but he rather often fails to find them to the full. Fishing, farming, and shooting are arts to be acquired young. Only if there are little girls in the family will he soon feel bound to keep a horse or two. He may become a good gardener, but only if he can get

an assistant, at any rate a day or two a week. He will be sure
to enjoy many hours of happiness and quiet, but leisure is not
quite so easy as it seems. It is there when it is wanted, but
sometimes too when it is not wanted. Charles Lamb's experience
at rural Enfield in 1830 is hardly unique: 'In the stagnation,
some molesting yearnings of life, not quite kill'd, rise, prompt-
ing me that there was a London, and that I was of that old
Jerusalem.' (*Letters of Charles and Mary Lamb*. Lucas. No. 817.)

Where to live on vacating the Deanery? As early as August
1927 on holiday at Painswick, the family amused themselves
by looking at houses, but nothing came of it. "I don't think we
have found the right one," the Dean wrote, "and to buy a
house three years before we want it would be unwise, as adding
so much to the cost." Retirement at seventy was evidently in
his mind. It was put off, but by the end of 1932 he had resolved
to resign in about eighteen months' time, though the place to
retire to had not been settled. Kent, where the family had many
connections in and around Canterbury, seemed attractive until
they came to think that the Dean would not be happy unless
he were within half an hour of Oxford, and he agreed that
there was something in that; but even this limitation left a wide
area to choose from, and there was the common difficulty that
men and women differ in what they require of a house that is
to be their home. One of the first houses they inspected was
about six miles from Oxford, and we have both the Dean's
impressions of this and Mrs Inge's: they visited it on 8 March
1933. The Dean's account runs:

> We saw Denton House near Cuddesdon, which we could have
> very cheap, for £2,500. It is a large stone house with extensive
> outbuildings and 15 acres. It is in bad repair, and there is no
> electric light. It might be made very nice with the expenditure of
> a large sum of money, but I think it would be troublesome and
> costly to keep up. It is also very isolated, nearly two miles from
> Wheatley Station, and buses on only three days a week.

It did not seem to occur to the Dean that they would be bound
to have a car.

Mrs Inge wrote in her diary:

It is a lovely late Stewart house with lofty rooms like our
beloved Deanery, and a glorious staircase of 1641, 2 panelled
rooms and spacious dining room wh. I could make into a lovely
study for WRI looking into wide stretching lawns ending in
mediaeval stone walls and beyond a paddock, thus preventing
any buildings coming near, and opposite the front entrance
lovely 17th century stables and roomy cottage, but O! the great
house is dirty and messy, and the 'Offices' would have to be
entirely remodelled and there is no electric light, but with dear
Vera Herbert's wise council it could be made into a lovely house
indeed. Tho' looking as though it were almost outside human
habitation, it is only $\frac{1}{4}$ hrs. ride in the motor fr. Magdalen Bridge!
The more I think of it the more I feel I shd. love this house.

But at a second visit "somehow the glamour had gone, and it
was dirtier and more miserable than ever."

These impressions show to some extent why the Dean
remarked later on their "interminable house hunting, especially
as Kitty and I do not always agree." The house was later bought
and restored by General Graham: the Inges made friends with
him and on a visit found the house and garden had had a great
deal spent on them; "but some of us find it just too perfect,
not quite a place to live in."

These extracts give a good idea of what they were looking
for. They liked very much Appleton Manor, but in the Dean's
absence on an Hellenic tour it was sold over his head. He liked
enormously Ewelme Old Rectory, but Mrs Inge did not like it.
At last she gave way, but with such distress that it was fortunate when it was bought by someone else while their solicitor
was bargaining for it. Of Stonehill House near Abingdon the
Dean ventured to write, "I think this will be our future home,"
till he discovered its proximity to a sewage works. He saw a
house at Deddington, which he liked better. Mrs Inge and
Catharine disliked it, and he gave way. A Tudor house at
Ramsden was impossible but—

August 14–15—much more promising is Brightwell Manor, close
to Wittenham Clumps, partly Tudor and partly Georgian, very
attractive but rather small. The reception rooms are not big enough.

Then my friend Dr Walker of the MCU wants to sell East Hag-
bourne Grange, two miles from Brightwell, a larger house. . . . I
hope we may fix on one of these two.

August 21–28. I think it is practically settled that we shall buy
Brightwell Manor. It is a most attractive house, but rather small.
I have written to Paul Paget and Seely to advise us as to adding
two or three more rooms. If I had had only myself to consider I
should have chosen a larger house, several are offered at about the
same price.

August 29–September 4. The only important event was our decision
to buy Brightwell. We met the two architects at Didcot, four or
five miles from the house, and drove over—the whole family.
The architects made a clever plan to alter the position of the
kitchen, and to throw out a new addition which will give us one
large room, enough for Catharine's piano. They were both
fascinated with the house, and thought we had made a very good
choice. I am to have for my study a small panelled room, over-
looking the orchard. Leading out of it is a room which can be
divided, the end separated from the rest to be a bathroom and
lavatory, and the rest my bedroom. Close by is an emergency
bedroom, which we shall call the book room. There is also a
large cupboard between the study and bedroom which will hold
a number of books, so that I shall not have to cover up the oak
panelling. We think the garden can be made very nice. . . . So
that is settled, thank goodness. I am beginning to wonder that I
endured to live in London so long.

September 4–9. The negotiations for Brightwell Manor are now
complete. We drove over again, with Sophy and Betty How. It
looked to me rather small; we shall feel rather cramped at first.
The contract is signed, and the deposit of £385 paid with Kitty's
money. The house is to be hers.

September 15. We lunched with John Seely and Paul Paget, to see
the plans for Brightwell Manor. . . . We like the plans very much,
and I think the house will now be quite big enough. The young
men are most ingenious—I think they enjoy working on such an
interesting house.

September 28. The legal business for the purchase of Brightwell
is now complete, and Kitty is the owner of the property.

October 13. The architects present terrible estimates—nearly £2,000 for the improvements at Brightwell Manor. We really must try to cut them down a bit.

It was almost a year after this when the Dean and Mrs Inge took up their residence at Brightwell. The farewells were said, the farewell parties given, the regrets expressed, the presentations made, and even the few who had sometimes wished the Dean away seemed genuinely to regret his departure. On 28 September they vacated the Deanery. "It is odd that I don't feel more sentimental over the move," the Dean wrote. "I think the fact is that I feel that my innings is really over, and I am only walking back to the pavilion." They were hospitably housed for a week by Archdeacon Sharpe. The next day was Michaelmas Day and the Dean celebrated the Holy Communion in the Cathedral for the last time. A week later they were gone.

The arrival at the new home was cheerful.

October 6. Kitty and I left 9 Amen Court and were met by the children [Catharine and Richard] at Didcot. Kitty was very much exhausted on the journey, but seemed better after we arrived. Those dear children have done wonders in five days, getting everything ready for us. The house, now the furniture is in it, looks twice as big as I pictured it; I cannot think how I ever supposed that we should be cramped in it. The new room is really beautiful; my study will be a bright and cheerful room; and the bedrooms are really very spacious. Our only servants at present are Mr and Mrs Tooze; they seem willing and good-tempered, but they have everything to learn about a gentleman's household. I am not unhappy at leaving the Deanery.

And a happy time was to follow. The next day was the Harvest Festival at Brightwell, and Dr Inge preached in the evening. He began as follows:

My friends, as I hope you will be, I count it a happy coincidence that my first day in my new home, where I hope, if it is God's will, to pass a peaceful old age, and prepare for a time when I must give an account of my stewardship, should fall on your harvest thanksgiving day, the most popular festival in all country districts. . . . I must confess that I do look forward to returning in my old age to those associations which are so much like my

earliest recollections, which must always have a peculiar sacred-
ness, as they take one back to one's first home and beloved
parents.

He turned out to be quite a countryman, and was pleased to
read about Inge of Brightwell in Burke's *Landed Gentry*, but he
was one of those fortunate countrymen who often go to town.
The first business was sorting out books; then to be called
upon and to return the calls. Unfortunately Mrs Inge had to go
away for a long rest, but Catharine filled her place very ade-
quately. They found their new acquaintances uniformly pleasant,
and soon made many friends : nine months after taking up residence they asked all they knew in the district to a garden party,
and one hundred and forty-six people came. Retirement was in
fact a decided success until the war clouded all. At the end of
1934, after three months at Brightwell, the Dean reflected that
the year had seen his last uprooting and the end of his active
life. "I have not the slightest doubt that I did right. Kitty's
health was alone a sufficient reason, though I was careful not
to put that forward. I really think I have done my work, and
may conscientiously allow myself a very quiet old age in real
retirement. I do not find the country at all dull even in this the
worst part of the year." A year later: "I am not sure that this
has not been the happiest year I ever spent. . . . I think we all
like our country house—I certainly do. I am afraid I did not
realise how great the relief would be to be free of Alexander
and the Minor Canons." A year later again (1936): "So ends
a year which Kitty and I think the happiest we ever spent."
On 4 (in error for 6) October 1938, he wrote, "It is just four
years since we first slept in this house. It has been a very happy
time, and I am deeply thankful for all the mercies we have
received since we came." But he could not be said to be in a
"real retirement." It was a pleasure to go about the country
dropping in on new friends, and to contemplate the country
scene. Old pleasures survived too : friends to stay—fifty of them
in 1935, sixty in 1937: and the old visits in the summer to
familiar homes mostly in Scotland and the North: invitations
to College feasts in Oxford, and more pleasurable still to King's,
where the Dean was received with greater and greater respect,
and to Jesus College too.

Since he was known, or thought, to be at leisure, many invitations to write articles and give lectures came in, and a great many were refused; but he accepted a proposal by Sir William Bragg that he should give four lectures at the Royal Institution, where he had given lectures on Plotinus in 1914. He delivered the new lectures in March and April 1935: the subject was 'The Living Past.' Journalism too was begun again, and at the end of February he was invited to contribute to the *Evening Standard* for an indefinite period at twenty-five guineas a week. He promised eight articles, and just a month later he wrote in his diary: "I am getting on swimmingly with my *Evening Standard* articles, two of them in one morning and evening."

He continued to write them for many years, gradually with less frequency. Three selections of them were published in book form in March 1936, October 1938, and November 1939. These volumes did not sell so well as the *Lay Thoughts of a Dean*, but this must largely be accounted for by the author being more and more regarded as a pacifist. For the third volume, *A Pacifist in Trouble*, he wrote an introduction in which he expounded his pacifism from the political and the Christian point of view. Since the book was published after the last war had begun it probably convinced no one: but at least it showed that the Dean in his eightieth year was as clear headed and insistent as ever. The smaller circulation was not due to lower quality. Indeed these volumes ought perhaps to be judged superior to the previous ones of like character. They are more relaxed, more leisurely, and often more thoughtful—naturally enough since they were written in the peace of Brightwell and not in the bustle of London, by a wise old country clergyman and not by a busy Dean. They show what can come of following faithfully what he recommended to his son Richard, when Richard still at Eton made his first attempt at authorship—"his Egyptian story" as Mrs Inge called it. She records that "when his father read it WRI told him to go on—it was worth working at. 'Make up your mind what you want to say, and then put it into the simplest language you can, that is the secret of good style: when I began I wrote very slowly, but use is a great help.'"

Over the years Dr Inge had certainly come to write faster, if less furiously. It is noticeable that in his first two years at Brightwell he was occupied with an anthology of the Christian Life which Longmans had asked for, and found it very dull work and wished he had not undertaken it. At the beginning of November 1935 he had not got quite enough material and did not know how to fill it up, but in December he added an introduction of about forty pages; "my extracts are not enough without it," which only shows that writing was less troublesome than compilation. The book was published in 1936 under the title *Freedom, Love and Truth*. At the time of George V's silver jubilee he wrote an article on the King while travelling in the Flying Scotsman from Edinburgh: he had finished it by the time he got to Durham. Shortly before he had written a lecture in two days. Later on in January 1940 he remarked: "I write very fast." He added, "and probably badly."

Everyday life, even if it is specially interesting, is not easy to describe. The record for May 1936 is a fair picture of the diversions of Brightwell: many other months would be much the same, at any rate in the summer:

May 1 [Friday]. The Private View of the R.A.

May 2. An amusing film at Reading called 'The Ghost moves West.'

May 4. To Bristol. The annual dinner of the Colston Research Society. I gave a twenty minutes address on 'English in Education.'

May 5. The new weed-killer is making havoc among the plantains.

May 9. Four guests to lunch. We played 'trente-et-un' afterwards.

May 10. To Oxford to lunch. The afternoon in the Union. I spent most of the time reading that wonderful periodical, the American 'Geographic Magazine.'[1] . . . I found to my surprise a very large framed photograph of the debating hall crowded with members. Underneath was 'Union Society, Visit of Dr Inge, 1922'!

May 14. Another perfect day; the apple blossoms, the fresh green leaves, the fields, a mass of gold and green, are very beautiful.

Married love

May 15–17. I am alone in the house . . . I have got through a good deal of reading—Eckermann's Conversations with Goethe is quite as interesting as Boswell. Eckermann has not Boswell's art, but he is never ridiculous as Boswell is, and of course Goethe, mellow and kindly in old age, is a far greater man than Johnson: The conversations are mainly about literature, art, and science; mostly very illuminating, though Goethe, perhaps from a vein of snobbishness, which occasionally appears, greatly over-estimates Byron as a poet and as a man. I have read again Loisy's 'La Naissance de Christianisme.' A very acute critic, often rather disconcerting, and a Christian, without a spark of religious feeling, and obsessed with a spirit of incredulity. Then I read again Lightfoot's Bampton Lectures, which after Loisy seem very reasonable and even conservative.

May 17. Dinner at Magdalen with Chapman of the Press: about fifteen were dining, including the President, Thompson, Cookson, Dixon, J. A. Smith. I do enjoy going back to this kind of society.

May 19. A very nice luncheon party at home. . . . After lunch I went to Cambridge via London, arriving just in time for dinner at Jesus, the Rustat Audit. I sat next to Quiller-Couch.

May 20. I lunched at Gatti's Restaurant with the Modern Churchmen's Union. About 70 were present.

May 21. I am reading Lodge's 'Plato's Theory of Ethics,' a good book. There were two men in Plato, a social and political reformer and a religious mystic. The combination of the two (and I don't agree with Burnet and Taylor that the Orphic strain is Socrates not Plato) is what makes him so uniquely important; Christianity inherited this fruitful dualism. The resulting doctrine that the perfect man sacrifices his bliss 'in heaven' to descend into the arena and help mankind brings him near to an incarnational belief: but his school, though they never quite abandoned this, became more mystical and detached from earthly interests.

May 23. We drove into Oxford for a squash in New College Hall, but I found it intolerable and flat.

March [*sic*] *24.* Gordon Selfridge and his grand-daughter Tatiana, who is seventeen, came to lunch. He is a very queer type—the American business man, entirely absorbed in his great game, but not, I should say, very fond of money for its own sake.

R   *Dean Inge*

May 27. Lunch party at home. [One of the guests "a rich lady."] The poor lady has had great difficulties about servants, and has fallen back on our Mrs Young. She gives her the ridiculous wages of two pounds a week.

May 28. The Kaiser, after a long interval, writes to me and expresses approval of my *Evening Standard* articles, especially the two about immortality!

May 29. I have written an Introduction to a book of Sutton of Christ Church on a new political theory.

May 30. G. B. Shaw sends me his three latest plays, in one of which he brings in my name.[2]

This looks like the record of a very pleasant month, but it is more stay-at-home than most months. In 1938 the Dean spent a hundred and thirteen nights away from Brightwell, twenty of them in London besides several expeditions for the day. In this year he went once more on an Hellenic tour with Mrs Inge and Catharine. They left Victoria on 14 February with London under snow: on the previous day the Dean had made certain resolutions:

> On my return I shall record how I have kept them. Since my retirement I have lived a very undisciplined life, taking things easily and letting myself go. Now, with God's help, I mean to be strict with myself. (1) To look after Kitty in every way, and to pay her those little attentions which women like. Never to speak impatiently. (2) To be courteous and considerate with all our fellow-passengers, even the bores, remembering that they have come to enjoy themselves, and that as Lunn's guest I have a certain responsibility for helping them to do so. (3) To keep a guard over my thoughts, to make them not unworthy, that this holiday may not, from the higher point of view, be wasted.

This is surely true humility in a man of seventy-seven, becoming almost as a little child. The promised record after the end of the cruise said, "It has been a very delightful holiday, but I have not quite kept my resolutions about being friendly to everyone." He had kept too much out of the way of one dignitary whom he didn't like, and of one lady whom he found it difficult to get on with, and one of the men at the same table as himself got on his nerves with his ceaseless prattle. "These, however, were only negative shortcomings; I made several new friends. We were a very pleasant and harmonious party."

On this cruise he found one interesting occupation. He read the four Gospels through in Greek and wrote down his reactions:

> My impression is that there was a large authentic collection of the sayings of Christ, many of them far above the capacity of the evangelists to invent or even understand, and that the piecing together has been done with almost incredible clumsiness. The interpretations are mostly quite childish.

The 1939 war, unlike the previous one, did not come as a surprise. In 1938, as is well known, the continuation of peace was only secured with the greatest possible difficulty. In September of that year the Dean thought we were "on the brink of a criminally foolish war," "dragged into war for a ramshackle republic, not twenty years old." He hailed the respite gained at Munich with enthusiasm, but for the rest of the year he was depressed. "I am painfully conscious of old age." "I am tired of life and have no wish to be tied to W.R.I. for ever." Reviewing the year he felt he was rapidly going downhill. At the same time he was still busy with his journalism: "I have managed, to my great astonishment, to go on with my weekly articles for nearly four years. I shall feel rather at a loose end when I have to give them up." The year 1939 began with a number of engagements in London. The month of April was occupied with another Hellenic cruise which proved to be "the pleasantest of all our cruises." Mrs Inge was with him. It certainly did the Dean good, though anxiety about public affairs intruded itself, particularly at Sparta, which incidentally the diary describes as "a smart little town." On reaching England they soon found the prospects of war being frequently canvassed. The Dean had his own view of the situation; in the middle of August he confided it to the diary in the following terms:

August 22. All this time public affairs are in a very anxious state. Many people think we are on the point of going to war with Germany over Danzig, which the Germans claim, reasonably enough, for the Reich. But as Hitler has shown that no reliance can be placed on his word, it is thought that he will resort again to his tactics about Bohemia and try to seize a great part of Poland. How we could stop him without the help of Russia I cannot imagine, and, as I have long suspected, Stalin and Hitler have an understanding. I wonder whether France also has been squared. Abuse of France in Germany was suddenly called off a few months ago, and we alone are daily insulted. I have some hope that the defection of Russia and the reluctance to fight in France, which has so much to lose and nothing to gain, may make war impossible; but I fear we are fools enough for anything. Ever since the perfidy of Hitler about Bohemia the war-party in England has been gaining strength. It includes nearly the whole of the Labour party, who gained materially by the last war and perhaps dream that they may do so again. I suspect that Jewish influence in the Press is being used against an understanding with Germany.

This appreciation of the situation, right or wrong, gains by appending another briefer comment to it, written down at the very end of 1939:

It seems to me that this is just a preventive war of the bad old kind. Whenever any continental Power threatens to upset the balance, we try to get up a coalition against it. So far, we have succeeded in the past. Continental nations think we are very clever: we think we are stupid, but ever so gentle and good.

It would serve no purpose to trace the course of his feelings, as the war proceeded. He was not wanting in courage, but he certainly was wanting in hope; but so were many others. In June 1940 he thought we had definitely lost the war: at the end of the year he could not see the remotest chance of winning it. In February 1941, "I am very miserable about the state of the world. Winston Churchill's heartening speeches are very clever, but he is not telling the truth. I do not see how we can win the war"; in March, "I fear we are done for"; in April, "We never had the slightest chance of winning the war." But in October a little change for the better. "I am a pessimist about the war, but the prospects of Germany do not seem bright." In March 1942 he was in favour of trying for a peace of agreement with Germany. A year later he was still much depressed about public affairs; only in August 1943 we read at last: "The war news is favourable."

But his activities were seemingly not much checked: the record of entertaining and being entertained still creates an agreeable impression, and visits to London for the usual meetings or on the way to Cambridge are still frequent. A fortnight at Keswick was an annual event. The bomb damage in general seemed not so great as he was led to expect. Reading and writing played a large part in his life as being the best distractions. At the end of 1941 he included in his summing-up of the year a depressing note. "I just read—mainly old books, and go to bed soon after ten." Not infrequently he read his old diaries, with interest and some surprise:

How I tormented myself when I was a master at Eton! Certainly schoolmastering was not my job, but I was not by any means such a failure as I thought. And I had spurts of extreme depression even at Hertford College. I wonder whether public affairs are not quite so desperate as they appear to me. I try to reason the matter soberly, but the outlook is very black.

Of the diaries themselves: "They are quite as interesting as the Creevey Papers, and may some day be published as a chapter of social history. What a strange life it was in London for a shy scholar!" That "some day" must certainly come, hardly yet, perhaps in fifty years' time.

But the classics chiefly consoled him, as they have consoled so many: Horace's Odes read with great delight, Tacitus and Thucydides; some plays of Aristophanes which he thought "might have been lost without much cause for regret": Ranging in another direction he read the Bhagavad-Gita through.

It seems to me the greatest of all philosophical poems. I am more and more attracted by the wisdom of the East. It is of course the same as the Orphic–Pythagorean–Neoplatonist religious philosophy. Not without reason do the Indians claim Pythagoras as an Indian sage, called in Sanskrit 'Pitta-Guru,' 'Father Teacher.' Of course the gospel of detachment is the only one that brings any comfort at a time of universal ruin: it is much more Christian than the Left-wing Christianity of the Socialists, deeply infected with the mirage of human perfectibility.

It is not surprising to find that a fortnight after this (6 June

1940, his eightieth birthday) he was reading Plotinus again: "It is an escapist philosophy; but so is Christianity, only redeemed by the law of love, and the lesson of the Incarnation." At the beginning of July he reported that he had read him all through, and he wrote down some criticisms that struck him, particularly that the mystical experience was not simply one of 'Withdrawal,' but of 'Withdrawal and Return.' Later on he was finding "comfort in Plotinus and Augustine, who both lived, as we do, when a civilisation was breaking up, and with Indian philosophy, esp. Radhakrishnan." He supplemented these great names with the mysticism of Aldous Huxley.

Although there was ample time for reading there, Brightwell seems, until the novelty wore off, to have moderated the Dean's zest for writing; he relaxed a little and it is significant that he noted on the first Christmas Day, when they listened to the King's speech on the new wireless, that it was a marvellous invention. His *Evening Standard* articles, a few long reviews and his Anthology were enough for his pen. At the end of July 1936, when a publisher had asked for a book, he thought he might manage one on Platonism, but nothing seems to have come of this, and he published no books except those in which his short articles were collected. It was the war that stimulated him to begin again. Before it had lasted a fortnight Longmans had asked for a book, and he accepted the invitation. "The work will take my mind off the horrible state of public affairs," he said. By Christmas 1939 he was busy with it. He seems at first to have called it *Between Two Wars*, but at the beginning of March it was finished and he thought he might call it *The Fall of the Idols*, the title under which it actually appeared. In notifying Longmans of this he said he doubted the wisdom of publishing it just now. Longmans took the hint and asked for some revision of the chapter on War. The Dean altered part of the chapter, but was not inclined to recast the whole of it, which, he said, expressed his views. In the middle of May Longmans said they did not dare to publish it in the present heated state of public opinion. But Putnam took it, and it came out, after some little delay, at the end of November, and was well received. "*The Times* has a very kind and intelligent review. . . . I think Longman must be sorry he did not take it, though

I don't think much of it myself." At the end of December Longmans lost everything by enemy action. Many of the Dean's really important books since 1911 went out of print automatically. "It is lucky," he wrote, "that Longman has not got *The Fall of the Idols*." Three thousand copies had been sold by the beginning of April.

The book consists of a short introduction and six chapters ranging from about five thousand to about twelve thousand words on Progress, Democracy, Economism, Pacifism, Humanism, and Religion. They contain some repetitions from earlier works almost word for word, which may be reckoned to have been reproduced from memory and not copied; they also contain many signs of new reading, and in many places almost the vigour of *Outspoken Essays*. The chapter on Pacifism is presumably the same as the chapter on War to which Longmans objected. What pruning it received one cannot say, but in its printed form it is the shortest chapter. It is also one of the best, viewing the matter from many angles; it may be that a conscientious objector would not find much in it to support him. The first chapter—on Progress—is not so good as the Romanes Lecture, but the times were not so favourable to a judicial view on this topic. The last chapter—on Religion—is, as readers of Inge had learned to expect, a very good one. In a man of eighty one does not anticipate much that is new, but there is not a little that is freshly put. He expresses some doubts about entropy, which did not assail him when he wrote *God and the Astronomers*, and he is clearer than ever that some things must be simply accepted and cannot be profitably questioned or their problems solved by us, as we now are.

> It is no disparagement to the reason to own that there are limits to the knowledge which it can give us. Goethe says: 'Man's highest happiness as a thinker is to have fathomed what can be fathomed, and to bow in reverence before the unfathomable.' As Meyerson has shown in his famous book on the philosophy of science, we must accept certain brute facts and values of which no explanation can be given. We do not know why the world exists. We cannot say that space and time are infinite, nor that they are not infinite. Both hypotheses land us in riddles which we cannot solve (pp. 252–3).

He claimed with greater plainness than ever that scientific knowledge is not the discovery of pure intellect, but depends on an arbitrary limitation of its fields, and on the other hand that religion puts on one side only at its peril the use of the intellect when its use is appropriate.

The deep depressions of 1941 produced nothing of note, though in August Benn published what the Dean calls "my angry pacifist pamphlet." But early in April 1942 the diary records an article which was to lead on to *Talks in a Free Country*. "I have written an imaginary conversation on 'Miracle, Myth and Mystery,' and sent it to the *Hibbert Journal*. Jacks is delighted with it, and I thought it rather good—So when Huntington of Putnam wrote to me asking for another book, I am inclined to accept, and write other conversations of the same kind. At any rate it will give me an object, and take my mind off sad thoughts." He wrote it very quickly. "*June 3*. I have finished my little book of 'Uncensored Talks,' and have sent it to Putnam. It is very senile." However, when it was published in December 1942, he gave away ten copies: "I confess that I rather like it when I read it."

He very well might do so. The new medium gave him new opportunities. He added eight conversations to the original one, all longer than it, but none of them more than thirty pages. They are not very like Plato's dialogues which when imitated have so often shown themselves to be inimitable, but they have some Platonic qualities. The characterisation is not very marked. (Except for a few leading characters the talk about characterisation in Plato is sheer imagination. Although diversity makes for good conversation, serious discussion is only possible if the participants all talk the same language.) The Talks do not aim at coming to a conclusion—they have an all-round look at the problem. They have charming little touches of scene and humour, but they are serious. All this is Platonic.

There is some old stuff in this new dress, and some new stuff. The war has by this time clearly led the author into an extensive study of foreign affairs. 'John, Jonathan and Fritz' dealing with the characteristics of the English, the Americans and the Germans is the newest of the Talks and perhaps the most entertaining. 'Escape,' the longest of them, shows an increased familiarity and sympathy with Eastern religion, though critical of its detachment. If the Dean called the volume "senile," it is senile only in the sense that it gives the impression of an aged judge listening carefully, occasionally directing the jury, summing up, but content to leave the verdict to them.

During the whole period now under review the Modern Churchmen's Union had been on and off in difficulties. Dr Inge, on retiring from the Deanery, had been followed as President of the Union by Dr Matthews, his successor at St Paul's, but the Union was largely run by Dr Major. He was thought to be offending the Liberal Catholics, whom many members, including Dr Matthews, wished to retain. At the end of 1936 these members started a rival magazine to the *Modern Churchman*, a quarterly called *The Way*. In January 1937, Matthews the President, E. St G. Schomberg the Chairman, Canon (Dick) Sheppard, the Master of the Temple (Harold Anson), the Archdeacon of Rochester (W. M. Browne) and Professor Norman Sykes all resigned from the Council. Dr Inge felt he ought to resign himself, but he shrank from wrecking the Society, and resolved to wait and see what Major had to say for himself. On 9 February a letter appeared in *The Times* signed by twenty-two members of the Union protesting against the action of Dr Matthews and his friends. Inge had refused to sign this letter, but on 5 May at a meeting of the Council he played a decisive part in getting Dr Norwood, the President of St John's College, Oxford, elected president of the Union, and objected strongly to the seceders whom he accused of "a wish to avoid theological questions and attend to the subjects which interest the young— i.e. socialistic politics." He condemned the second number of *The Way* as frankly political and revolutionary.

The Union now continued calmly on its course, but in November 1940 Inge was again inclined to resign: "Some of the younger members have really no interest in Liberal theology, and wish to commit the Society to a kind of sloppy socialism, totally alien to the objects for which it was founded. . . . The Society has achieved the greater part of its objects in safeguarding freedom of thought and speech in the Church, and perhaps it had better die." It did not die, however, though in April 1942 the political clique was still, in Dr Inge's view, wrecking the

Union. But the Union held out, and at the annual conference in 1943 he himself was sufficiently reconciled to read a paper on 'The National Church as Teacher of Christian Truth' which was well received, and the attendance at the conference was very satisfactory.

Inge was always frightened of politics in religion, and the war aggravated this fear. Although William Temple was a friend of the family, his little book of *Thoughts on the War* got the Dean worked up to a great pitch: "I have never known such a pitiful downfall of what was once a fine and candid mind." In February 1941 he criticised an article by the Archbishop in a volume called *Christianity*, for omitting what he himself thought mattered. The list is interesting.

> Not a word on the important things—the great advance in biblical and historical scholarship, the acceptance by the Churches of the main conclusions of natural science, the consequent abandonment of the traditional orthodoxy, the decline of rationalism, the revival of the *philosophia perennis*, mainly by R.C. scholars, the secession of a number of men of letters to Rome, the decline in church-going and the attempt to improve Anglican church-services; the continued strength of Anglo-Catholicism, and the risk of a new Evangelical party; the rapprochement between the C. of E. and the Free Churches, etc. All that interests the Archbishop is the flirtation of a certain group to which he himself belongs with Left-wing politics.

He thought Temple's appointment to Canterbury "a disastrous choice," and when he died he only entered in his diary: "A great grief to Kitty. I must get new Trustees of my marriage settlement." But the diary at this period is very brief.

As the war went on it isolated Brightwell, and the Dean sometimes wished they had gone to live in Oxford. The death of Mrs Inge's mother had made her house in Banbury Road available. After describing a large tea-party at Worcester College in some detail he wrote in his diary (7 March 1941): "I must confess that I sometimes wish we had decided to live in Oxford, where there is so much delightful society." Compared to it he found the country people dull, and the war finally broke up the family circle.

A family gathering at Brightwell, now that the children were grown up, had in fact never been frequent. The Dean had not been in the house a fortnight before he remarked that it was "rather disgracefully large for three people," meaning by the third person Catharine. Craufurd was in England in 1933, but now back in India. Edward was on leave, but his work was in the Sudan. Richard was just going up to Magdalene College, Cambridge: the three young men were rarely in the same place at the same time: the war brought Craufurd and Edward together in Calcutta, when they had not seen one another for nine years. The numerous relatives in Oxford came out to Brightwell quite often, but only for brief visits. For Richard's twenty-first birthday, 6 December 1936, there was a notable gathering for dinner and round games. "We are indeed a happy family—thank God for it," the Dean wrote afterwards. Subsidiary members of the household with affectionate names were Perseus and Andromeda, the big and the small motor-cars, and Trixie and Trudie, the white Highland terriers.

Richard, contrary to family tradition, took up rowing at Cambridge and stroked the Magdalene First Eight, which caused his father to go to Henley for the first time when he was seventy-seven years old. This was Richard's last term at Cambridge where he gained a First Division, Second Class in History. He went then to Westcott House to prepare for Holy Orders, and was ordained on 18 December 1938 with a title at Horsforth near Leeds. He read the Gospel at his ordination in Ripon Cathedral: in the evening the Dean preached at Horsforth, and recalled that he himself had spent the days of his childhood in a Yorkshire parish. Looking back on his visit to Horsforth he wrote: "I liked all that I saw immensely. I am sure Richard, if he is spared, will be a very useful man in the Church: everybody loves and trusts him."

It was true, but Richard was not spared. When our fortunes in the war were very low, he thought things out and decided that he must join up as a combatant. It was a terrible blow to his father, the more so as he was convinced that we had lost the war. He urged the Bishop of Ripon to forbid it, but Richard said he would rather renounce his orders than refuse to be a combatant. Before the end of June 1940 he had formally joined the Air Force, and had his first solo flight in November. On 23 April 1941 he was killed in an accident at Cranwell as an instructor. He was practising low flying with another officer, P/O. H. R. Lanchester. The Dean printed an account of him as an Appendix to the *Diary of a Dean*. He was buried with military honours at Brightwell. "All my hopes are now in my children, and Richard is the dearest of all to Kitty, and, next to Catharine, to me." "We have decided to be ourselves buried here next to Richard's grave."

Edward's war was very different. A letter from him received on 10 October 1939 told how promptly he had resigned his post in the Sudan and was on his way home to join the army. He arrived in November and by the beginning of 1940 had obtained a commission in the Somerset Light Infantry; and after fifteen months was due to go overseas. This no doubt decided him to propose marriage to Miss Diana Paine, and they were married at Sanderstead on 12 May. In the interval between the engagement and the marriage Richard had been killed. The Dean and Mrs Inge took to Diana very much: "a charming girl, the more we see of her, the more sure we are that Edward has chosen well." In August she went to stay at Brightwell: "She is quite charming with her old father-in-law." Meanwhile Edward had gone overseas, to the Eastern Mediterranean it was thought. He proved an excellent soldier. He was wounded, but by August 1942 he was a Major and on the H.Q. staff in Iran.

Craufurd all this time was immobilised in India, and Catharine was doing war work in London and elsewhere. She was near enough to come home, but presently Brightwell ceased to be her home. In May 1943 she told her parents she was half engaged to Derek Wigram, a master at Bryanston School, and in the middle of August the engagement was made public, and they were married in Brightwell Church on 11 January 1944. Dr Temple, the Archbishop of Canterbury, performed the ceremony. In May the Dean paid them a most enjoyable visit at Bryanston and found Catharine "a self-possessed married woman, as good a hostess as her mother." He liked all he saw of the boys and masters. In 1946 Mr Wigram was made

Headmaster of Monkton Combe School, and he and Catharine still live in that delectable valley.

Thus the Dean and Mrs Inge were left alone for a time, and Mrs Inge during the summer of 1944 had had frequent and serious heart attacks. But the war had reached the beginning of its end.

20

The Last Years

Cicero on Old Age argues for the Immortality of the Soul: de Sen.
XXI. 77.

It is my belief that the immortal gods have put souls into
the bodies of men in order to create beings who would care for
earth, but at the same time take note of the orderly motion of
the heavenly bodies and imitate its controlled stability in their
own lives. It is not only reason and argument that have brought
me to this conclusion, but the impressive testimony of the great
philosophers. I used to be told at lectures that Pythagoras and
the Pythagoreans are as good as fellow countrymen of ours
(they were called the Italian philosophers); and that they never
doubted our having souls that are derived from the divine
Spirit of the Universe. Furthermore Socrates was pointed to
by the Delphic oracle as the wisest of all men, and what he said
on the last day of his life about the immortality of the soul was
brought to my notice. Need I say more? When I consider the
rapidity with which the soul thinks, the extent to which it
remembers the past and anticipates the future, the many arts,
sciences, and discoveries of which it is the originator, then I
feel convinced that what is so wide in its range cannot die. And
further, since the soul is always in motion, and its motion is
not given it from without, but it moves of itself, I am certain
there will never be any end to its motion, unless it abandons
itself, which it never will do. And again, since the soul by its
nature is simple and not complex, and admits no intrusion of
what is incompatible with itself or unlike, it cannot be separated
into parts and, if that is so, it cannot die. I take it to be a strong
argument in this connection that men know most things before
they are born, because when they are still children and are
learning difficult lessons, they grasp an immense number of
things and seem not to be getting to know them for the first

time, but to recollect and remember them. This is Plato almost
word for word.

At last the war ended. Outwardly it did not make a great
difference to life at Brightwell. Mrs Inge, in spite of ill-health,
had not made more concessions than she was obliged to the
rigorous conditions of the war years. But the long strain of
anticipating defeat which only towards the end of 1944 changed
to the almost equally dreary prospect of a disastrous victory
or stalemate, seemed to tell permanently on the Dean. In spite
of all appearances he persisted in regarding himself as ruined
and the country as in a dismal decline. A month after the
Germans surrendered he had his eighty-fifth birthday. His
reflections on it were not festive: "As far as I know I may live
to be ninety: but I have no wish to cumber the ground any
longer. These two wars will do nothing but harm: they will
extinguish the educated and cultivated classes all over Europe."
Perhaps he was being half envious when a few days after on a visit
to Eton he remarked on the "marvellous portraits of Eton
boys by Reynolds, Romney, etc.—such proud, confident faces,"
and a little later at a meeting of the Trustees of the National
Portrait Gallery he saw "the Kitcat portraits, recently acquired,
very fine heads of eighteenth-century noblemen, for whom life
had no problems." Was he thinking their times better than his
own? The Socialist victory in the General Election at the end
of July elicited some moans and (what is very rare) an absence
of syntax: "The prospect is most alarming. For Churchill himself I think it is good luck. He retires in a blaze of glory and
there are no more laurels to be won. Humble pie to Russia,
and the repudiation of pledges which never ought to have been
given; and a financial crash in the near future."

But as ever he solaced himself with writing. He had been
engaged in the last fifteen months of the war with a book on
the Religion of a Platonist. He did not think it would come to
anything, but it kept him busy, and by August 1944 he had
finished the first draft of it. "But it cannot be published till the
war is over," he wrote, "and I do not think it is worth publishing at all"; so it seems to have been laid aside, though we
shall hear of it again presently.

But in April 1945 he suggested Origen for the next British Academy Lecture on a Master-Mind; there and then he was asked to give the lecture himself. He had already given his lecture on Plotinus in 1929 under the same auspices: nobody had ever been invited to give a second one before. 'Origen' was delivered on 20 March 1946; characteristically he had finished it by the middle of the previous August; few authors have been so consistently up to time or in front of it. For delivery he had to shorten what he had written. His comment was: "Not bad, but I fear rather senile and second rate. It can't be helped at my age." The lecture is in fact full of interest, and not least as a sort of briefer Confession of Faith. The Plotinus lecture had been something of the same sort, but less discursive. Here we have admiration for Clement of Alexandria, almost as much as for Origen, and not a little of Buddha, rebirth, time, entropy. To Origen is attributed "an eclectic Platonism," that some would attribute to the lecturer himself. Of the contents of Dr Inge's mind in his later years this lecture may be taken as an epitome.

The Dean was close on eighty-six years of age when he gave it. He might have been expected to relax, but strikingly enough a period of great literary activity followed. In May 1946 Professor E. O. James, then of King's College, London, invited him to write a book of sixty thousand words on Christian Mysticism. He accepted the offer: "I think I can do it, and it will take my mind off public affairs, which are desperate." In a month's time he was able to say: "I am getting on swimmingly with my new book, writing the first draft at 1,000–1,500 words a day. I find that many pages of my book on the Religion of a Platonist, which I decided not to publish can be incorporated." He sent the book to be typed in August, and in November it was in the hands of the publisher, who asked for a few changes and additions on the ground that it was "too advanced" for the readers he had in mind. It was submitted again before the end of January 1947 and was published in the following November as *Mysticism in Religion* (Hutchinson, n.d.).

While he was finishing off and adjusting this book, he was also engaged upon another which Putnam had asked for. In his diary the Dean calls it his Penguin, but this seems to be only

(*Photo: Allan Chappelow, M.A., F.R.S.A.*)

Ninety years old

a nickname: perhaps he thought it worthy of no more than a paper cover. He already had the proofs of it in September 1947, and it came out in February 1948, under the title *The End of an Age*. It was a large octavo in blue cloth, singularly unlike a Penguin.

That these two books should appear within a space of four months is remarkable. *Mysticism in Religion* as published came to about eighty thousand words, and covers the whole large field indicated by the title. Two chapters at least (VI on 'Symbolism and Myth,' and VII on 'Greek Mysticism') may be assumed to come from the Religion of a Platonist, and there is a good deal of repetition from former writings. The Plotinus lecture of 1929 and a paper on the 'Philosophy of Mysticism' published in a periodical in 1938 are reprinted, but these insertions fall naturally into their place. What is newest is an increased attention to Russian mysticism and Eastern religions. The whole effect is of an overall treatment of what had been the author's lifelong study and meditation. To a reader who has read his previous works it comes as a kind of legacy of all he had stored up: to a new reader who wished to be introduced to the best of Dr Inge's mind and teaching it might be the right book to recommend. The Preface describes its scope: it is concerned with four principal problems: how far can the inner light supplement or even supersede external authorities? what is the real self? the meaning and status of the world of space and time; the meaning and value of symbols. "I cannot see how these difficult problems can be dispensed with," the Dean wrote, "if, as I say, we take the mystical experience quite seriously as a revelation of ultimate truth." And in this book the author does take it quite seriously.

The other book, *The End of an Age*, is similar in form to *The Fall of the Idols*, an introductory essay and six papers of forty pages, more or less, on man in society. Most of the book was new, but an article on 'Escapism,'[1] reprinted from the periodical *Philosophy*, October 1940, is perhaps the best part of it. The writing as a whole is as clear as ever, and interesting in quite the ordinary sense. The outlook is pessimistic, but the Dean seems to have felt this himself, for he wrote in the brief Preface: "The next fifty years are likely to be a very difficult and dangerous time; but the body politic generates anti-toxins as well as toxins, and the volume of Toynbee's *Study of History* on 'Challenge and Response' is a good tonic against pessimism."

The last chapter of this book, 'The Population Problem,' begins with the words "Vital statistics and eugenics have long been a favourite hobby of mine," and eugenics had certainly been his first interest outside the classics, and it was one of the last to be displayed in print (and in his diary too).

He only published one more volume, and that was a compilation, *Diary of a Dean, St Paul's, 1911–1934.* It proves the quality of the diaries as literature, and the picture it gives of society and public life shows the reader of 1960 how far things have moved from what they were half a century ago and less. What it does not show very fully is the Dean's character and feelings, except in the tributes which he paid to his wife and to his son Richard after he had lost them. These give a strangely different impression from the rest of the diary as published. In a number of places the Dean inserted extracts from Mrs Inge's diaries, or new reflections on what he had written in his own.

While he was compiling this book it appears that he was also engaged upon another. At the end of 1948 he says: "I am getting on with my two books, and hope to have them both off my hands next month." Two months later he says, "My two books are now off my hands: Margaret Cloudsley has typed the Diary for me. I have not heard from Putnam about the other book." A postscript runs: "(He wrote declining it.)"

During all this period of busy authorship he was still contributing to the *Evening Standard.* In September 1946 an article on the Nuremberg trials "made a little commotion," and in November he has to write, "In fact I think I have been sacked." But he was wrong: he continued to be asked for articles by the editor, and in his ninety-second year he was still at it. A request for four articles in November 1951 produced two on politics, one on the new B.B.C. hymn-book, and one on 'Sunday Sports.' He never wanted for a subject for a short article, though he often feared he was drying up. When he was asked by the Society of Individualists for twelve articles of about nine hundred words each for them to send to the newspapers, he did not pledge himself to twelve articles, but he jotted down some subjects which occurred to him: "Incentives, Revolutions, Future of Domestic Service, Community Life in Derelict Country Houses, Religion in the Churches, the Revival of Superstition, Climates of Opinion, the Future of Democracy and Socialism, Eugenics, Great and Small Powers, Asia and Europe, Liberalism, Pacifism, Romanticism, Happier Times, Collectivist Christianity." No risk of drying up just now.

He often contributed to a work by various hands. One of these contributions deserves to be recorded. For a book called *What Life Has Taught Me*, edited by Sir James Marchant in 1948 (Odhams, n.d.), he wrote five pages of lively reminiscences and opinions. "One thing I have certainly learnt—not to have a good opinion of myself."

Once when the Dean and Mrs Inge were reading her diaries, he remarked that "they show Kitty's love of London, which I never shared." It was not, however, entirely for her sake that he continued to visit London. He still took a great interest in the meetings of the Trustees of the National Portrait Gallery, and in the elections at the British Academy. He still visited the London Library, went to Nobody's Friends, still gave lectures or attended them, dined out with pleasure. In November 1947 they stayed in Lord Beaverbrook's flat in Arlington House for four nights and had a full programme of engagements. The next year their activities were restricted through the Dean having a prostate operation, very serious at his age. He was in hospital most of May, all June, and the first days of July. Only in September did he recover his strength and was able to walk without sticks. They made just one short visit to London at the end of October. But in the following spring, April 1949, they went once more to Lord Beaverbrook's flat. Mrs Inge had been a fortnight resting in the Acland Home at Oxford, and now fully rested she wanted to have a week in her dear London. The Dean secretly hoped that the doctors would forbid her to go, but they did not. They arrived on 20 April; he went to some of his usual engagements, and Mrs Inge abated none of the social round in which she so much delighted. The

following postcard from her to Catharine gives a picture of
the visit:

c/o Lord Beaverbrook, Arlington House, W.1.

Friday, Apr. 22, 1949

I am ashamed not to have thanked you both for yr. generous
invitation, but Derek's message in red ink wh. looked *so* important
arrived just as we were starting off! We shall love to come on
Sat. 7th–11th—when alas! I must return as I am entertaining the
V.I. that afternoon. We will be packed and ready by 4 o'cl. so
that whenever it pleases Derek to come he will not be kept waiting.
We are having a wonderful Little 'Season.' Father is happy and
well, & attending meetings in between. We were royally entertained by John and Paul Paget at the Ladies Annexe to the
Athenaeum, and met Sylvia Lyall, Lady Margaret Watney's d.
Dean of West: & Mrs Don, & such a good lunch, & then to
Tommy Cotton, & both to tea at the Ritz, & a quiet evening—&
to-day lunch with the Leo Amerys—& we give a tea-party here
on Sat. Mr Oliver Locker Lampson, Rosalys and Rose Macaulay,
so it will be quite a brilliant little party! Lunch with Rosalys on
Sunday & then to tea at Lambeth. Irene is having a distinguished
lunch party of 12 to meet us on Tuesday & Mr Kimber invites
to lunch on Monday when we discuss *the book*!² Loving M.C.I.

About one o'clock in the morning on the following day Mrs
Inge died. Lord Beaverbrook's servants did not dare to tell the
Dean. Craufurd was summoned from Brightwell and broke the
news to his father, who has described it all with the simplicity
with which he faced every personal misfortune:

April 23. At 8.30 Craufurd suddenly appeared and said: 'I am
the bearer of very bad news. Mother died in the night.' It was
absolutely unexpected. She saw Dr Cotton two days ago, and he
gave a very encouraging report, and she was looking better after
her rest cure, than she has done for a long time. It seems that she
had a heart-attack in the small hours, and telephoned to the
Middlesex Hospital, who sent a nurse and then a Dr Davies, who
found her unconscious. I am sure, if she had known she was
dying, she would have wished to say goodbye to me. Craufurd
was most kind in making all needful arrangements, and we drove
home at 1.45. Catharine was already there. I knew my darling's
life was threatened, but the doctors gave me reason to hope that

my call might come first. I have now nothing to live for, and I am afraid I am *not* so near my end as I could wish. No one ever had a better, sweeter, more loving wife than God has given to me.

From what I hear now, I think she passed suddenly into a state of coma. She probably had no warning at all.

The funeral was at Brightwell on the following Wednesday, 27 April, and there was a Memorial Service in St Paul's on 3 May. "Then Derek, Catharine and I went to Monkton Combe. My dear children make life tolerable for me. . . . On Sunday I preached to the boys and gave them an Easter sermon about death. I managed to get through with it. . . . I have answered about 100 letters. . . . On Friday Catharine drove me and Richard [her son] to Brightwell."

Life was resumed. It was a lonely and rather silent life. Craufurd managed the running of the house and garden admirably, but he had to go to London to his work in the Anglo Persian Oil Company five days a week, and came back late and tired. The Dean highly appreciated him and calls him "a model son," but he knew they had not much in common. "He never reads my books, preferring very light literature, and I know nothing of oil, music, and gardening." In many ways he continued his old way of life in pretty good health, and with his mind unimpaired. He had still nearly five years to live, but the diary grows briefer and was suspended in August 1949 until February 1951, and at the end of 1951 it ceases altogether.

Some events stand out: in the family the birth of Edward's twins, and very pleasant visits to Catharine and Derek at Monkton Combe: celebrations each year on 6 June; the Dean says in fact that "the chief event of 1950 was the great garden party for my 90th birthday, which my children arranged for me. Kitty would have been delighted with the cordial telegrams from King George and Queen Mary."

Outside engagements grew fewer; but he continued until 1952 a custom that had grown up lately of preaching annually at Pusey House in Oxford: it surprised him to find himself there: he drew a great congregation. One of his latest appearances of importance in public was to preach the Gore Memorial Lecture in Westminster Abbey on 15 November 1951. He chose for his subject 'The Mind of St Paul.' The circumstances were rather curious. Dr Don, the Dean of Westminster, had invited his former colleague, Canon Lewis Donaldson, to give the lecture. As Donaldson had been one of the earliest and most active members of the Christian Social Union in which Bishop Gore was so much involved, this was appropriate enough. But Donaldson was now ninety years of age and presently asked to be excused. Dr Don then asked Inge to give the lecture, who was just three months older than Donaldson. He undertook the task and achieved it, and the lecture was published by the S.P.C.K., "very nicely got up," the Dean said. It was the last event in his life which he recorded in the diary which he had kept since 1888, and on the opposite page characteristically enough he had pasted a newspaper cutting giving statistics of the Births, Deaths, and Marriages in England and Wales for the last quarter of 1950. He was still interested in the population question which had first attracted his attention some seventy years before.

He was writing for the press to the very end. By the beginning of 1951 he had come to the conclusion that it was useless to think of writing another book, but he did a number of short articles and reviews. In July 1951 Professor R. H. Lightfoot asked him to review an Italian work in four volumes on Plotinus. He did it: "I have found an Italian dictionary, and can make it out quite easily." In the *Hibbert Journal* of October 1952 he reviewed two more books on Plotinus, one by Professor A. H. Armstrong, and the other by Professor Pistorius of Pretoria. The *Modern Churchman* for March 1954 contained an article by him of nearly three thousand words entitled 'Liberalism is not Dead.' The next number of the same periodical had also a short article which had reached the editor only four days before his death. It is entitled 'The Leaping Spark,' and is a final testimony to the reality of the mystical experience. The first name it mentions is Plato, the last is Paul.

Mr Warner Allen, his neighbour at Brightwell for the last ten years of his life, has given a delightful little picture of the Dean at work: 'The visitor might find him in his study, even after his ninetieth birthday, with a school exercise book and a pencil, writing an article or revising a book already published or perhaps boldly embarking on a new volume, and chuckling over what he was going to say to stir to the discomfort of thinking those whose brains were bemused by automatically repeating the catch phrases of the day' (*The Times*, 17 March 1954).

Naturally he passed a great deal of time reading, and his comments on some of the books he read show the old critical, questing spirit at work. They give an insight into the problems his mind was running on, and mingled with his remarks upon his habits and infirmities afford a good notion of his latest years.

February 12 [1951]. I have just resigned my Trusteeship of the N.P.G. After all I was appointed as Dean of St Paul's, not as a retired parson, and I am getting very feeble, especially on staircases and in getting out of chairs. I had a very kind letter from Lord Ilchester, the chairman. Worst of all, my eyes are no longer good, and at 10 p.m. I have read enough for the day. . . .

I shall be well content when my call comes, but I believe I may live for some time, since Lord Moran, the King's physician, whom my new friend Mr Stirling Gilchrist brought to see me in the summer, found that my arteries are still those of a middle-aged man. I am living at low pressure and reading mainly old books. . . .

February 18. I have been reading Henson's Autobiography again. It is very human and lovable, but a touch of pride and reticence would not have hurt him. 'Yesterday I was Bp of Durham, to-day I am nobody at all.' A wise man smiles and keeps these thoughts to himself. Then he must needs plunge combatively into every controversy; only once he has the sense to hold his tongue, at the abdication of Edward VIII. I am told that his letters contain severe criticisms of his friends, including myself. One thing is clear—he ceased to be a *thinker*, and so became a yes-man among the bishops. What wretched guidance the bishops have given— Essays and Reviews, Colenso, and now the O.T. and miracles!

February 22. The wettest February on record—nearly 5 inches. I have been reading Trevelyan's essays, which are extraordinarily good. The one on the 'Middle Marches' of Northumberland is brilliant. He says that the difficulty of communications has done more for liberty than Magna Carta. That is interesting, but it cuts both ways. The robber baron was not a pleasant neighbour. He criticises Toynbee's 'challenge and response.' Many challenges have evoked no response, or one quite unexpected. Chance decides most things—e.g. the accident of a great man, e.g. St Paul. But I think Toynbee's main point is 'no challenge, no response.' He is still a progressist, and regards a stable equilibrium as failure. Recurrence for him is pessimism. And yet there is great truth in his main point.

February 25. Keyserling on 'Immortality.' The self is much more than the conscious individual. In proportion as we overcome isolation we are sure of our immortality. Modern philosophy has made too much of consciousness, which is only a device of nature to meet changing environment. There are so many degrees of individuality that the concept is quite vague—e.g. the insects in a hive, and the living germs in our bodies. All this is very good but he speaks of women like Aristotle, and he does not emphasise that without duality there can be no love and no devotion. In prayer the I and Thou relation is never transcended, and in human love subject and object are never fused. A very good point is that men will give their lives freely for friends, religion, country. This proves that monadic personality is not ultimate. May not this be the answer to the new 'Existentialism'?

March 18. George Tyrrell once said that some day nothing might be left of Christianity except the Pauline Christ-mysticism and the law of love—I have been moving in this direction, willing to blot from the page 'unborn to-morrow and dead yesterday.'[3] What happened 2,000 years ago cannot matter to us now, and there has been no revelation of the future. I firmly believe that οὐδὲν ἀπολεῖται τῶν ὄντων; 'Quod Deo non perit sibi non perit' (Augustine); 'non est potentia ad non esse' (Aquinas); but the rest is blank while we live here.

Stebbing on Jeans and Eddington is severe and irritable; she does not do justice to Eddington's Quakerism, and the philosophy of ultimate values.

Eton is asking for a million pounds for various improvements, including a swimming pool! The Thames was good enough for us. I should not subscribe even if I had any money. . . .

May 6. I have been exercised to hear of the new fashions in philosophy at Oxford and Cambridge, which I cannot understand. Cambridge actually elected the Austrian refugee Wittgenstein to the professorship of philosophy, and Oxford has elected Gilbert

Brightwell, 6 June 1950

Ryle, another 'logical positivist.' As far as I can make out this school has no use for philosophy or religion—Plato, Aristotle, Aquinas, Kant, Hegel all 'talked nonsense'; I read Urban's book on Logic and Language. He is of course hostile to logical positivism, but hardly makes it intelligible. He fully accepts evolution, and makes the interesting point that man is an 'amphibium' because he is distracted between two evolutionary trends— aggressive isolationism and sociability. He does not bring out sufficiently that the great danger is in the compromise between the two—the unit neither the unicellular particle nor humanity, but the false group-idolatry of creed, class, nation. This is better emphasised in Aldous Huxley's Perennial Philosophy, a very remarkable book, in which the author accepts the philosophy of mysticism in an Indian form rather than a Christian. I once told Julian Huxley that the Roman priests would end by capturing his brother. They may do so, but he is nearer to Buddhism in its Mahāyāna[4] form than to Catholicism.

Old men are apt to nod over their books, but here is an old man wide awake enough, as he reads on, and with these extracts from the diary, the longest series in this book of many extracts, the story may well end. Not actually happy, but content, he lived on when the friends and relations of his own generation had gone before. His hopes were in his children and his grandchildren, and in those particular assurances of the indestructible and eternal which he had made more and more secure in his own mind. In the middle of February 1954 he had an attack of bronchitis which he could not shake off, and he died at Brightwell on the 26th of the month.

Dean Matthews, his successor at St Paul's, in the address which he gave at the Memorial Service on 16 March in the Cathedral began and ended with the following words:

The body of William Ralph Inge, formerly Dean of St Paul's, lies in the churchyard of the country parish, to which he retired in 1934, with those of his beloved wife and son. We can understand that he wished this to be, though we may feel some regret that his tomb is not in this Cathedral with those of John Donne and Milman.

William Ralph Inge was a great man, a unique man. We shall not look upon his like again. It is sad to know that we shall not hear his voice again commenting, in his individual and forceful fashion, on the topics of the day. It is sadder that we shall have no more penetrating discourses on the great themes of Freedom, Love, and Truth, the three values and ideals which he always venerated and tried to serve. He is added to the roll of deans who have shed lustre on the office and to the roll of those who have added to the treasures of learning and wisdom in our English tongue. May he rest in peace and may the Eternal Light, for which he so earnestly sought, rest upon him—and in that light may he see light.

Epilogue

We will come back to where we started—Lord Oxford and Asquith's opinion: 'He is a strange, isolated figure, with all the culture in the world, and a curiously developed gift of expression, but with kinks and twists both intellectual and temperamental.'

Strange he certainly was: so full of brains, so full of passion; so social and so shy; so confident in opinion, so depressed by adverse criticism; so bold and so unhopeful; so affectionate and so detached.

Isolated he was in several senses; cut off very considerably from the circles to which he belonged by his deafness and by being too easily bored, by being over-critical of many who in the main thought as he did; isolated from the Church of England and all organised religion by his indifference to ritual and his eclectic orthodoxy: his undoubted ability to give a lead neutralised by his preference for single combat; isolated by being like nobody else at all.

'*All the culture in the world*'—but not quite all if mathematics is a part of culture, for he had it not, nor if a fastidious taste is a part of it, for his feeling for art was conventional. But if culture comes from a study of what has been thought and taught in the past with one's own thoughts added in abundance, then surely all the culture that a single mind could accumulate in the course of a long life was there. The classics, the mystics, the ancient Fathers, the scholastic philosophy, the Anglican divines, the outlook, if not the method, of modern science, the political thought of many thinkers from Plato to the consumptionists all furnished a mind, which went on to furnish itself with acutest criticism and reasoned conviction about government, morality, and religion, those three great pillars of civilisation and culture.

'*And a curiously developed gift of expression.*' What Lord Oxford called 'a gift of expression' would now often be called 'a gift of communication,' and this gift was developed in the Dean in the sense that he conveyed to others what he thought and meant with much less loss than the use of words normally entails. It was easy to make sense of what you read of him and to be confident that it was the sense he intended. For a man of learning he may be reckoned to have had a relatively small vocabulary, with just a scattering of rarer words, mostly adjectives such as "anabolic," a borrowing from biology, "dysgenic," which he was the first to use, or "existential," which he used a good while before it became fashionable. Speech was a less effective gift, unless the conditions and his mood were favourable. On serious matters he usually read from a script, and was not always well heard; but if he was heard, his sermons were impressive from the great simplicity and earnestness of the preacher, and if he was feeling gay, he could be very amusing. Perhaps, when Lord Oxford said his gift of expression was *'curiously'* developed, he had in mind its range, or perhaps he meant that he never failed to say something striking, and rarely failed to say something provocative, quite often without provoking. At times he was taciturn; it has been suggested that this was when he feared that others would be talkative; he liked to display his wit (which was inexhaustible) when he was likely to be listened to.

'With kinks and twists both intellectual and temperamental'—little things but conspicuous, not to be described in sum, but by instances almost at random. On the intellectual side we meet with his depreciation of Bishop Butler, the author of *The Analogy of Religion*, his dislike (even horror) of William Temple's politics, his admiration of Sir William Watson as a poet, his confidence in eugenics. As to temperament his irritability was sometimes unconcealed, his odd economies fairly persistent; his invincible prejudices against Roman Catholicism, church music, and taxation were undiminished almost to the end; everywhere was unexpected adherence to opinions based on pure intuition, and this heightened by their being incorporated into genuine philosophical striving after truth.

On the other hand there are traits of a different kind: his great interest in cricket, his great love of Eton, where he had

lived for nine not particularly happy years, his success with
little children, his great surprise at finding that people were
fond of him.

If there is any distinction between 'kinks and twists,' the
twists will be the strains he put upon himself by self-contra-
diction, as by his claim for simplicity with his rejection of
asceticism, or his dutiful attendance at service in St Paul's with
his protests against the waste of time involved in it, or in an
ampler field his want of orthodoxy alongside of his admiration
of St Thomas Aquinas, or his own approximations to the Continental Modernism which he attacked so vigorously. The kinks
will be the admixture of epigrammatic half-truths into serious
disquisitions upon serious subjects. Often his epigrams were
devastatingly true.

But it is all of this that makes him so 'really interesting.' That
is Lord Oxford's conclusion, *'Still, he is one of the few ecclesiastics
in these days who is really interesting,'* only this seems to suggest
that he is interesting in spite of his kinks and twists. But surely
without them he would have been much less interesting, much
less famous, and much less lovable. His writings by themselves
would have given him a distinguished name, and would have
made a varied and valuable mark in English letters, but, as
C. C. J. Webb wisely observed of his theology, and it is true
of much else, 'His contribution has been himself' (*Journal of
Theological Studies*, October 1954).

His influence is not easy to estimate. On what is called the
business of the Church he had no influence except in his support
of English Modernism and the freedom it won for deviations
of belief without penalty. In theology he had a great place as
the expositor of mysticism. He wrote on its history and claimed
a place for the mystical experience as the basis of religion and
ultimately of reality. To a wide circle he introduced the chief
mystical writers, who, previously unknown, have become for
many the staple of their devotional life. Going on from this he
has played no small part in the present widely diffused interest
in religion and the healthy taste for the free discussion of it. In
philosophy he made a substantial contribution to the study of
Neoplatonism, and he wrote trenchantly against pragmatism
and the elevation of the Will above the Intellect, though he felt

obliged to draw attention quite often to misplaced intellectualism in religion. In psychology he emphasised the study of the individual as a unit and not as a collection of faculties. But attention has now drifted away from these controversies, and his philosophical writings may be read in future for the history they embody rather than for any conclusions they arrive at.

It is as a religious writer and a great craftsman in prose that the Dean will be known. He deserves a permanent place in religion and in literature. And his writings are such that those who read them are bound to grow inquisitive as to his life and character, and they will not be disappointed when they discover this great lover of truth, ever grappling with it and with himself, so tormented, so irritable, so gifted, so intelligent, so dutiful, so affectionate, so unexpected, so successful, and all the time some kind of a saint.

THE MEMORIAL PLAQUE AT CRAYKE

A Plaque on The Cottage at Crayke marks it as the birthplace of Dean Inge. The inscription runs as follows:

Here on June 6, 1860, was born William Ralph Inge, D.D., K.C.V.O. Dean of St. Paul's 1911–1934; scholar, philosopher, writer, who died at Brightwell Manor, Berkshire on February 26th, 1954.

The Plaque was unveiled by Mr Craufurd Inge. Dr Garbett, the Archbishop of York, gave the following address:

'It is very fitting that this house should bear a plaque commemorating the fact that it was the birthplace of one of the most famous Englishmen of his time. Dr Inge had many happy memories of this village. Some years ago I had a letter from him in which he spoke of the beauty of its view over the Vale of York with the Minster rising from it like a ship crossing the ocean. On another occasion he wrote of the happiness of a childhood spent in a country vicarage.

'He was one of the best known Englishmen of his time. His books were not only widely read in this country, but they had a wide circulation on the other side of the Atlantic. They were among the few books written by an Englishman which appeared on the bookstalls of the railways on the Continent. He was famous not only for his writings, but also for his epigrammatic and often caustic comments on persons and events which were widely quoted.

'He became known through a combination of courage and genius which expressed itself in perfect English prose. He brought to bear on contemporary events a brilliant and critical intellect and did not hesitate to express the conclusions he had reached, however unpopular they might be.

'The very resentment evoked by some of his more sweeping utterances made men question views which they had too easily accepted. At a time when progress was the watchword and generally regarded as inevitable he challenged this assumption.

'His claim to a place among the English thinkers will not, however, rest upon his outspoken essays or on newspaper articles, but on the solid contribution he made to theology by his writings on Christian mysticism. His Bampton Lectures on this subject had a great influence on theological thought; they opened to many a forgotten way of approach to God. By these lectures, by his book on Plotinus and other writings on mysticism, he revived in this country a rational mysticism and strengthened the faith and devotion of many.

'But those who had only known Dr Inge through his outspoken essays or the theological writings would gain a very inadequate conception of his character. He reveals himself most of all in some of his devotional books.

'They are a perpetual source of spiritual refreshment and help their readers to ascend the mount of vision. They have given help and inspiration to large numbers of ordinary men and women who have never read the other books.

'They show that beneath a reserve which was sometimes frightening, there was sympathy and tenderness. I know nothing of its kind more moving than his tribute both in Latin and in English to his little girl who died at the age of eleven.

'This tablet commemorates one who died at a great age, honoured by his fellow countrymen as a scholar, philosopher, writer and Christian.'

This report of the speech is from *The Easingwold Advertiser and Weekly News* of 13 November 1954 with the permission of the Proprietors.

The Revd. W. F. Cotton, the rector, very kindly showed me the Plaque and much else of interest at Crayke.

ETON v. WINCHESTER

From W. R. I. at Eton to his parents, 29 June 1879

We have been very lucky in the weather for our match. It was quite
fine (except for one little shower) for two whole days, a thing which
has not happened before this half, and the match was a great success.
I think the Winchester match is the jolliest thing in the whole Eton
year. It is always played either here or at Winchester, and so we are
always their guests or they ours, which makes the match much
more of a "friendly game" than the match at Lord's. You will see
by the papers that the match was very fairly even, and it would
probably have been more so had the Winchester eleven been more
used to the ground. Upper Club has been such a swamp most of
the half that it is much slower even than usual, and the chalk at
Winchester always plays very fast even in rainy weather. Both the
first innings were very small, but on the second day the ground
was much drier, and consequently more runs were got. The
Winchester fielding was as usual a treat to witness, ours as usual
atrocious. The College representative unfortunately did not distinguish himself, as he only made 4 and 5, and missed two catches.
There was a tremendous crowd of people on the field, and Walter[1]
and I did not find each other out till the match was over. However
we had nearly all the afternoon together, and I shewed him over
my room etc., and then we went to the Castle, and St George's,
which he had never seen before. At 6.15 p.m. we went to the dinner
in hall, at which all the Winchester fellows were invited, and our
eleven, eight, and Sixth Form. After the dinner the Provost[2] rose
to say grace, and as everybody thought he was going to make a
speech, they clapped and stamped and cheered for about 5 minutes
before the poor little man could make them understand. Afterwards
he did make a speech, and then the Warden of Winchester[3] and the
Captains of the two elevens[4] spoke, and the Winchester fellows went
back to the station, very uproarious as usual. About 4 years ago
they bagged the station bell at Basingstoke on their way back, and
rang it at intervals all the way to Winchester till the officials were
perfectly furious. I believe they threw it out of window near
Winchester, and it was found soon afterwards lying in a field. I

am afraid we were just as bad last year, when the match was at Winchester.

1 Walter W. How, his cousin.
2 The Provost of Eton, C. O. Goodford.
3 The Warden of Winchester, G. B. Lee.
4 The Captains of the two elevens:
   Eton, C. T. Studd;
   Winchester, C. T. Weatherby, who was a master at Eton (with W. R. I.) 1884–86, and died 15 June 1886.

THE WORKS OF W. R. INGE

The following lists do not include the hundreds of articles and reviews which Dr Inge contributed to the press, unless they were re-issued in book or pamphlet form. Nor have I attempted to trace papers which have only been printed in the Proceedings of learned Societies. Even within these limitations the lists make no claim to be a bibliography in any proper sense. There are probably considerable omissions of which I am not aware. But I have tried to indicate the extent of the Dean's output, and where necessary the size of his contribution to any particular volume. Otherwise I have only given enough information to enable the reader to identify a work in a Library Catalogue or order it from a bookseller. Of a good many of the items only second-hand copies are available.

A. SCHOLASTIC WORKS

1880. Senarii Graeci Praemio Porsoniano dignati Shakespeare *Timon of Athens*, Act III, Sc. V, Idem Graece Redditum.

1882. Carmen Graecum Numismate Annuo dignatum "Nunc seges est ubi Troja fuit"/Epigramma Graecum Numismate Annuo dignatum/ Poema Latinum Numismate Annuo dignatum Diocletianus imperio se abdicat.

1888. *Society in Rome under the Caesars.* Hare Prize at the University of Cambridge. 276 pp.
Selections from Cornelius Nepos, ed. O. Browning. 3rd edn. revised by W. R. I.
Eton College Latin Grammar for use in the higher forms. F. H. Rawlins and W. R. I.

1889. *Selections from Lucian.* W. R. I. and H. V. Macnaghten.

1890. *Selections from Valerius Maximus.*

1891. *Scriptores Romani*, ed. W. R. I. and others.

1899. *Nova Anthologia Oxoniensis.* Items no. 41, 64, 73, 138. Greek Elegiacs by W. R. I.

B. MAIN WORKS PUBLISHED IN VOLUME FORM

1899. *Christian Mysticism.* (8) Bampton Lectures.

1904. *Faith and Knowledge.* (20) Sermons.

1905. *Studies of English Mystics.* (6) St Margaret's Lectures.

1906. *Truth and Falsehood in Religion.* (6) Lectures to Undergraduates.
Personal Idealism and Mysticism. (6) Paddock Lectures.

1907. *All Saints' Sermons.* (22) Sermons.

1909. *Faith and its Psychology.* (10) Jowett Lectures, expanded.

1911 *Speculum Animae.* (4) Addresses at Corpus Christi College, Cambridge.

1912. *The Church and the Age.* (4) Addresses at Sion College.

1915. *Types of Christian Saintliness.* (3) Addresses at Sion College.

1918. *The Philosophy of Plotinus*, 2 vols. (22) Gifford Lectures. 511 pp.

1919. *Outspoken Essays*, First Series. 281 pp.

1922. *Outspoken Essays*, Second Series. 275 pp.

1924. *Personal Religion and the Life of Devotion* (Paula's Book). 96 pp.

1926. *The Platonic Tradition in English Religion.* (4) Hulsean Lectures.
Lay Thoughts of a Dean. (45) Short Articles collected.
England. Vol. VII in a series entitled 'The Modern World.' 290 pp.

1927. *The Church in the World.* (8) Collected Essays.
Protestantism, in Benn's Essex Library. 160 pp.

1929. *Assessments and Anticipations.* (31) Short Articles collected.

1930. *Christian Ethics and Modern Problems.* 394 pp.

1931. *More Lay Thoughts of a Dean.* (37) Short Articles collected.

1933. *Things New and Old.* (8) Addresses to Undergraduates.
God and the Astronomers. (6) Warburton Lectures, expanded.

1934. *Vale*, an autobiographical farewell to St Paul's. 127 pp.

1935. *The Gate of Life.* (12) Sermons.

1937. *A Rustic Moralist.* (58) Short Articles collected.

1938. *Our Present Discontents*. (50) Short Articles collected.

1939. *A Pacifist in Trouble*. (51) Short Articles collected.

1940. *The Fall of the Idols*. (6) Essays.

1942. *Talks in a Free Country*. (9) Dialogues.

1947. *Mysticism in Religion:* the subject of 1899 worked over and extended. 165 pp.

1948. *The End of an Age*. (7) Essays.

1949. *Diary of a Dean, St Paul's, 1911–1934*. 224 pp.

C. PAMPHLETS AND SINGLE LECTURES AND SERMONS

1907. *Death the Fulfilment of Life*. University Sermon: Cambridge. 11 pp.

1912. *Authority and the Inner Light*. The Liverpool Lecture. 32 pp.

1914. *Plotinus*. Essex Hall Lecture. 49 pp.

1920. *The Idea of Progress*. Romanes Lecture: Oxford. 34 pp.

1922. *The Victorian Age*. Rede Lecture: Cambridge. 54 pp.
'*The Jews*' (An Answer to Hilaire Belloc's 'The Jews'). Reprint from *The Jewish Guardian*. 7 pp.

1924. *English in Education*. Birkbeck College, 1924. 18 pp.
Liberalism in Religion. Papers in Modern Churchmanship. 15 pp.

1926. *Christian Mysticism*. Anglican Evangelical Group Movement Pamphlet, 15 pp.
Science and Ultimate Truth. Fison Memorial Lecture. 32 pp.

1929. *Plotinus*. British Academy Lecture. 27 pp.

1930. *The Social Teaching of the Church*. The Beckly Lecture. 93 pp.

1932. *The New Twilight of the Gods*. Aberystwyth. 31 pp.

1933. *The Eternal Values*. Riddell Lecture. 39 pp.

1934. *Greeks and Barbarians*. Presidential Address to the Classical Association. 16 pp.

1935. *Platonism as a Rule of Life*. An Oration before the Union Society of University College, London. 22 pp.

1936. *Liberty and National Rights.* Herbert Spencer Lecture. 38 pp.

1937. *Modernism in Literature.* English Association's Presidential Address. 14 pp.

1938. *Dean Inge indicts the Red Government of Spain.* Speech, 1938 ('Famous Churchman hits out'). 3 pp.
The Price of Progress. Rickman Godlee Lecture. 31 pp.

1941. *Possible Recovery?* Society of Individualists Post-War Questions No. 5. 30 pp.

1946. *Origen.* British Academy Lecture. 23 pp.
Ultimate Values. See 1941: No. 28. 16 pp.

1948. *The Twilight of Freedom. See* 1941: No. 30. 12 pp.

1951. *The Mind of St Paul.* Charles Gore Memorial Lecture, Westminster Abbey. 20 pp.

D. WORKS TO WHICH DR INGE CONTRIBUTED

1902. *Contentio Veritatis.* By Six Oxford Tutors. W. R. I.: II, The Person of Christ, 59–104 pp.; VII, The Sacraments, pp. 270–311.

1905. *The New Testament in the Apostolic Fathers.* Oxford Society of Historical Theology. W. R. I.: Ignatius, pp. 63–83.

1908–1921. Hastings's *Encyclopedia of Religion and Ethics.* W. R. I.: 1908, Alexandrine Theology; 1911, Ecstasy; 1913, Logos; 1917, Neo-Platonism; 1921, Synderesis.

1909. *Cambridge Biblical Essays,* ed. H. B. Swete. W. R. I.: IX, The Theology of the Fourth Gospel, pp. 251–88.

1911. *Facing the Facts,* ed. W. K. Lowther Clarke. W. R. I.: The Universities, pp. 171–202.

1914. *Lay Views of Six Clergymen,* ed. H. B. Colchester. W. R. I.: I, Causes of the Decline in Church-going, pp. 3–31.

1915. *The Faith and the War,* ed. F. J. Foakes Jackson. W. R. I.: V, Hope Temporal and Eternal, pp. 101–21.

1920. *Ruskin the Prophet,* ed. J. H. Whitehouse. W. R. I.: Ruskin and Plato, pp. 25–43.

1923. *The Claims of the Coming Generation*, ed. Sir James Marchant. W. R. I.: The Right to be Well Born, pp. 1–14.

1926. *The Study Bible*, ed. John Stirling. Hebrews: H. L. Goudge and W. R. Inge.
Science, Religion and Reality, ed. Joseph Needham. W. R. I.: Conclusion, pp. 345–89.

1928. *If I had Only One Sermon to Preach*. 20 Sermons ed. Sir James Marchant. W. R. I.: The Eternal Values, pp. 175–84.

1929. *The Anglican Communion*, ed. H. A. Wilson. W. R. I.: Evolution and the Idea of God, pp. 251–60.

1930. *Points of View*, ed. G. Lowes Dickinson. W. R. I.: Second of seven Broadcast Addresses (delivered 7 October 1929), pp. 35–48.
What is the Real Hell? W. R. I.: First of thirteen articles, pp. 1–12.

1931. *Science and Religion*: Twelve Broadcast Addresses. W. R. I.: No. XI (delivered 7 December 1930), pp. 141–57.

1934. *To the Memory of Ruskin*: Nine Addresses, ed. J. H. Whitehouse. W. R. I.: No. 2. 5 pp.

1935. *The Causes of War*, ed. H. J. Stenning. (8) Broadcast Talks. W. R. I.: I. pp. 13–22.

1938. *Our English Bible*: Six White Lectures in St Paul's Cathedral, ed. E. N. Sharpe. W. R. I.: What England owes to the Bible.
United Christian Front, ed. Sir Henry Lunn. W. R. I.: The Psychology of Revolution, pp. 44–7.
Asking them Questions, Second Series, ed. R. Selby Wright. W. R. I.: What do we mean by 'Leading a Christian Life'? pp. 1–6.

1947. *God, King and Empire*, A Trilogy by W. R. Inge, Walter Elliot, Quintin Hogg. W. R. I.: God, pp. 9–24.
Has the Church Failed? ed. Sir James Marchant. W. R. I.: Institutionalism on Trial, pp. 94–104.

1948. *What Life has taught me*, ed. Sir James Marchant. W. R. I.: pp. 1–13.

1952. *The Philosophy of Sarvepalli Radhakrishnan*. Fragments of a Confession by S. R. followed by 23 Descriptive and Critical Essays. W. R. I.: No. 6, R. and the Religion of the Spirit, pp. 325–31.

E. WORKS FOR WHICH DR INGE WROTE AN INTRODUCTION

The number of pages indicates the length of the Introduction, not of the whole book. An asterisk denotes that Dr Inge compiled or edited the book as well as writing an Introduction.

*1904. *Selections from the German Mystics*. 56 pp.

1905. T. G. Upham. *Life, Religious Opinions, and Experience of Madame Guyon* (Re-issue). 2 pp.

1912. *The Parting of the Roads*, ed. F. J. Foakes Jackson. 12 pp.

*1913. *The Life of the Blessed Henry Suso*. 25 pp.

1923. *The Coming Renaissance*, ed. Sir James Marchant. 3 pp.

1926. W. R. Bowie, *The Inescapable Christ*. 5 pp.

1930. *Benjamin Whichcote, D.D., Moral and Religious Aphorisms*. 8 pp.

*1931. *Everyman's Bible*. 47 pp. Introduction issued separately 1935.

1932 *Lyra Mystica*, ed. C. C. Albertson. 15 pp.

1933. *The Post Victorians*. 5 pp.

1935. *Jesus Manifest*, D. Merezhkovsky, translated E. Gellibrand. 2 pp.

1936. C. W. H. Sutton, *Farewell to Rousseau*. 6 pp.
Freedom, Love and Truth. 38 pp.

F. POSTHUMOUS WORKS

1958. *Goodness and Truth*. (22 Sermons) ed. A. F. Judd, with a brief memoir by W. R. Matthews. 190 pp.

1959. *The Awakening of the Soul*. Lectures on Mysticism (delivered 1912), ed. A. F. Judd. 61 pp.

Notes

Preface

1 Earl of Oxford and Asquith. *Memories and Reflections*, 1928.

I

1 *The Letters of Sydney Smith*, ed. Nowell Smith. O.U.P. Letters 244, 246.
2 Mrs William Inge's eldest brother, Ralph's "Uncle Willy."
3 Lillywhite's *Guide to Cricketers, 1862*: 'Daft, Richard, born at Nottingham, Nov. 2, 1836. Another brilliant star from the North, and who, as a batsman, no one can surpass from any part of the globe. His defence is perfect, and his easy style of tackling the best balls bowled is wonderful, and is seen almost every innings, and appreciated by his many admirers. Not only is he a master of the willow, but cannot possibly be excelled in the field, especially at long-leg or anywhere "out" in the field.'
4 Presumably the famous W. G. Grace, though his brother E. M. Grace would also be known to Ralph by name. Both are in *D.N.B.*
5 "Uncle Willy" was noted for his silence in the Combination Room at King's (*see* p. 27). Archdeacon Theodore Churton was rather silent, and his son T. Percy Churton (b. 1895) a very silent schoolboy.

II

1 Shakespeare. *Julius Caesar*, V, i, 168.
2 In an article in the *Strand Magazine* reprinted in *Assessments and Anticipations*, p. 20.
3 K.S. stands for King's Scholar. (The king is Henry VI.)
4 1877 in the original; it should be 1878.
5 In his diary at 12 May 1917 the Dean wrote: "I have been reading masses of my old letters, which Sophy sent from Oxford. Apparently I wrote home nearly every day from Stoke House or Eton. The early letters are astonishingly mature and well expressed. They are on the whole cheerful in tone, and do not betray much of the chronic psychalgia or mind-ache from which I have suffered all my life."

He seems to have made a selection of these letters, and as they are nearly all Sunday letters, it is likely that he wrote "daily" above in mistake for "weekly."

III

1 The Little-go is the entrance examination for matriculation at Cambridge, corresponding to Responsions at Oxford. It was formerly quite common to enter either University before passing the examination, though no terms could be counted towards a degree before it had been passed. Inge had not passed it and was afraid he would fail in mathematics, though the standard would not be high.
2 "We sat up till the small hours with a shaded candle (for 'lighting up' was against rules)." (*Assessments and Anticipations*, p. 17.)
3 S.T.C. stands for Sanctae Trinitatis Confraternitas.

IV

1 Charlie is his brother, K.S. at Eton, January 1883–July 1887.
2 *Eton College Chronicle*, 19 October 1885.
3 The examiners were A. A. Tilley of King's and J. S. Reid of Caius.
4 *Society in Rome under the Caesars.* John Murray, 276 pp.
5 *Assessments and Anticipations*, p. 20.

V

1 Some of Mr Justice Vaisey's compositions which have survived have only very slight corrections or suggestions upon them. But it may be that his compositions could scarcely be bettered.
2 This was Mr Norman Whatley's opinion.
3 In 1891 Sir Frederick Leighton, afterwards Lord Leighton, was P.R.A.: other painters in vogue were Millais, Orchardson, Poynter, Sant, Marcus Stone, Alma Tadema, Dicksee, Herkomer: among the architects Alfred Waterhouse, G. F. Bodley, Norman Shaw: as sculptor Alfred Gilbert. There were altogether 2,102 items, many of which would be 'skied' near the ceiling. The exhibition would probably now excite interest and in some quarters ridicule, but at this period it had great prestige in London. In Oxford the R.A. is possibly always thought "very poor."

VII

1 *Christian Mysticism*, 1899, p. x.

IX

1 The Vice-Chancellor was Stuart Donaldson, Master of Magdalene.
2 See *Truth and Falsehood in Religion*, p. 111.
3 *Personal Idealism and Mysticism*. Preface to the 3rd Edn., p. vii and p. 67.

X

1 *The Times* obituary notice, 27 February 1954.
2 The various members of the family were distinguished as (i) the Dean's elder daughter *Catharine*, (ii) her mother *Kitty*, (iii) her maternal grandmother '*Mother Kate*,' (iv) her first cousin, the daughter of Dr W. A. Spooner, Warden of New College, *Catherine*, Mrs Campbell Dodgson.
3 Ecclesiasticus 37^{14}.
4 Montagu John Rendall was appointed Headmaster of Winchester in succession to Dr Hubert Murray Burge, made Bishop of Southwark.
5 *Speculum Animae*.

XII

1 Canon Jones must be Thomas Jesse Jones, Residentiary Canon of Llandaff. There was another Canon Jones in Convocation at the time, Lloyd Timothy Jones, Hon. Canon of Peterborough and Vicar of Northampton. But the speech was about industry in Glamorgan.
2 Synderesis is defined in the New English Dictionary as 'a name for that function or department of conscience which serves as a guide for conduct': as distinct from syneidesis which is conscience 'concerned with passing judgment on acts already performed.'
3 *Lay Thoughts of a Dean*, p. 82.

XIII

1 Apart from 'Our Present Discontents' only one, 'The Future of the English Race' (IV), was written after the war.
2 See the extract from *The End of an Age* on pp. 257, 258

3 The short extracts from the 'Confessio Fidei' which follow are taken from *Outspoken Essays*, II, pp. 2, 3, 35, 10, 12, 13, 15, 20, 26, 45, 50. The longer extracts are from pp. 24 and 25, 14 and 15.

XIV

1 In March 1935 the Dean gave an 'Oration' before the Union Society of University College, London, on 'Platonism as a Rule of Life.'
2 See the Plotinus lecture as reprinted in *Mysticism in Religion*, pp. 106, 107.

XV

1 *Paradise Lost*, X, 891.
2 *The Modernist Movement in the Roman Church*, A. R. Vidler, p. 97.
3 The controversy was precipitated by the publication of Harnack's *What is Christianity?* There is a good succinct account of what Harnack took Christianity to be and Loisy's answer to Harnack in *Protestantism* (W. R. Inge, 1927) under the heading Developments of Protestantism in Germany.

XVI

1 In 1935 the Dean provided the Bishop of London with another Lenten book by collecting some sermons under the title *The Gate of Life*.
2 Although *England* appeared in various shapes and sizes, this page reference is correct for all copies before the Sixth (so-called Popular) Edition of 1938. The reference there is to pp. 130–6, the change being due to a new Preface. Chapter I now begins at page 13.

XVII

1 The names of these newspapers and periodicals are printed in italics to display their variety. They are not underlined in the diaries.
2 *The Challenge* was the organ of the Life and Liberty movement. The first number came out on 1 May 1914. William Temple edited it from July 1915 to October 1918. It only lasted a few years longer.

XVIII

1 I am assuming that the average age of an undergraduate's father will be round about fifty. The Dean was close on seventy-two when he delivered these lectures, and he had a son of seventeen at Eton.

XIX

1 The Dean noted down in his diary on several occasions how much the American *National Geographic Magazine* interested him and gave some description of what he had found in it.
2 The three plays will be *The Apple Cart*, *Too True to be Good*, and *On the Rocks*.

XX

1 The article on 'Escapism' really belongs to 1940, so it is prior to 'Escape' in the *Talks in a Free Country*, 1942. The two, in spite of the similarity of title, overlap very little. The subject is one which was much in the Dean's mind. He was fond of the texts 'Our citizenship is in heaven' (Philippians 3^{20}) and 'how they desire a better country, that is, an heavenly' (Hebrews 11^{16}). He was equally fond of quoting Plotinus' exhortation to 'flee to our dear country.' In the Talk entitled 'Escape' one of the four talkers is Pundit Bhagavan Chandra, who contributes contemporary Indian thought, with which the Dean made himself increasingly familiar in his old age.
2 "The book" is the *Diary of a Dean* published December 1949.
3 *Rubaiyat of Omar Khayyam*, stanza 57.
4 He actually wrote Mayarana.

INDEX

An asterisk after a page number indicates an extract from the work in question.